TERESA MARIE BECK
JACQUELINE MECCHELLA BUSHWACK
SHAYNA MICHELE STEINFELD
editors

her story

LESSONS IN SUCCESS FROM LAWYERS WHO LIVE IT

Cover design by Tahiti Spears/ABA Design

Printed in the United States of America.

25 24 5 4 3

Library of Congress Cataloging-in-Publication Data

Names: Beck, Teresa, editor. | Bushwack, Jaqueline M., editor. | Steinfeld, Shayna M., 1964-, editor.
Title: Her story : lessons in success from lawyers who live it / edited by Teresa Beck, Jaqueline M. Bushwack, Shayna M. Steinfeld.
Description: Chicago : American Bar Association, 2017.
Identifiers: LCCN 2017018193 (print) | LCCN 2017018393 (ebook) | ISBN 9781634257596 (ebook) | ISBN 9781634257589 (softcover : alk. paper)
Subjects: LCSH: Women lawyers—United States—Biography.
Classification: LCC KF299.W6 (ebook) | LCC KF299.W6 H47 2017 (print) | DDC 340.092/520973—dc23
LC record available at https://lccn.loc.gov/2017018193

Discounts are available for books ordered in bulk. Special consideration is given to state bars, CLE programs, and other bar-related organizations. Inquire at Book Publishing, ABA Publishing, American Bar Association, 321 N. Clark Street, Chicago, Illinois 60654-7598.

www.shopABA.org

CONTENTS

FOREWORD

This book shares women lawyers' wide diversity of experiences as they have overcome obstacles, reached goals, and led lives rich with opportunities, challenges, and successes. It does not enter the debate about having it all, climbing ladders or jungle gyms, or leaning out or in. It avoids the unattainable image of a woman precariously balancing on a tightrope in favor of telling real stories about real professional women being managers of their careers and families. Here the contributors share real stories, of real women lawyers, managing the varied aspects of their lives. What works for one of them may not work for all. If you take away one lesson from the many shared, we hope you, your practice, and your personal life will be the better for it.

This book's genesis is the belief that to change the workplace for the betterment of all women, there's not just one model, but rather story, after story, after story of happy and successful women. We are grateful for the contributors who have generously shared their stories in order to encourage both their colleagues and those women who are newer to the practice of law to hang in there and to make choices that work for each of them. We are also grateful for the years of hard work and dedication by the coeditors of this book, Teresa M. Beck, Jacqueline Mecchella Bushwack, and Shayna M. Steinfeld.

We hope you will learn, laugh, cry, and be inspired.

Heather White
Sabrina Beavens, Hailyn Chen
Robin Perkins
Cochairs, The Woman Advocate Committee

PREFACE

Her Story: Lessons in Success from Lawyers Who Live It is designed to encourage, teach, and provide insights to fellow attorneys about successfully managing daily lives and careers while climbing the ladder of success and ascending into executive roles. Our message is both positive and uplifting. It is a compilation of stories about achieving success while juggling career advancement and the curveballs of life, and doing so with strength and grace. *Her Story* tells the real story about real lawyers' lives with abject honesty as told by the lawyers themselves. These are not sensational stories but amazing ones. These are stories about lawyers overcoming obstacles, reaching goals, and leading lives that are full to the brim and rich with challenges, successes, and opportunities. These are stories of hope and lessons learned; stories with advice and unique perspectives. The stories are of and by women who enjoy their careers, whose eyes light up when they talk about the joy of the practice of law and the joy of their personal lives, and who understand that telling their story is important in order to encourage both their colleagues and those lawyers who are newer to the practice of law to hang in there and make their lives work for them and those who will follow.

Her Story is designed to encourage further discussion on topics that we all face but seldom speak about. Each chapter ends with Reflection questions to facilitate discussion in a book club, roundtable, or meeting setting. Enjoy the book from start to finish or by picking out a chapter or essay of interest. The book is divided into eight chapters with topics from career management, to developing a plan for success, gaining momentum, keeping values straight, building endurance, professional goals, maintaining perspective, getting back up, and finally, going the distance.

In an effort to inspire women attorneys everywhere, the Work/Life Management Subcommittee of the American Bar Association's Woman Advocate Committee embarked on this project to broadcast to a larger audience these positive and inspiring stories of real women attorneys. Collectively, these stories provide true examples of how attorneys are managing the interplay between thriving careers and enjoyable, full lives. Individually, these stories take you on a journey through personal challenges and struggles while at the same time offering a plethora of advice and guidance on all aspects of career development. These are real stories with views of what really matters when we step back from day-to-day challenges and set our eyes on the big picture. This is what happens when we deliberately define our goals with inspiration and focus.

We have discovered that these stories are really the stories of the professional workforce at large in the twenty-first century. It is our deepest hope that this collection of powerful, encouraging, and uplifting accounts of the profession will encourage lawyers everywhere, and our counterparts in other professions, to remain in their professions and advance in their careers, deliberately. Although managing career advancement and life is not exclusive to women, *Her Story* focuses on the stories of successful and accomplished women who have managed these issues, have managed them well, and have successfully developed amazing careers along the way. We suspect you will find that these stories have a certain magic in them, and we are excited to be on this thrilling journey with you.

Please reach out to the ABA Litigation Section's Woman Advocate Committee and let us know what you think after you read *Her Story*. We would really appreciate your feedback. Thank you.

Teresa M. Beck
Jacqueline Mecchella Bushwack
Shayna M. Steinfeld
Editors

ABOUT THE EDITORS

Teresa M. Beck is a partner in the California, Arizona, and Nevada civil law firm of Lincoln Gustafson & Cercos, where she defends a wide range of clients in litigation and provides advice on an extensive array of legal topics. She is active with the Claims and Litigation Management Alliance, where she is a member of many committees and a frequent speaker and author of articles on a long list of litigation-related topics, the most popular of which is the litigation strategy known as "Reptile." She is also active with the Defense Research Institute. Ms. Beck is also very involved with the American Bar Association where she cochairs the Work/Life Management Subcommittee of the Section of Litigation's Woman Advocate Committee. She is a board member of the National Conference of Women's Bar Associations, and she cocreated the GOOD Guys program (GOOD = Guys Overcoming Obstacles to Diversity), designed to engage men in diversity efforts and end the stagnation in women's advancement in the workplace. She is also active with the National Diversity Council. Ms. Beck has been recognized by many organizations for her legal skills, including Martindale Hubbell (she is an AV-rated lawyer), and she has been named Best of the Bar and a San Diego Top Lawyer for consecutive years. She is a 2017 Super Lawyer. She recently won the National Diversity Council's Diversity First award. Her local women's bar organization, Lawyers Club of San Diego, awarded her the Belva Lockwood award in 2014. She lives with her husband and three children in San Diego.

Jacqueline Mecchella Bushwack is a partner in Rivkin Radler LLP's Complex Torts & Product Liability, General Liability and Medical Malpractice Defense Practice Groups, where she defends property owners, construction management companies, construction contractors, convenience store chains, pharmaceutical companies, hospitals, physicians, adult care facilities, and others in suits alleging premises liability, violations of New York State's Labor Law, product liability, medical and dental malpractice, nursing home negligence, and toxic exposures. She is on the board of directors for the North Shore Child & Family Guidance Center and chairs its Business Advisory Council. Prior board experience includes serving on the Board of Trustees of Albany Law School as the recent graduate trustee from 2007 to 2010. She is actively involved with the American Bar Association, where she cochairs the Work/Life Management Subcommittee of the Section of Litigation's Woman Advocate Committee and serves as the subcommittee chair of Book Projects. She is also an active member of the USLAW Network and the Long Island Center for Business & Professional Women. She was selected as one of Long Island's "50 Most Influential Women" by *Long Island Business News* for 2014. She is a member of the firm's softball and volleyball teams. She lives in Long Island with her husband and two young children.

Shayna M. Steinfeld, board certified by the American Board of Certification in both Consumer and Business Bankruptcy Law, is president and shareholder of Steinfeld & Steinfeld, PC, where she practices with her husband, Bruce, a Fellow of the American Academy of Matrimonial Lawyers. She is a past-president of the Atlanta Bar Association, the Georgia Association for Women Lawyers, a cofounder and past-president of the Georgia IWIRC (International Women's Insolvency and Restructuring Confederation) Network, a past-chair of the Sole Practitioner/Small Firm Section of the Atlanta Bar and the Bankruptcy Sections of both the Atlanta Bar and the State Bar of Georgia. She is past-chair of the bankruptcy committee of the ABA Family Law section and is currently actively involved with the Work/Life Management Subcommittee of the ABA Section of Litigation's Woman Advocate Committee, serving as a subcommittee chair of Book Projects. She has received many accolades, including "Section of the Year" and "Outstanding Woman in the Profession," and is regularly named a "Georgia Super Lawyer," one of the top fifty women and one of the top one hundred lawyers in the state. A graduate of Emory (BA, JD, and MBA), she frequently lectures and has authored many publications, including *The Family Lawyer's Guide to Bankruptcy*, which is published by the ABA Family Law Section and is in its third edition. She has been married for twenty-six years and has three sons, a graduated mechanical engineer and two business students at Georgia Tech.

ACKNOWLEDGMENTS

ABA Litigation Section, Woman Advocate Committee

Editors

Teresa M. Beck, Esq., Lincoln, Gustafson & Cercos, San Diego, CA

Jacqueline Mecchella Bushwack, Esq., Rivkin Radler, LLP Uniondale, NY

Shayna M. Steinfeld, Esq., Steinfeld & Steinfeld, P.C., Atlanta, GA

Associate Editors

Kelley Conaty, Esq., Sidley Austin LLP, Dallas, TX

Erika Kleinschmidt, Esq., American Arbitration Association, Dallas, TX

Maurine Wall Laborde, Esq., Wall Bullington & Cook, LLC, New Orleans, LA

LaKeisha R. Randall, Esq., State Farm Mutual Automobile Insurance Company, Atlanta, GA

Amy M. Stewart, Esq., Estes Okon Thorne & Carr PLLC, Dallas, TX

Virginia K. Trunkes, Esq., Borah, Goldstein, Altschuler, Nahins & Goidel, P.C., New York, NY

Janet Wallace, Esq., Adamski Moroski Madden Cumberland & Green LLP, San Luis Obispo County, CA

Creative Assistance

Laurie J. Bloom, Director of Marketing and Communications, Rivkin Radler LLP, Uniondale, NY

A Special Thanks to ABA Litigation Section, Woman Advocate Committee Cochairs (Past and Present)

Sabrina Beavens, Esq., Heather White, Esq., Hailyn Chen, Esq., Robin Perkins, Esq., Beatrice "Beatty" O'Donnell, Esq., Erica L. Calderas, Esq., Patricia O'Prey, Esq., Anne Marie Seibel, Esq., and Paula Hinton, Esq.

The Woman Advocate Book Committee coeditors wish to thank everyone who has given their time to *Her Story* over the past three years. *Her Story* has been a work of love that has been in the works for several years under three different sets of Women Advocate Committee chairs within the ABA Litigation Section, and without all of their support, the support of the Woman Advocate Committee as a whole, and the support of the Work-Life Subcommittee, *Her Story* could not have taken form and come together. We would also like to extend our thanks to the many essay writers, editors, associate editors, spouses, children, partners, associates, secretaries, paralegals, and all the others who provide daily support in the lives of working mothers who also litigate, without which *Her Story* could not be told and published. Thank you so very much to all of you for all you have done. Although we are unable to specifically name everyone who provided their helping hands, know that we appreciate everyone who has touched, guided, and assisted with *Her Story: Lessons in Success from Lawyers Who Live It.* Thank you.

Teresa M. Beck
Jacqueline Mecchella Bushwack
Shayna M. Steinfeld

1

CAREER MANAGEMENT MATTERS

The Case for Fostering Work-Life Balance among Employees

Introduction

In this chapter, Nan Joesten, principal of Rapid Evolution LLC, asserts that businesses, including law firms, "need to look no further than their bottom line when evaluating what's in it for them to help their attorneys manage how their work fits into their life," and senior associate general counsel of Wal-Mart Stores, Inc., Alan Bryan, explains that "it is absolutely critical that law firms, indeed the legal profession, start making work-life balance a priority." The essays in Chapter 1 present the case for fostering and encouraging successful work-life management among employees. Read about how these issues are affecting today's legal workforce in terms of retention and attrition and how the millennial generation, both male and female, is a driving force for change.

Understanding the Generational Shift and the Increasing Importance of Quality of Life in the Practice of Law

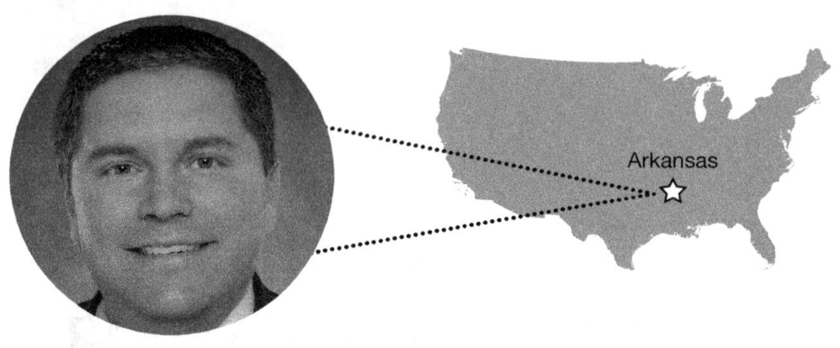

His Story

Alan Bryan

Career

Senior Associate General Counsel—Legal Operations and Outside Counsel Management.

Education

J. William Fulbright Senior Scholar and Phi Delta Theta International Fellow from the University of Arkansas. Graduated *cum laude* from the University of Arkansas School of Law. Managing Editor of the *Arkansas Law Review*.

Best Advice

Be kind and respectful to everyone, no matter who they are, no matter what they can do for you, and no matter how you feel.

Personal

Married (six years) with two children: Luke, four, and Reagan, two.

For more information about Alan

www.linkedin.com/in/alan-bryan-2080332

Remember *The Jetsons*? It was the 1962 follow-up to Hanna-Barbera's cartoon, *The Flintstones*. It only lasted one season, but *The Jetsons* left an indelible mark on American culture, and not only through its catchy theme song and years of syndication. Today, it gives us insight into what the creators thought life would look like 100 years in the future—in 2062. It was fairly prescient; just over fifty years after the show aired, we see that *The Jetsons* correctly predicted future conveniences such as video chat, talking alarm clocks, robot vacuums, flat screen televisions, and even tanning beds. One thing the creators did not get correct, at least not yet, is the way we work.

Show devotees will recall that family patriarch George Jetson regularly complained about working a handful of hours each week at Spacely Space Sprockets, where his primary job duty was repeatedly pushing one button on a gigantic computer. It is true that technology has made working more efficient, but it also has led to an expectation of 24/7 responsiveness. The number of hours we work per week has steadily gone up. Increased work hours and expectations of availability have hit our personal lives hard. The legal profession, which has always required long hours, has been hit particularly hard.

More than ever, it is time for law firms, legal departments, bar organizations, and the entire profession to recognize "quality of life" as an important aspect of being a lawyer. The profession otherwise will lose out on the highest qualified talent among our future high school and college ranks because they will choose other career paths. Any lure of becoming a lawyer will be clouded by the prevailing belief that those walking into the profession will face a life with a nose constantly to the proverbial grindstone. A career not offering flexibility is no longer acceptable to those who expect more than hard work to fulfill their lives. Inevitably, a tremendous talent gap will emerge in the legal profession.

Is This Only a Generational Consideration?

I leave it to others to fully deconstruct the generation becoming the majority of our nation's workforce. Enough has been written about them, however, to conclude several things. Money and higher salary are consistently *not* at the top of the list of things younger workers look for in a career. Instead, and perhaps to their credit, members of the millennial generation entering the workforce place more importance on their time. They derive satisfaction from fulfilling work and will put in time and interest to get it. They also want to work on different terms, primarily during different hours and in different places, than we have in the past. Employers will need to provide more flexibility in the ways their employees work to entice new talent. This applies especially to law firms. Attorneys entering the workforce, as they observe contemporaries in other industries, will want the flexibility of setting their hours and working at places other than a desk.

Millennials want employers to provide training, experiences (not just experience), and inspiration in the tasks they perform. Some who read this may scoff at these desires as the fanciful aspirations of youth. Beware of dismissing them. If new generations of workers, including attorneys, do not feel a sense of purpose or relevance, they will simply leave for a new job. Loyalty to an employer has and will take a backseat to personal fulfillment. Think about the time and investment put into developing these attorneys, and then the cost of finding and developing their replacements. When considered in real dollars, these desires cannot be ignored. Rather, fulfilling these goals should be part of the "package" offered to these recruits.

But is it fair to consider work-life balance only in terms of the perceived desires of younger generations? Hardly. Think about the world today compared to that of fifty years ago. In the 1950s, 1960s, and 1970s, the vast majority of two-parent households had one breadwinner and one stay-at-home parent. It is no longer the single parent who faces the near-impossible task of juggling a full-time job with caring for children and a household. Today, more two-parent households have two full-time breadwinners. Both generational desires and economic realities now must be considered as part of any realistic recruitment plan for law firms and other employers.

Why Law Firms Have to Make the Greatest Changes

This combination of changing career expectations and households in which all able adults are working must now be considered when designing a law firm work culture. To compete for the highest-caliber talent coming out of law schools, law firms will need to offer attorneys either flexible or reduced-hour options. They will need to recognize that being seen sitting at a desk for long hours, at night and on weekends, no longer defines a "hard-working" lawyer. They must adjust business models to compensate attorneys for output and calculate that output not merely by reference to hours billed. They must find a way to compete for legal talent or it will go elsewhere.

The legal profession does require work outside normal hours on occasion, but it should not be a profession that demands so much of our time that we cannot achieve balance—having success at work plus a fulfilling and enjoyable life outside of it. Within law firms, at least two common factors can derail that aspiration of work-life balance: the billable hour and the unspoken "face time" requirement.

The billable hour remains the primary form of quantifying and valuing legal work. Connecting any task to an amount of time entails that time controls the value of that task: the greater the time, the greater the value. Moreover, the value of the individual attorney is measured by a yearly requirement for billable hours. Because the amount of time in any day is finite, the more you increase the amount that must be billed, the less of the rest of the day you have. As overhead costs and profitability per attorney expectations have increased, so too have hourly billing requirements and the pressure on individuals to bill more hours. Family and home life inevitably suffer from this pressure.

Beyond billable hour requirements, flexible work schedules often take a backseat to being seen in the office. "Out of sight, out of mind" has been used often to explain why attorneys on flexible schedules receive fewer high-profile assignments and remain on a flat career path. This must end. It is an excuse that has not been limited to more recent generations. For some time, this phenomenon has disproportionately affected women attorneys who are more likely to work flexible schedules. Despite a near equal number of women entering law schools for decades, the number of women equity partners in large law firms has remained shockingly stagnant—and low—for the past decade. In part, that is because many women who want to start families must chose flexible schedules or temporarily leave the law firm setting or the profession entirely. It leads, respectively, to fewer plumb assignments and failed reentries at law firms. Millennials entering the legal profession are now asking the question women lawyers have been asking for years: "Will I jeopardize my career by starting a family (or otherwise working on a flexible schedule)?" Law firms will continue to fail women, and lose the next generation of potential attorneys, unless they become purposeful in finding flexible paths for those who choose lives beyond law books.

Why "Quality of Life" Should Have a Place in Law Firms and Recruitment of Attorneys

Allowing attorneys to work outside the office and historical working hours makes good business sense. It allows them to enjoy family, recreation, or other interests. That greater satisfaction at home leads to happier and more productive workers. Furthermore, it leads to less burnout and attrition. It is a fool's concept to set unreasonable work expectations on attorneys only to see them leave a firm that has invested in their training and development, and then have the firm spend even more on a replacement. Of course, if firms are willing to admit that attorneys are merely profit centers to be discarded or forced to leave, then it makes sense. It might not help, however, to mention that philosophy in a recruiting pitch.

A law firm making a play for the best and brightest coming out of law school should instead be touting how attorneys can have a career and a personal life—and still succeed! The past model of dangling "prestige" and pay will not work as broadly as it once did. The partnership lottery tickets are just not paying like they used to, and younger generations have become wise to the fact that a law degree offers its holder myriad choices. They wisely know fulfillment can be found beyond a career, so they are demanding that their careers provide fulfillment too. The younger generations realize that our time is finite and that we should not spend the vast majority of it with our heads down at a desk. Like it or not, that is the sentiment. Perhaps we should nurture this inclination instead of maintaining a failing model of attaching success to time spent on matters or at an office. In other words, we should be flexible in our thinking and also in our schedules.

Millennials have been labeled "entitled," "spoiled," "needy," and "self-centered" for daring to believe they can dictate how and where they work. Those labels might be shortsighted, and I am sure most of that generation would agree with that (this from a gen Xer who did not appreciate his generation being labeled "malcontent slackers"). Not to defend millennials in other respects, but as a whole, they may be onto something we older generations have not fully considered, and that is particularly the case in the legal profession. Advances in technology, how and where we are able to work, and the desire for a balanced life, all lend themselves to reconsidering how we practice law. Today, it is working to live, not living to work. If employers do not recognize this, they will miss tremendous opportunities to staff firms with first-rate attorneys. Moreover, it will not just be the millennials who rebuke the lifestyle. Slowly, throughout the profession, men and women will realize there is a better way.

In fact, all of them have new alternatives offering a nonstandard way of using a law degree, and those options are growing with new forms of law firms and legal service providers. The ascendance of low-overhead, legal service providers, increasingly used by clients, has created a viable and legitimate way to practice law on one's own terms. The twenty-first-century law firm faces abundant challenges already. Competing for clients and talent in this environment is near the top of the list. Law firms should adapt to the alternatives by altering the construct of a typical law practice to better conform with reasonable and increasingly widespread expectations of work-life balance. Law firms should adopt new policies to help recruit talented attorneys from younger generations but also to keep the attorneys they already have.

Here are some practical steps to consider:

- **Have a clearly *written* flextime policy.** A flextime policy should be in writing to be fully understood and uniformly followed. Written polices provide transparency and prevent resentment. They also avoid the inevitable hesitation by attorneys to use flexible work arrangements, which is created by the confusion of an unclear or unwritten policy.

- **The flextime policy should make clear that it applies to *everyone*.** Any policy directed at only one group invites an unwarranted stigma. For instance, never should a flexible work arrangement be offered only to single parents. Yes, single parents need flexibility in how and when they work, but so does everyone else. Singling out a group in a policy can even cause hesitation by that group to utilize the policy for fear of others resenting the "special" treatment received.
- **Flextime must be taken from the top down.** A firm's leadership must understand that it sets the tone. If firm leaders are not working flexibly, those down the line will not do so either for fear of alienating or not impressing the boss. If the boss is working on a flexible schedule, his or her subordinates feel more comfortable doing so. As the old adage goes, actions indeed speak louder than words.
- **The dangers of perception over reality must be recognized.** An attorney may be in the office from 6:00 a.m. until 3:00 p.m., and then work again at home for three more hours after picking up the kids, having dinner, and enjoying family time. Another attorney may work from 8:00 a.m. until 8:00 p.m. every day. The perception is that the former attorney is slacking and the latter attorney is hard working, although both worked the same amount of time. Firms should recognize that presence during traditional business hours is not necessarily indicative of work ethic.
- **In addition to working flexibly, attorneys must not be afraid to work on their own terms.** We must retreat from the belief and expectation (including those we put on ourselves) that technological capabilities mean we should be available at all hours on all days. Although technology has made life and communication easier, we have established an unspoken expectation that requests and questions must be answered immediately. We are tethered to our cell phones and laptops due to this expectation. The constant feeling of connectivity has increased stress on the balance between home and work life. We should be zealous advocates when acting as attorneys, but then we should set it aside to be fully engaged in our personal life.

The aforementioned suggestions are the precursors to changing the recruitment philosophy of law firms. Setting a foundation by way of policy and practice, much like when building a house, must be the first step in making necessary changes. An environment of accepting work-life balance and the "flexible" practice of law must be present before a law firm can make quality of life one of its primary recruitment tools. It is absolutely critical that law firms, indeed the legal profession, start making work-life balance a priority.

The Jetsons imagined a world full of innovations that would define our lives in 2062. Although many of its premonitions have come to fruition, its vision of work as a part of life thus far has been incorrect, at least compared to what most practicing lawyers experience. We should not wait another five decades or so to make a change for the better.

The Millennial Generation: An Emerging Force of Change

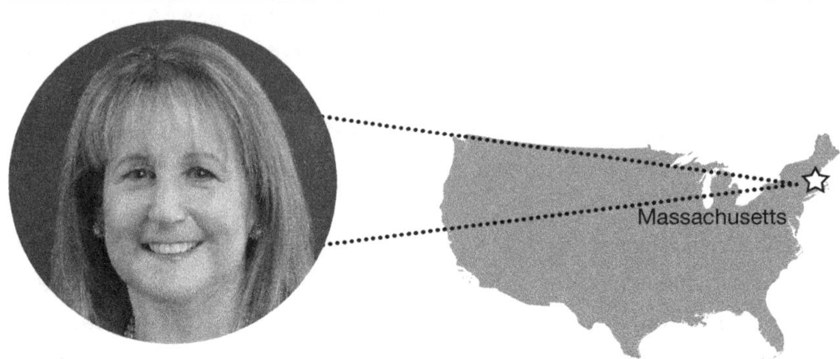

Her Story

Lauren Stiller Rikleen

Career

President, Rikleen Institute for Strategic Leadership. I provide speaking, training, and consulting services on strengthening multigenerational issues; women's leadership and advancement; and unconscious bias.

Education

Brandeis University, BA, *magna cum laude*; Boston College Law School, JD.

Best Advice

Be kind to others. Try not to let the craziness of your work-life challenges prevent you from enjoying the journey along the way.

Personal

Married to Sander Rikleen, a litigation partner at Sherin & Lodgen, with two millennial children.

For more information about Lauren

www.RikleenInstitute.com

Similar to the work-life struggles faced by my generation, millennials are confronting the same work-life challenges that have been discussed in law practice for decades. This time, however, there is reason to believe the future may look different. As a generation comprised of both women and men striving to integrate their professional responsibilities and personal and family needs, there may be a real opportunity to activate change.

More than a dozen years ago, I gave a presentation at the MIT Workplace Center, and I had an opportunity to reflect on the state of working parents. I expressed how easy it had always been to connect with other working parents about our mutual work-family challenges, as we all have in common our deep desire to do what is best for our families while performing with excellence at work.

In those 2004 remarks, I also observed that as an equity partner in a law firm I had participated in many partnership elevation discussions, and I had spoken with colleagues in many other firms about the promotion process. I stated: "I often hear the criteria of 'total commitment' as a critical quality that an associate needs in order to become a law firm partner. I worry about what 'total commitment' means and how this criteria impacts how one can parent and lawyer at the same time."[1]

This 2004 presentation incorporated what I had learned from a project initiated six years earlier. In 1998, in my role as president of the Boston Bar Association, I had the opportunity to create a task force charged with analyzing the changing nature of law firm practice, the concomitant increase in the demands on lawyers, and the growing intolerance for anything that appears to take time away from a law firm economic model built on a demand for hours billed.

The final report of that task force was groundbreaking for two reasons. It marked the first time a major bar association detailed the financial cost of ongoing attrition. Second, it identified the myth of meritocracy that pervades the law firm success narrative. The task force report noted that the language of meritocracy incorrectly creates a perception that the quality of a person's work is the only determinant of his or her professional merit. When

1. Lauren Stiller Rikleen, *From Here to Flexibility in Law Firms: Can It Be Done?* MIT Workplace Center, Spring 2004 Seminar Series.

examined more closely, meritocracy relies on the comfortable idea that merit is defined by the quality of one's legal skills, responsiveness to client demands, commitment to the firm, and teamwork. These qualities may indeed be components of merit, but they also are correlated with long hours and the sacrifice of personal and family time.

In effect, as the task force report noted, meritocracy has come to mean a lifestyle that regularly pushes all nonwork obligations aside as a symbol of one's commitment to the law firm.[2] In other words, you are judged well in a deemed meritocracy if—in addition to excellence in your performance—work is seen as your highest priority and the first choice among all other conflicting demands.

Fast forward to today. The legal profession has become even more demanding as the combined forces of globalization and technology fuel seemingly endless demands for accessibility, billable hours, and client development. Although many firms have adopted various policies over the years, such as maternity and paternity leave and alternate work arrangements, few have achieved a stigma-free environment in the implementation of these written opportunities.

Enter the generational shift that has the power to finally bring about the change that has been talked about for decades.

Millennials grew up watching their boomer parents struggle through a rapidly changing economic climate. The children of boomers observed their parents enduring some very difficult changes along their career paths. In many workplaces, hard work was rewarded with layoffs, the request to do more with fewer resources evolved into an expectation, and a hard-driving workplace culture forced early retirements and responded to years of loyalty with diminished retirement benefits. One study reported: "Unlike their Boomer parents, Millennials are not workaholics. They believe in a clearly defined work/life balance, and they expect companies to have policies in place to help them achieve

---

2. Boston Bar Association: Report of the Task Force on Professional Challenges and Family Needs, *Facing the Grail: Confronting the Cost of Work-Family Imbalance* (1999).

this. . . . They are less willing to pay dues, and are unlikely to pursue the delayed gratification of a gradual promotion track."[3]

Globally consistent data supports the fact that, as a generation, millennials expect to follow a career path that allows them to integrate all aspects of their lives. Work matters, but attention to family and personal needs matter as well.

This outlook is not new. Rather, it mirrors the focus on work-life integration for which women have advocated in the legal profession for decades. The gender-neutral data that has emerged with respect to the newest generation to enter the workforce led me to write *You Raised Us, Now Work with Us: Millennials, Career Success, and Building Strong Workplace Teams.* Millennials are demonstrating a concern for living a whole life in which multiple priorities can be managed, and that seems to be embedded in their generational DNA.

In today's workplace, where dual-earner families are the norm, young men and women are pursuing gender flexibility in caretaking and breadwinning roles, as well as a stable family structure. As one professor wrote: "The tensions between changing lives and resistant institutions have created dilemmas for everyone. . . . In the place of fixed, rigid behavioral strategies and mental categories demarcating separate spheres for women and men, gender flexibility involves more equal sharing and more fluid boundaries for organizing and apportioning emotional, social, and economic care."[4]

Research suggests that millennials reject a definition of success measured by income and long hours. "They see success as including the opportunity to participate fully in the lives of their families. And they are not embarrassed to include among their key priorities the need to exercise and maintain friendships. Further, they will seek workplaces where the growth and development of employees are a strategic focus and where a culture of inclusion and respect is a priority."[5]

---

3. Consumerlab, *Young Professionals at Work*, Ericsson Consumer Insight, at 4 (April 2013), *available at* http://www.slideshare.net/Ericsson/youngprofessionalsatwork-130410234032phpapp02.
4. Kathleen Gerson, The Unfinished Revolution: How a New Generation Is Reshaping Family, Work, and Gender in America 6, 10 (Oxford University Press 2010).
5. Lauren Stiller Rikleen, You Raised Us—Now Work with Us: Millennials, Career Success, and Building Strong Workplace Teams 212 (American Bar Association 2014).

The research leads to an inescapable conclusion that millennials should not be judged by outdated notions of face time as a proxy for commitment. Moreover, this is a generation that eschews the concept of technology as a tether. Rather, millennials see technology as the tool that can facilitate a redesign of the workplace—one that offers opportunities for attention to family and personal commitments without sacrificing productivity.

Boomers and gen Xers have every incentive to develop the next generation of future leaders. In so doing, they also have a tremendous opportunity to influence their own legacy. The Boston Bar Association task force report concluded with these words of prediction, warning, and hope: "As we stand on the edge of a new millennium, our decisions with respect to professional commitment and work-family balance will profoundly affect the nature of law firms, the course of the profession, and the lives and families of those of us who choose law as a career. How will we be remembered?"[6]

To my boomer and gen X colleagues, I hope we choose to be remembered for, at long last, fostering a workplace culture that will allow our millennial children to demonstrate their merit through excellence, and where they can serve as admired role models through their unquestioned commitment to all of life's priorities.

---

6. Boston Bar Association, *Facing the Grail: Confronting the Cost of Work-Family Imbalance* (1999), *available at* https://www.bostonbar.org/prs/reports/facingthegrail0699.pdf.

The Importance of Flexibility in the Workplace

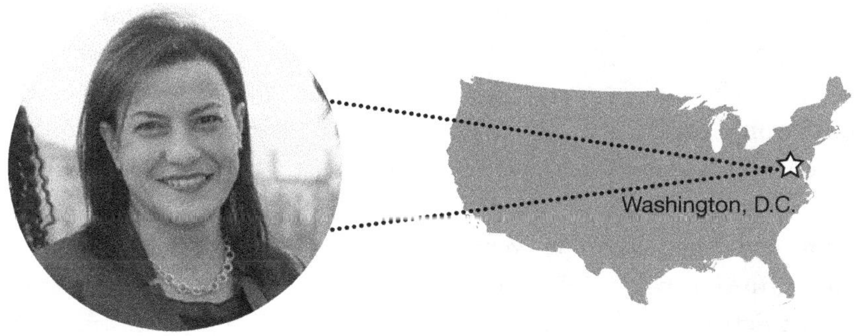

Her Story

Manar S. Morales

Career

Manar is a national thought leader in women's leadership, diversity, and workplace flexibility. She serves as president and CEO of the Diversity & Flexibility Alliance—a think tank dedicated to helping organizations create inclusive cultures that leverage diversity and flexibility to attract and retain top talent. Manar began her career as an employment litigator representing clients in all aspects of labor relations and employment law. She has litigated in federal court, before federal administrative agencies, and in arbitration. In addition, Manar served as an adjunct faculty member at Georgetown University teaching classes in Labor, Employment, and Entrepreneurship.

For more information about Manar

www.linkedin.com/in/manar-morales-1800a37

The simple truth about workplace flexibility is that, when implemented properly, every aspect of a law firm benefits including clients, associates, partners, recruiting, the bottom line, and myriad other less tangible aspects. As our workforce evolves and the percentage of independent-minded millennials increases on both the firm and client sides, workplace flexibility becomes even more of an imperative. We are all familiar now with the cold fact of shrinking law school class size, which makes the competition for top talent even fiercer. Now, more than ever, a flexible work model is essential to recruit and retain top talent.

A firm without an overarching work-life management approach manifested as a flexible work policy has a built-in canary in the coal mine—attrition. Losing top talent is problematic; losing top talent across the diversity spectrum is even more so. An unavoidable truth, however, is that women are most often affected by the lack of a holistic flexibility policy, and low retention numbers for women are a strong indicator that such options are lacking. In particular, research shows that women of color are affected disproportionately by a lack of flexible work options. That said, both men *and* women greatly benefit from a successful, flexible workplace, and ultimately, their firms do as well.

Your Clients Are Already There

Clients are often further ahead of the curve in embracing evolving models of workplace flexibility than the firms they employ. They expect their law firm teams to be diverse and accomplished, and they expect the firms they choose to offer flexible options to retain the top—and diverse—talent they expect. There is a greater demand for transparency regarding staffing on particular client matters. Sending a nondiverse team to represent your firm in a new business pitch is a red flag to clients that your firm is not going to offer the kind of diversity they seek. This is especially true given the rise of women and people of color among general counsel and on in-house teams. Clients want to know that firms they employ have flexibility policies in place to ensure that the attorneys they value stick around. Law firms pride themselves on touting their top talent. Clients choose to work with firms that offer a depth and breadth of talent. More important, clients ultimately hire attorneys, not firms. Studies show that when firms lose their key attorneys, they damage their client relationships through matter disruption, loss of knowledge of the client's business, and ramp-up costs associated with staffing matters with new attorneys.

Don't Fear Flexibility

Fear and misperceptions about embracing a flexible workplace abound. Firms assume offering part-time and full-time flex options will be too costly, that this approach won't work when billable hours equal dollars, and ultimately, that flextime options are "nice to have" as opposed to vital to the firm's bottom line. Firms assume people won't work as hard and that commitment to the firm will decline. Yet available data show that flexible work increases productivity, talent retention, and engagement. Moreover, employers have developed creative ways to build a sense of workplace community even when people are not physically present with each other every day.

Another common worry is that the "floodgates will open" and everybody will jump on the flextime bandwagon, and no one will come into the office. That bleak vision has never become a reality. Everyone needs *some* flexibility regarding when, where, and how they work, but not everyone needs the *same* type of flexibility. For instance, many people need and want to work full-time because working reduced hours is not feasible. Even though there are huge benefits to having a telecommuting policy (including real estate cost-savings and emergency preparedness), not everyone wants to work remotely all of the time.

Ironically, it's sometimes easier for "poor performers" to hide in plain sight at the office and appear to be effective team players by simply being there. Firms that have an inflexible face time expectation often don't realize that it can mask poor performance. Just because someone is in the office all day/every day, sitting at a computer, doesn't mean he or she is working effectively and delivering a high-quality work product. Work product from telecommuters is often more scrutinized, and poor performers can be more easily identified within the framework of a telecommuting policy.

Most law firms are built on an attrition model and recognize that attrition is not necessarily a bad thing. All too often, however, firms use this mind-set to resist a flexibility strategy and fail to discern the difference between good and bad attrition. What flex options do is ensure that regrettable attrition—when high performers leave—is minimized by providing viable options for success to a wide range of top talent.

The truth is that flexibility options (both part-time and full-time flex) are critical talent retention tools. When evaluating whether or not to incorporate flexibility, firms should view offering these options not only as an employee benefit but also as a business initiative that helps firms retain their top talent.

Choose to Embrace Flexible Options

Successful flexibility initiatives should be open to everyone and involve both part-time and full-time flex options. Let's be very clear in emphasizing that flexibility *does not mean just reduced hours.* Flexibility encompasses a range of full-time and part-time options and can be crafted to meet everyone's needs. Changing the culture of the firm to embrace this approach is key. The sense of entitlement that flexibility is an option needs to positively pervade the firm. A strong, flexible workplace is one in which flex options are not gendered (are tailored for everyone, not just women), are de-parented (open to all, not just parents), and are destigmatized (an appealing option for all). This is called a *holistic flex approach*, and it's key to your firm's success.

As daunting as it may seem, your firm can move toward holistic flex policies that address all needs by offering both part-time and full-time flex options with no negative impact on hours or the way work is completed. Annualized hours, flexible start and stop times, fluctuating hours—all these approaches strengthen your flexibility strategy and enhance its chances of success. My years of experience in the flexibility field have taught me that every practice group can handle a flexible work environment; it just looks different from group to group. For example, in mergers and acquisitions, it's hard to offer flextime in the middle of a deal. But a realistic flex option could be one deal on, one deal off. The same is true for litigation. A viable flex option for these types of groups is annualized hours. In other groups, it's possible to manage and offer flex options on a weekly basis.

Formalizing your flex policies is essential so that providing flexibility doesn't amount to a special exception to the rule. With set policies, firms can establish standards, enable people to be successful within flex work options, and performance criteria can be tied to flextime. Finally, with a formalized flex policy, your firm shows it values flexibility at an institutional level. It becomes a tangible part of the culture of your firm, and potential employees and clients can see and believe in it.

Commit to Making It Happen

Over the years of implementing these types of programs within law firms, I've seen incredible success. When that happens, firms are delighted at the win-win of happy lawyers and happy clients. I've also seen the resulting failure when strategies and policies are distributed with great fanfare only to have no further attention or action. Implementation must be realistic and ongoing so people will embrace the flex policy; the strongest policy is only as strong as its implementation. There's no sense in investing the hours and effort to develop policies that will benefit no one.

As detailed in the Diversity & Flexibility Alliance's Flex Success Framework, the critical areas of implementation—leadership support, training, career development, measurement, and assessment—look different for every firm but are essential for successful holistic flexibility initiatives.

Rolling out the program from the top down, with buy-in from all partners, gets things started in the right direction. Training is the next step: partners must learn to assist their teams in exploring flex options; supervisors must learn to ensure those they manage are empowered to adopt these policies; and individuals must learn how to be effective within a holistic flexibility environment. Accountability is a two-way street in this context. Are employees performing within the new flex structures? Are supervisors supporting employees and guiding them appropriately? Are practice leaders not just abiding by flexibility guidelines but encouraging their adoption? What happens to those who are not supporting the adoption of these policies?

Talent development should be an aspect of performance evaluations, and support of flexibility initiatives is an integral part of talent development. Failure to support these initiatives should have consequences in the performance review process. Firms should determine up front how these negative consequences manifest (from compensation to advancement) based on their culture and success metrics.

An easily overlooked aspect of offering a flexibility model is the importance to all employees of career advancement. Employees taking advantage of a part-time flex option want to grow their skill sets and advance in their careers too. Mentoring programs and opportunities for continuing education are meaningful ways to keep professional development moving forward. Everyone should grasp the importance of proportionality. For people working within a full-time flex model, advancement should continue as for any full-time employee. However, if someone is operating at a seventy-five percent schedule, it's important to realize advancement could take place at a commensurately slower pace (although individual initiative and experience will certainly play a role in this process). Does this mean firms may need to be more thoughtful about how work is assigned? Possibly. Does this mean there is a burden on the person leveraging a flexible strategy to be more strategic and effective? Possibly. But, long term, both of those approaches are better for everyone.

On an ongoing basis, measuring and assessing the impact of these policies assures ongoing learning and improvement; systems must be developed to do just that. Tracking the progress of those using flextime policies and their successes are important. It ensures that they are advancing and garnering the right kind of assignments. Highlighting successes of individuals working within holistic flex strategies should be an ongoing process as well. By doing so, the firm identifies flex role models who can inspire others. Conversely, ongoing evaluation and learning from what is not working helps strengthen policies as they become more tailored to the needs of the firm and its talent. From a quantitative perspective, measuring the overall impact of these policies helps reinforce their continuing value to the firm.

Ultimately, the most successful holistic flexibility options are ones that take into account and support the needs of both the organization and the individual. With thoughtful strategies and committed implementation, a law firm can become a place that supports a range of professional goals for a diverse range of top talent. The cycle this creates over time provides tangible benefits. Attorneys are able to fulfill professional goals while maintaining more control over their days; their commitment to the firm grows, resulting in increased client satisfaction and loyalty; and firms will flourish.

What You Can Do

If your workplace offers a flexibility model, you have a responsibility too. Rather than passively absorbing flexibility offerings, you will benefit most by thinking and prioritizing first. *Taking the time to figure out what you want your life and your career to look like is essential to ending up where you want to be.* Once you have a vision and a framework, you can be more strategic in your choices regarding how to work flexibly: what types of work you take on; how you leverage your time in the office; and how you spend your time working flexibly. Ask yourself, *what is your overall vision of success*? Think from large to small. Define success for every aspect of your life—work, family, health, and professional development. Commit to it. Don't be so concerned with the *how*, and keep your commitment to the vision. So many times, we stop ourselves by thinking "This won't work" or "I have to figure out exactly how this will work." Once you know your vision of success—what your "having it all" looks like—you'll begin to see opportunities across every aspect of your life that will help support that vision. This includes how to effectively use a workplace flexibility model.

People need to have support in their personal life to truly make this approach work. Firms offering flexibility options are opening doors on the work side, but you must be responsible and engaged. Be strategic with what you delegate, how you manage your time, and what you're willing to own versus support. Firm citizenship is still important. Choose to spend your time in a way that is of high impact. Make strategic decisions about work assignments and volunteering for committees within the firm. Maximize the time you are in the office by meeting with partners and associates. Be seen actively seeking the assignments you value most, and actively network—it's *your* responsibility to remain top of mind.

Apply this same thinking to your personal responsibilities. Look for ways to outsource low value/low impact tasks. Being as efficient as possible at work and at home will ensure you can advance more in both areas. Be unapologetic about what is important to you. Take stock of what needs to get done on a daily basis, and define what success looks like for you.

If you know how you want to appear—as a partner, as an attorney, as a citizen of the firm, and as an individual—and if you've defined what success looks like, then you can use that definition to develop a path to what needs to happen to further your overall goals.

Concrete Benefits to Employers of Successful Work-Life Management in the Workplace

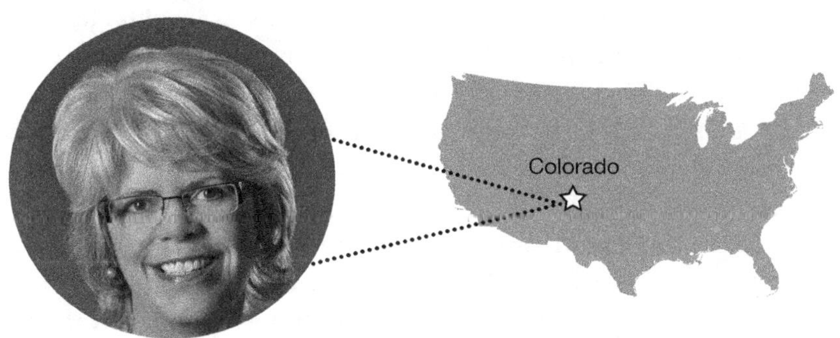

Her Story

Nan E. Joesten

Career

Principal and founder of Rapid Evolution LLC. Executive coach and consultant to law firms and attorneys on accelerating professional development and leadership skills.

Education

University of Colorado Boulder, BS Chemical Engineering; University of California Berkley (Boalt Hall) Law School, JD.

Best Advice

Never stop growing!

Personal

Nan and her husband, Hank, live in the mountains above Boulder, Colorado, where they enjoy backpacking with their dogs, skiing, snowshoeing, and sampling craft beers and red wine with friends.

For more information about Nan

www.Rapidevolutionllc.com

Businesses—including law firms, which are in the business of making money by serving their clients effectively—need to look no further than their bottom line when evaluating what's in it for them to help their attorneys manage how their work fits into their life. Having the ability to hire the right lawyers, who can sustainably deliver ever-increasing value to clients, is invaluable, and a winning combination that is all too difficult for legal service providers to either find, maintain, or both.

Let's start with the premise that the cost to law firms of unwanted attrition is high. A report from the National Association for Law Placement and the Massachusetts Institute of Technology states that half of all attorney departures from law firms are unwanted by those firms.[1] The lost productivity is readily quantifiable. The departing attorney spends substantial time handing off files to others in hopes of creating a smooth transition, and others in the office spend substantial time reassuring clients that there will be no negative repercussions to their matters due to the impending departure and getting the replacement lawyer(s) up to speed on the new projects they will now be handling. The hit to the bottom line of losing a valued attorney skyrockets when adding the cost of having to hire a replacement, when necessary, bringing that new employee or partner up to speed, and integrating him or her into the organization.

Why do lawyers leave? Although many factors contribute to job satisfaction, retention, and career advancement, there is plenty of evidence showing that offering employees strategies to succeed in balancing the demands of a high-stress work environment and avoiding burnout, and a subsequent decision to leave the work setting, are key advantages for employers. Catalyst, the leading nonprofit organization expanding opportunities for women in business, reports that many companies using employee surveys find that work-life balance and flexible work arrangements are extremely important for their employees, particularly

1. Debra Cassens Weiss, *How to Curb the Law Firm Exodus? Study Looks at Traits of Those Most Likely to Leave Law Practice*, ABA JOURNAL (2014), *available at* http://www.abajournal.com/news/article/how_to_curb_the_law_firm_exodus_study_looks_at_traits_of_those_most_likely.

for younger professionals who come into the workforce expecting flexibility as a matter of course.[2] This is confirmed by a study of CPAs at large accounting firms, which showed that the intention to stay with the firm long term was stronger for professionals with a flexible work arrangement than those with a more traditional work schedule.[3] Although it's not always clear what role work-life balance may play in an attorney's decision to move on, or not to join an organization in the first place, data from many large corporations and consulting firms confirms a strong link between workplace flexibility, retention, and the bottom line. For example, Deloitte's implementation of flexible work arrangements saved an estimated $41.6 million in potential turnover-related costs in 2003 that were avoided when employees stayed with the firm.[4] At Bristol-Meyers Squibb, one in five employees hired in the last three years stated that flexibility was a factor in their decision to join the company.[5]

Beyond the generalized data on retention, recruiting, and work-life management, there is another related factor that employers disregard at their peril. To the extent a lack of employer support for work-life management disproportionately affects women, the result is that fewer women will rise up through the organization to take on senior leadership roles. Countless studies show the relative dearth of women equity partners in our country's largest law firms, and the same is true at the general counsel level. The price these institutions pay for the lack of women at the top is not well documented, but there is no reason to think that the proven outcomes in the business world would not be similar in the legal profession. Performance improves when more women lead. A study

---

2. *Benefits of Flexible Work-life Arrangements*, Catalyst (Oct. 14, 2016), *available at* http://www.catalyst.org/knowledge/work-life-prevalence-utilization-and-benefits.
3. Louise E. Single & Elizabeth Dreike Almer, *Research on Women's Advancement in Accounting*, AICPA, at 1, *available at* http://www.aicpa.org/career/womenintheprofession/downloadabledocuments/research%20on%20women%20advancement.pdf.
4. Amy Richman, Arlene Johnson, and Karen Noble, *Business Impacts of Flexibility: An Imperative for Expansion*, WFD Consulting (Feb. 2011), *available at* https://www.wfd.com/PDFS/BusinessImpactsofFlexibility_March2011.pdf, at 10.
5. *Id.*

of the S&P 1,500 companies found that companies in which strategy focused on innovation performed better with female representation in top management.[6] In the world of start-ups, a company's odds for success increase with more female executives at the VP and director levels.[7] There is a clear connection between financial performance and gender diversity on corporate boards. Most recently, Catalyst has shown that companies with sustained high representation of women on their board of directors (defined as at least three women board members in at least four of the prior five years) dramatically delivered better financial results than companies with sustained low representation of women.[8]

A law firm's bottom line is well served by attorneys who are able to successfully manage the demands of their work with the priorities in their personal life. Those individuals tend to have more passion for the workplace and a greater desire to contribute to the overall work environment and morale. The *Harvard Business Review* reports that a survey of 20,000 people at all levels worldwide across a wide array of industries found four core dimensions must be satisfied to create long-term high performance at work: renewal (physical), value (emotional), focus (mental), and meaning and purpose (spiritual).[9] HBR.org pointed out that "when leaders actively support more sustainable ways of working in these four dimensions, the result is a significant positive impact on employees' engagement, stress levels, retention, and job satisfaction."[10] Although that seems intuitively obvious, the surprise is that it was not even necessary to meet every one of the core needs to see

---

6. Cristian Dezső and David Gaddis Ross, *Does Female Representation in Top Management Improve Firm Performance? A Panel Data Investigation*, 33 Strategic Mgmt. J. 2, 1072–89 (Sept. 2012), *available at* https://www0.gsb.columbia.edu/mygsb/faculty/research/pubfiles/3063/female_representation.pdf.
7. Dow Jones and Company, Inc., *Women at the Wheel* (Sept. 2012), *available at* http://www.goldenseeds.com/content/PDFs/WomenPE_report_final.pdf.
8. *Companies With More Women Board Directors Experience Higher Financial Performance, According to Latest Catalyst Bottom Line Report*, *available at* http://www.catalyst.org/media/companies-more-women-board-directors-experience-higher-financial-performance-according-latest.
9. Tony Schwartz & Christine Porath, *The Power of Meeting Your Employees' Needs*, Harvard Business Review at 1 (June 30, 2014), *available at* https://theenergyproject.com/key-ideas.
10. Tony Schwartz & Christine Porath, *Your Boss's Work-Life Balance Matters as Much as Your Own*, Harvard Business Review (July 10, 2014), *available at* https://hbr.org/2014/07/your-bosss-work-life-balance-matters-as-much-as-your-own.

significant improvement. When employees felt that any one of these four needs had been met, they reported a whopping thirty percent higher capacity to focus, almost a fifty percent higher level of engagement, and a sixty-three percent greater likelihood to remain at the company.[11]

Attorneys wish to bring a sharp focus to work that they feel is valued and meaningful, while notoriously struggling to maintain a healthy role for their work within the context of daily life. Client demands often exceed the ability to meet them, and exercise, sleep, and vacation are regularly sacrificed on the altar of client service. Opportunities for relaxation and renewal can be fleeting in a 24/7 world of "always on," but savvy legal organizations recognize the benefits of helping lawyers do just that. In the HBR survey, only twenty percent of the respondents said their supervisors encouraged them to take "renewal breaks" during their workday, but those respondents were fifty percent more engaged, more than twice as likely to stay with their employer, and twice as healthy overall.[12]

To take advantage of the bottom line value achievable by encouraging lawyers to embrace a balanced life, law firms must reexamine the historical billable hour culture in which performance is still measured in large part by the number of hours an attorney logs, rather than by the value those hours create. Consider the typical expectation that an associate attorney should bill at least 1,900 hours annually. If a mythical Big Law attorney actually takes four weeks of vacation and ten holiday days, she must bill an average of forty-one hours in every one of the remaining forty-six weeks of the year, assuming she misses no time for illness, a child's illness, doctor's appointments, or the like. If the attorney is also expected to contribute to nonbillable but necessary activities such as recruiting, mentoring, service on internal firm committees, or business development, it does not take long before another 300 to 500 hours of time is sucked up, especially when including the nonnegotiable need to keep abreast of developments in the attorney's area of expertise. For partners, the numbers are larger still, and it is easy to see why it is difficult to effectively integrate work into one's life when work requires more

11. Schwartz & Porath, note 9, *supra.*
12. *Id.*

than half of an attorney's waking hours, if she can even get a full night's sleep.

Organizations that offer flexible work schedules, reduced-hours opportunities, and support to enhance attorney productivity have the edge when it comes to attracting talent, but only when no stigma is associated with using these programs and they actually work as advertised. A workplace model based on attorneys (mostly men) with caregiver support from stay-at-home spouses is hopelessly outdated because seventy percent of today's children live in homes where both parents work.[13] The millennial generation will soon be the largest share of the U.S. workforce. That demographic reality means that successful legal teams won't be able to *not* hire millennials, and they must adjust to the changing marketplace if they hope to attract the best and brightest attorneys.

More than half of the respondents to the Hartford's 2014 Millennial Leadership Survey identified flexible work schedules as the number one benefit an employer can offer to retain younger employees.[14] Whether that looks like the ability to work remotely one or two days each week, to move to a part-time schedule to accommodate the need to raise children or care for elderly parents (or both!), or to take paternity leave to help care for a newborn, millennials are looking for different ways of integrating work into their lives than their parents did. This is particularly so for two-career couples who see their careers as being equal in priority, as is increasingly common among millennial professionals. Being able to have flexibility in their work, and the time they commit to it, while still advancing over time to positions of greater responsibility, is what many attorneys, especially parents with primary caregiver responsibilities, have been seeking for years. Employers who care about their bottom line will find ways to help the millennials be the generation that actually does it.

---

13. News Release, *Employment Characteristics of Families-2015*, Bureau of Labor Statistics, U.S. Department of Labor, (April 22, 2016), *available at* http://www.bls.gov/news.release/pdf/famee.pdf.
14. The Hartford, *The Future of Leadership By The Numbers*, (2014), *available at* http://www.thehartford.com/sites/thehartford/files/millennial-leadership.pdf.

Moneyball Hiring: A New Paradigm for Finding and Retaining Quality Lawyers

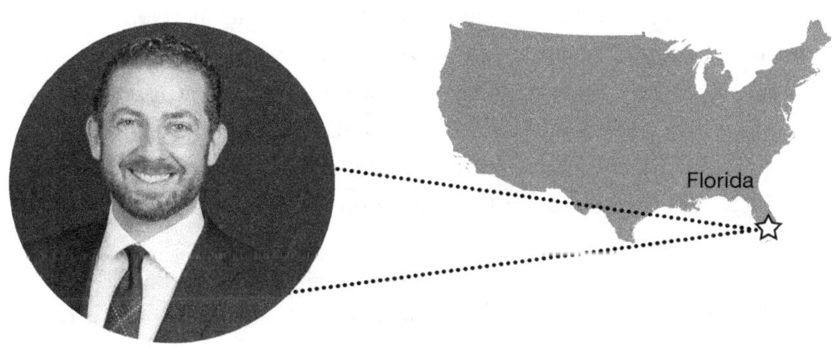

His Story

Joshua Frank

Career

Currently general counsel for Dicom Transportation Group and St. George Logistics. Formerly GC and head of HR for Garda Cash Logistics, and GC for DHL.

Education

University of Pennsylvania, BA (1993); Georgetown University Law Center, JD (1997).

Best Advice

Developing an area of expertise and doing quality work are very important, but it's also necessary to work on your people skills and understand your clients to maximize your value as a trusted advisor.

Personal

Married (eighteen years), three children ages fourteen (boy), twelve (girl), and nine (boy). I enjoy running and crossword puzzles, when not spending time with my family.

I've always loved baseball, so when *Moneyball* was published in 2003, I devoured it. Since then, analysts have attempted to apply the lessons from *Moneyball* to a variety of other contexts, everything from other sports, to sales, to medicine, and, yes, to the legal profession. Even in the articles that reference *Moneyball* and the legal profession, I've never seen *Moneyball* referenced in the context of expanded opportunities for women. Yet *Moneyball* is the best shorthand explanation I can provide whenever the question arises regarding my commitment to sometimes unorthodox hiring practices, and the successful employment relationships and careers that have resulted.

As a brief background, *Moneyball*, written by Michael Lewis, explains the seemingly unlikely success of the Oakland A's, a team with a small fraction of the payroll of the other teams that usually were successful. In a nutshell, the A's general manager (Billy Beane) used statistics different from those that had been used for decades in baseball to find valuable players in the marketplace who were significantly undervalued by other teams. The main reasons the other teams undervalued these players were because of adherence to baseball tradition and the fact that no significant changes or advancement in the statistics teams used or how teams evaluated players had been made in decades.

The legal profession has not significantly changed its hiring criteria or practices in generations. Like the A's in baseball, I've been able to use this to my advantage to find outstanding lawyers that law firms and other in-house legal departments overlook in the hunt for top talent.

A lot of lessons can be, and have been, drawn from *Moneyball*. For me, the most revelatory part of *Moneyball* was the A's ability to draft or trade for players that other teams undervalued. Billy Beane's big realization was that he could use the same information available to everyone, but look at it in a different way, to try to find players who were otherwise being overlooked by every other team in baseball. For example, baseball teams traditionally valued high school players instead of players who went to college, but apparently never analyzed whether high school players were more likely to do better than college players over the span of their respective careers. Beane conducted that analysis and realized that players who played in college were as or more likely to succeed as players who went directly from high school to the pros. Even more ludicrous, baseball scouts focused on "body types" and often looked down on prospects who didn't have traditional athletic builds, discounting them as potential players. Beane was able to use these antiquated notions, and many others, to build a sustainably successful team on a fraction of the budget of the biggest spending team in baseball.

In my career, I haven't worked for the types of companies that lawyers would traditionally aspire to join or for companies in particularly desirable geographic locations. Yet I have been tasked with hiring talented lawyers to come work with me. As I make hiring decisions, I think of companies that most lawyers would want to work for (because of compensation, location, type of industry, career opportunities, etc.) as the equivalent of the Yankees in baseball, who had virtually an unlimited budget to spend on players. I ask myself, how can I compete with these companies for top talent without being able to offer much of what other companies may be able to provide? It would be very difficult for me to try to compete head to head for the same legal talent. Instead, like Billy Beane, I try to find undervalued lawyers in the marketplace who are as good as, or better than, those traditionally evaluated as the best lawyers to hire.

Like baseball's search for talent at the turn of the century, the legal profession has not substantially changed its hiring practices in decades.[1] Applicants try to get into the highest-ranked law school and then work to get the best grades in those schools. This strategy makes sense because almost all of the large law firms that recruit on campus look at GPA (and sometimes law review) as the main point of consideration for potential candidates. Students at top-twenty schools take advantage of "blind" interviews, in which the firms cannot choose who they interview. At most law schools, though, firms preselect the candidates they see based almost exclusively on grades. This all occurs, of course, during the first few

1. This discussion of the legal profession is focused on larger law firms and larger in-house legal departments where these practices are most prevalent and ubiquitous. That said, the same practices are frequently followed to at least some extent throughout all parts of the legal profession. This may explain in part why our profession continues to struggle to keep diverse lawyers in active practice.

weeks (or sometimes before school starts) of the second year of law school, so it is based entirely on grades from the first year of law school. Successful candidates who get jobs at these law firms become summer associates the following summer, and in most cases they are made offers of employment after the summer is complete. In short, this process is based almost entirely on the rank of the school one attends, and one's grades in the first year of law school.

This system gives rise to many questions. Is there really any correlation between one's ability to get top grades in first-year law classes and being a good lawyer? Is there a distinction between transactional lawyers and litigators in which a correlation might exist for one and not the other? Is the perfect combination a candidate from both a top school with top grades, or is it sufficient to have one or the other? If someone has neither of these, is there some other factor that's a great predictor of success, either in the technical aspects of lawyering or in generating business?[2]

Law firms are ready to invest hundreds of thousands of dollars in each potential associate in their firms. Although these firms have the resources to potentially answer many or all of these questions, they continue to blindly ignore trying to figure out the answers to these seemingly relevant questions. It is understandable why firms do this. Like baseball teams historically, selection bias and the availability heuristic have a very strong gravitational pull, especially in the context of difficult decision making.[3]

---

2. Spoiler alert: To the extent people have tried to evaluate these issues, they've found grades to be slightly (at best) correlated with success in firms and overall in legal careers, but many other traits or attributes are much better predictors of success for lawyers coming out of law school. *See, e.g.*, Steve Gibson, William Henderson, Caren Ulrich Stacy, & Chris Zorn, *Moneyball for Law Firms*, AM. LAW DAILY (Oct. 2011), *available at* http://amlawdaily.typepad.com/amlawdaily/2011/10/moneyball-for-law-firms.html.

3. In *Moneyball*, Lewis hypothesized that part of the reason Beane was able to avoid these common pitfalls was because he had been a highly coveted recruit coming out of high school, and gave up an opportunity to go to Stanford to start his professional baseball career. One of the main attributes scouts loved about Beane was his body type—he just "looked" like a star baseball player to them. Despite being a top draft choice, Beane spent very little time in the major leagues, and his career fizzled out after only a few years. So, when scouts talked about preferring high school players to college, or about the importance of body types, as the best criteria to determine successful prospects, Beane knew from personal experience that these criteria were not necessarily good indicators of future success.

A successful partner at a large law firm, or a general counsel, might think to himself, "I went to a top school and got top grades, and I'm successful, and many of my partners have similar backgrounds, so there must be a strong correlation!"

Of course, correlation is not causation, and it ignores the fact that he (and most of his partners) was one of a small fraction of associates who made it through to full partnership at a large firm or who became general counsel of a large company. Moreover, there are a significant number of lawyers who have very successful careers by any measure, who neither attended top-ranked schools nor got good grades in law school, further eroding the strength of the potential correlation.

The statistics on women in the legal profession are atrocious. Almost as many women as men attend and graduate from law school, and women represent almost half of the summer associates and junior associates at firms.[4] Yet women represent only seventeen percent of the equity partners in law firms, and only four percent of managing partners. The in-house statistics are similar: women represent twenty-one percent of the general counsel in the Fortune 500, and only seventeen percent of the general counsel in the Fortune 501–1,000. Women of color are equally underrepresented in both high-level positions in law firms and large companies, especially when compared to their numbers coming out of law school.

These statistics give rise to new questions: Are top law schools doing a poor job of selecting students to attend their schools? Are large law firms only able to make good decisions on candidates for employment with respect to men? What happens to all of the women who go to work at these large firms, are trained by the firms, and then leave? Are they not as good as the lawyers who survive and eventually make partner?[5]

A few years ago I had a problem. My Labor and Employment department desperately needed another lawyer. In the "make vs.

---

4. *See* American Bar Association, *A Current Glance at Women in the Law* (July 2014), *available at* http://www.americanbar.org/content/dam/aba/marketing/women/current_glance_statistics_july2014.authcheckdam.pdf. All statistics in this section are taken from this report unless otherwise noted.

5. The dysfunctionality of law firms is an important topic that should be analyzed; the end result of that dysfunctionality is what is addressed here.

buy" world of in-house legal, we could save the company significant money if we brought someone on board, but we were not sure we needed someone full time and we tried never to overhire.

Around the same time, my daughter was entering elementary school and became fast friends with a girl named Mia. As often happens, my wife and I became friendly with Mia's parents. As it turned out, Mia's mother, Julie, was an employment lawyer working part-time for a local company on an "as needed" basis. Soon thereafter, Julie told my wife that there was a new general counsel at her company who did not like Julie's arrangement, and, as a result, Julie was looking for somewhere else to work. Julie asked my wife, "Where am I going to find a company that allows me to work a completely flexible schedule on a part-time basis?" My wife asked me if my company might be interested, and I brought Julie on board soon thereafter. Because of her desire to work a flexible schedule, we paid Julie hourly. She was thrilled to have a job that allowed her the flexibility she desired, and we were thrilled to find a top-shelf lawyer to handle all of our overflow work in the employment area. Needless to say, the arrangement has worked out fantastically both for the company and for Julie.

When people ask me how they can find someone like Julie, I jokingly say, "at the elementary school carpool line," which is only a slight exaggeration. After attending a top law school, Julie went to work as an associate at one of the bigger firms in her city. When she wanted to start a family, the firm was completely inflexible about her desire to take time off and potentially work part time thereafter, so Julie eventually found a local company to take her on a part-time basis. This was a *Moneyball* moment—a well-trained lawyer looking for work but unable to find a traditional job because of her desire for a flexible schedule.

Over the last few years, several other situations have occurred in which my department has accommodated a lawyer's personal situation to allow him or her to work for my company, and in the end, the company has benefited tremendously. One lawyer could not move when the company moved its headquarters, and we allowed her to stay in her preferred geography. Another lawyer needed to move away from headquarters for personal reasons, and we were able to accommodate him as well. There is a lawyer who is going through a difficult divorce involving child custody issues, so she cannot travel even though her role would normally include some travel. We've had a lawyer who needed to work from home a couple of days a week, which we were able to easily accommodate. Another lawyer, with a special needs child, asked to work part of the year in another country where she could get her child specialized care for his condition. We have accommodated all of these requests.

To be clear, the success rate I've had with the lawyers described above has been 100 percent; they have all been able to meet (and usually exceed) the demands of their jobs and to manage their personal issues as well. They are loyal, committed, show a strong work ethic, and have a desire to do great work. These are all of the best characteristics that managers hope to find in their employees. Not surprisingly, all of the lawyers described above went to good schools, were hired and trained by big law firms, and are appreciative of the opportunity to do meaningful work despite their "limitations," whether geographic or temporal.

I also want to mention the importance of technology in this discussion. Advancements over the last five to ten years have made it easier than ever for people to work from anywhere, at the hours most convenient to them, and still be able to do the highest quality work. Whatever "rules" may have existed for a successful lawyer more than ten years ago should be tossed; ubiquitous high-speed WiFi, smartphones, video chats, home printers and scanners, and the like have made physical presence in an office as unnecessary as it has ever been. This makes the statistics cited above even more distressing because it should be easier than ever for law firms and large companies to accommodate lawyers who do not have the desire or the ability to do face time in the office. If you have good people who are self-motivated, and you trust them, there is no reason in this day and age for them to be physically present to be key contributors to a firm or in-house legal department.

Personal obligations outside of work may limit a lawyer's time in the office, hours or days he or she can work, or ability to travel. Sometimes these limitations mean that those lawyers are not considered for jobs for which they are otherwise eminently qualified. Like the overlooked prospects in *Moneyball*, these lawyers are everywhere, looking for a great work environment that will allow them to use the skills they spent years learning without sacrificing their personal lives. Yet the more I speak to people on this topic, the clearer it becomes that most law firms and in-house legal departments have not figured out how to successfully integrate these types of lawyers into their practices. This is as much, if not more, the firms' and companies' losses as it is of the lawyers, because my experience is that lawyers like these succeed if we are willing to be a little flexible, think outside the box on what defines an actual job requirement, and make a real effort to look for nontraditional candidates in nontraditional places.

If someone asks why a certain process or policy exists, it is an axiom in most organizations that the worst answer is "because that's the way it's always been done." Yet that seems to be the overriding reason hiring and retention practices in the legal profession haven't substantially changed in decades, despite advancements in data analysis and technology, and despite the fact that there is little to no correlation between the current system and maximizing the potential of the largest number of lawyers to have successful careers in the long term. Law firms are wasting tens of millions of dollars in the aggregate, training lawyers who may never be able to fully utilize the skills they are learning; and both firms and in-house legal departments are potentially missing out on incredibly talented lawyers, all because of strict adherence to an antiquated system.

As millennials become a larger segment of the working population of lawyers, they are looking for a better balance in their lives between work and personal time. Although the unorthodox *Moneyball* approach I have taken to hiring and retention has mostly, though not exclusively, benefited female lawyers,[6] this approach will in the end benefit everyone—men and women, lawyers of color,[7] and countless others who may otherwise not

6. In point of fact, my companies have actually benefited as much or more from this approach.

7. Studies have shown that both women and lawyers of color (both men and women) have a higher likelihood of having obligations outside of work that may inhibit their ability to work in a traditional way.

continue to practice law because of the arbitrary restrictions the profession often puts on how lawyers practice their profession. The firms and companies that learn this lesson sooner rather than later, like the A's in baseball at the turn of the century, will have a decided advantage in the war for talent for years to come.

REFLECTIONS

1. Does your firm offer flexible work options? If so, are these policies supported by the management and ingrained in the firm's culture?
2. What policy do you wish your firm would change to be more accommodating of both junior and senior lawyers who seek improvements in their quality of life? What is the best argument that the firm should adopt such a policy to improve its bottom line?
3. Have you found that flexibility in the workplace encouraged you to remain at the firm in a particular difficult time? How has it helped you?
4. Did flexibility affect your decision to join, stay, or leave a firm? Have you noticed colleagues leaving either the firm or the legal profession due to a lack of flexibility?
5. Does flexibility play a role in recruitment at your firm? How so? If not, do you think it would help in recruitment or retention of highly qualified attorneys?
6. How can and should millennials balance expression of their values (importance of work-life balance, etc.) with the values that law firms seem to project regarding the importance of the billable hour and face time? Are some strategies employed by millennials likely to be more successful than others as they advocate for workplaces that better meet their needs?
7. Are you a millennial? Do you identify with the authors' comments regarding millennials and the importance of quality of life as a priority?
8. Have you found that the issues concerning quality of life and being present for life outside of the office are not necessarily gender specific but are shared by your millennial male colleagues as well?

2

PREPARING FOR THE LONG ROAD AHEAD

Redefining Balancing versus Managing and Developing a Plan for Success

Introduction

The phrase "work-life balance" has been around for decades. As Anne Marie Seibel learned and suggests, "to succeed long-term you must banish all visions of balancing" and instead "consider yourself a 'manager.'" Being an effective manager includes defining what success means to you and developing a deliberate plan to achieve it. Mother Teresa noted: "Yesterday is gone. Tomorrow has not yet come. We have only today. Let us begin." It is, therefore, critical to pay attention to the marching of time and to plan where you are going and how you plan on getting there. The essays in this chapter explore the individualized nature of the term *success* and provide stories and advice for developing goals, creating a plan, and maintaining perspective.

Balance versus Management: Redefining the Interplay between Work and Life

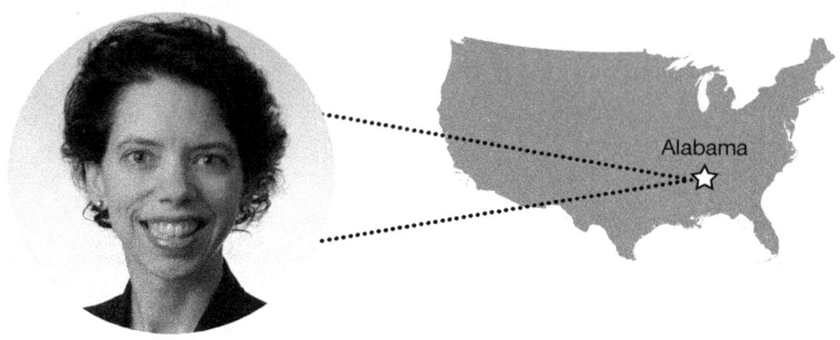

Her Story

Anne Marie Seibel

Career

Complex litigation partner at Bradley Arant Boult Cummings LLP in multiforum and multiplaintiff litigation.

Education

University of Virginia, BA; Bonn University, Fellowship; Vanderbilt University, JD.

Best Advice

Anticipate the needs of the partners and clients with whom you work and always keep them updated regarding their cases. When they wake up in the middle of the night worrying about their cases, you never want them worrying about what is on your plate.

Personal

Anne Marie and her husband, a research physician, have two children.

For more information about Anne

www.bradley.com

Busy job, busy family, and busy mind. What is a busy female lawyer to do? Popular culture would suggest that you must become an expert in "balancing." What are the first images that are summoned at the idea of "balancing"? A tightrope walker, someone teetering on a seesaw, a magician straining to keep spinning plates from falling off, a mom holding a baby in one hand with a computer in the other, or lady justice trying in vain to prevent the scales from tipping? With those as your goals, you are bound to feel as if you are perpetually failing—and no wonder. If one grain of sand on one side of the scale can tip the scales and one missed step can send you falling off the tightrope, you are constantly on alert to fail miserably at any moment.

As I learned from my dear friend Paula Hinton, to succeed long-term you must banish all visions of balancing. We put enough pressure on ourselves each day; there is no need to exacerbate the challenges by setting unattainable goals. There is a much better way to view these daily challenges—consider yourself a "manager." Managing requires assigning limited resources to competing projects. Resources include your time, energy, money, and support network. The challenge of allocating resources is the same challenge you face in law practice; thus you know how to do it already.

The good news is that you likely already are managing your life—it is just that you are being told you need to "balance," not manage. Examples of evaluating difficult options and managing toward an end are all around us. It is curious that management is ubiquitous in the professional world, but the concept of balancing is reserved for working mothers. The coach who substitutes a rookie for an injured player isn't accused of failing to balance the goal of winning the game with the need to respect the veteran's health. Rather, he is respected for making a decision as a manager. The same goes for a lawyer making tough decisions about which potential jurors to strike. There's no expectation that the result will be a perfectly balanced jury. Rather, the goal is to manage to make the best decisions given the options at hand. There is no good reason that it is only for working women that we set "balance" as an unattainable goal.

What does changing the dialogue from *balance* to *management* mean in practice? First, stop spending energy trying to walk a tightrope between your home and work obligations; rather, spend time allocating the available resources to cover the responsibilities you have. By doing this, you are better able to immerse yourself in the task at hand, knowing that other responsibilities are in other good hands.

Rather than focusing all of your effort on staying perfectly balanced at every moment, consider your path forward as a long-term effort you can manage. You don't have to achieve everything at once. There's no specific timetable by which you have to achieve anything. I've seen how hard this is, in particular for high-achieving women. These women are used to being at the top of their class with the sky being the limit. It is not easy to get out of the mind-set that you must do what you did in school—rise to the top, move up with your class, and get good grades. In private law practice, that often means moving up to partnership ranks and equating good grades with compensation. With time, however, you will see that you don't have to progress along that path to succeed. In contrast, there are as many different definitions and paths to success as there are lawyers. Here, the most challenging management comes into play: managing your own expectations and developing reasonable definitions of success. This is a challenge, and one I'm still tackling, but it is worth the effort.

Not surprisingly, one of the important management tasks comes in relationship to having children. For many, this is the first time they are faced with true competition for their professional ambitions. It is challenging to grasp the reality of what it means to undergo a physical change that requires diversion of time and effort from professional goals. This may be the first time for many women when being a woman has put a limit on what she can achieve. Often this comes at a time when career opportunities are also opening up. It is naturally difficult to think about any opportunity at work passing you by when you are focused on becoming a mother. This feeling is heightened by the image of stepping on an out-of-balance seesaw that has "mother" on one side and "career" on the other. As opposed to this counterproductive imagery, consider a conductor asking the wind section to play more loudly while the strings provide the background. All you are doing is adjusting the mix at any given point in time. It doesn't prevent the symphony from being beautiful in the end. It is easier to see motherhood as a decision to reallocate resources if you aren't looking at the opportunities you have over the next three months but rather at what you want to achieve over a long career. Over that longer time span, it doesn't matter if the guy down the hall gets a few more opportunities while you are out on leave. If you only focus on the short term, however, those trade-offs cut harder. The challenge is to let go of the constant drive to be number one "right now" and focus on what you want to achieve in the long term.

Having children also provides a crash course in managing the unexpected. The phone rings, and the baby is sick at school. Or you've packed up and are ready to pick up the children, and the phone rings with a client emergency. If you consider this development as causing a scale to tip very far in one direction, everything is off balance. Instead, instantly turn on your management skills, surveying the options for picking up the baby, covering your day's calls, and planning for the next day at home. Your ability to handle these surprises will increase over time as you learn that there isn't a single perfect management solution. You need to survey your options quickly: Who other than you can handle the work issue? Who else is available to pick up the baby? Once you've evaluated these options, you make the best decision available to you at that time on the facts presented. Sound familiar? Sure, this is what you do every day as a lawyer.

As with any good manager, selecting the team is important. Over the years, my colleagues and I have watched many promising lawyers decide that things were too off balance to continue pursuing their professional goals. We've become pretty adept at predicting the course. The primary factor that we've identified in staying in the game is choosing a spouse or partner who is a co-manager instead of a hindrance bouncing on the other end of the seesaw knocking you off balance. This can present itself in micro and macro ways. If you and your spouse or partner both work full-time and all of the daily grind at home falls to you, it is an impediment to managing competing demands. In some cases, the pressures are worse, as when a partner notes, "if you didn't work, we could have a home cooked meal every evening." Coming home to guilt for pursuing your professional goals is a surefire way for those professional goals to fall to the wayside. And that guilt only multiplies when you have a child.

In contrast, finding a true partner in management can make all the difference. For example, one successful professional recently told me that one of the most important phrases her partner uttered was "what are *we* going to do for dinner?" That's a simple example of how being a "we" can take the pressure off. Practically, when you are running through the options when the baby is sick and the deadlines are pressing, it helps when your partner is a viable option to step in on the home front. Perhaps more critically, on the inevitable day(s) when work and home obligations collide to such an extent that you want to give up, what you need is a partner who asks what can be taken off your hands and reminds you of the professional satisfaction you ultimately get from work. Those days will come. If the test is whether you are staying balanced, you'll always fail. If the test, however, is whether you can manage through it, you can pass. You won't always get an A+, but passing is what matters.

Of course, your chances of managing successfully improve in a work environment in which some semblance of respect exists for life outside of work. The unpredictability of life and law practice is a given. Those in your work environment, however, should be part of your team. I always tell our young associates to look around them and get to know their colleagues. I am eternally thankful to have colleagues on whom I have called in moments of life emergencies and who have immediately taken every work-related item off my plate. I am equally grateful for the times when work colleagues have stepped in and helped with home responsibilities during a work crisis. That support system is a necessity. But it is worthless if you aren't willing to use it; if you aren't willing to ask for help, you aren't managing.

It is also important to recognize that building that support system requires some amount of vulnerability about the demands on your time and the willingness to make hard calls in managing your responsibilities. It also requires respect for the fact that obligations and schedules (both yours and your colleagues) change over time. For example, when I was a young associate with limited home responsibilities, I could arrive early and would stay late when my medical resident husband was on call. When I first had children, my work schedule needed to shift to fit the day care schedule. I also carved out time midday to nurse the baby at lunch. Once the children were in school, I had to give up the early mornings at work in favor of drop off for school. It was difficult for me to adjust to arriving at work only to find others thinking that I had been sleeping in while they had been hard at work. As I became more confident in my role at work, I was more willing to disclose the hard work I had been doing in the hours between waking and reaching my desk. The tendency to isolate work and home as two worlds to be balanced separately is less productive than integrating the two so that there is a healthy respect for your responsibilities in each.

Finally, develop genuine networks of support—not comparison. Women lawyers are notorious for beating themselves up for not being able to give 110 percent to all efforts at all times. One may think she is failing because the woman down the hall has more trial experience. That woman may think she is failing because trial took her away from her children. Such comparisons are not productive, and they feed the notion of unattainable balance in contrast to management of a long-term plan. I've found it helpful to interact with professional women of varied life experience and age. Speaking to teachers or others with very rigid schedules, for example, helps you appreciate the flexibility inherent in everyday law practice. It is likewise helpful to learn from women whose children are grown. They will tell you about the benefits their children believe they received from being in a household with a working mother. You'll also hear the challenges faced by those without a career when their children went away to college. It is from those mentors that I have learned to appreciate management of a career over the long term. In contrast, if you only speak to women who are going through the same life stages you are, you don't receive this benefit.

Whatever you do, be a force of change. Don't ask others how they are balancing work and home. When they ask how you are balancing it all, be sure to answer, "I'm managing just fine, thank you."

You've Got to Have a Plan

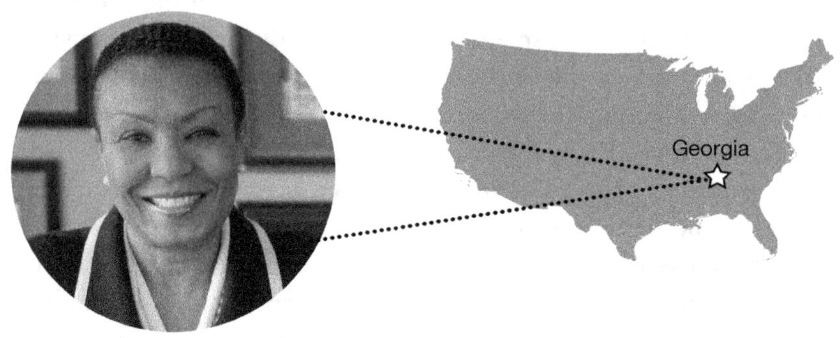

Her Story

Chief Justice Leah Ward Sears (Ret.)

Career

Partner at Schiff Hardin LLP, where I lead the law firm's Appellate Group.

Education

Cornell University, BS; Emory University School of Law, JD; University of Virginia School of Law, Appellate Judicial Process.

Best Advice

You can do anything you set your mind to do. You just have to do it.

Personal

Married (eighteen years), with two adult children.

For more information about Justice Leah Ward Sears

www.schiffhardin.com

"A goal without a plan is just a wish."
—Antoine de Saint-Exupéry

People often ask me how they can achieve the perfect "work-life balance." I always wonder if people realize the right work-life balance is very personal and is unique to the seeker. There is no uniform answer to balancing your professional and personal life. However, in my personal experience, achieving an acceptable work-life balance required me to prioritize and have a plan. Having become a Georgia Supreme Court Justice at the age of thirty-six—the first woman and second African American on the court—some may say I have achieved success. However, my path has not been an easy one. Early on, I dreamed and planned on being a super lawyer, kind of like Linda Carter as Wonder Woman, but with the partner power suit as my costume and well-presented oral arguments as my weapons. Happily, for the most part, I have achieved my goals. But what people rarely see is the hard work it took for me to get here and the various tilts in my work-life balance. I can honestly say I did not get where I am by a series of serendipitous events or perfect moments. Like most women in the legal field, I've had to work hard to be considered a serious contender. No matter what I accomplished, it was always the result of having a plan.

Living in Savannah, Georgia, during my formative years and yearning for the freedom to be an adult, I crafted a plan to work and study hard to enter college early. I applied myself, took extra courses, and applied to Cornell University when I was just seventeen. At Cornell, I took classes and joined certain groups in anticipation of law school. I sacrificed and studied when others were going out. I was deliberate in choosing friends; limiting myself to those who were thinkers and pushing the envelope on intellectual stimulation. I prepared as much as I possibly could for law school with a solid educational foundation and an established quest to learn more.

Although I planned to enter law school immediately after undergrad, I quickly discovered that life doesn't always go according to plan. I didn't plan on love happening and throwing me a bit off track in my well-thought-out quest to become an attorney.

Newly married, I took a slight detour and worked as a newspaper reporter to support my husband in his blossoming career as a 1st Lieutenant in the U.S. Army. This detour took me to live in places that I didn't expect, but it was also a blessing because it reminded me that even though I had fallen in love and gotten married young, I still could not ignore my dream of becoming an attorney and all of the planning I had done to realize that dream. When my husband was transferred to Atlanta, at the first practical moment I entered Duke University School of Law and then Emory School of Law. Balancing school and a new marriage was incredibly hard, but I was determined to work my plan and excel in law school. I approached law school with such fervor that it became a type of therapy for me to do well. When I graduated and was one of the select few to be offered a job at a big Atlanta law firm, I knew it was the result of diligent planning and hard work.

When I started working in Big Law, my plan was to move up the ranks quickly, which I knew would not be easy for an African American woman. If I applied the same equation of hard work and deliberate action, I thought I could eventually become the Wonder Woman of law I had dreamt about. However, life intervened yet again, and I had to reevaluate my plan.

During my time as an associate, I made the unbelievable decision to have a child (gasp). Believe me, during those times, women in the legal field didn't dare wear pants or even mention children. The plight of being a woman lawyer was all very draconian in the late 1970s and early 1980s. One day my child, as all children predictably do, fell ill. This illness wasn't just a runny nose or a fever from teething; this illness landed my six-month-old son in the hospital. As an associate at a large law firm, I didn't think I could just up and leave. I had to finish my work and make sure my partners had what they needed before I left. While my husband stood guard at our child's bedside, I was finishing cite checks and briefs. It was a fact of life that went with my plan. But when I saw my son in that hospital bed with IV tubes inserted in the side of his head, I knew the personal life I wanted was not possible with the legal career I planned. In that moment I decided to make a change.

I suppose that is a part of life's beauty. One day you are headed in one direction, but life's twists and turns lead you down another path to a completely different kind of happiness. As soon as my son recovered, I went back to the drawing board and started researching other careers in the legal profession that would allow me to reach my legal pinnacle without sacrificing my family in the process. I quickly figured out that becoming a government lawyer, specifically a judge, would be most beneficial to my family and my plan. Once I determined my goal, I created a plan. I started working on political campaigns and put myself in the path of people who made judicial nomination and appointment decisions. I established organizations, took up causes, networked until my face hurt from smiling, and put my name and a good work product out there until I was recognizable. I was appointed to my first judicial seat at just twenty-seven years old, not through a series of fortuitous events but through solid proper planning. I haven't looked back since.

Some may think that once I became a judge I stopped planning because I had reached my goal. But the reality is that once you reach your goal, you realize there are greater possibilities. So I got a new dream. I decided to leave the city court bench and run for a superior court seat, a higher court. For those of you who haven't run in an election, believe me, it requires planning beyond any planning that has ever come before. I mapped out a plan to visit certain churches, communities, local fairs, and anything that would make an impact in between. And through that strategic planning, I won my election.

Once I was on the Supreme Court of Georgia, I didn't stop planning there either. I worked hard to build relationships with my colleagues to try to get them to see my way on a particular case. Building those personal relationships and working hard to draft solid opinions got me to the seat as Chief Justice. Even now, in private practice, getting here was the result of a new dream and even more planning. As the coordinating partner for the Atlanta law office of Schiff Hardin LLP, I have plans to make a great impact here.

For women just starting out in the legal field, or for those who have been around for a while and are searching to make a new mark, I offer the following advice: Don't expect your dreams to fall in your lap. Always set a goal, and then create an action plan to achieve that goal. In other words, be deliberate!

I have learned that it is important in this ever-changing legal field, filled with high demands, to remember that we arrived where we are with a plan, and at no time is it smart to drift away from some kind of plan. You see, things rarely happen by happenstance. Even though not everything gained is always earned, everything earned is almost always a result of a deliberate plan. So how do you plan?

First, have a dream. Your dream should be something that excites you, propels you forward, makes you feel magical, and makes long hours and sleepless nights worth the effort. Your dream should not be something that was given to you by someone else or a preordained path for your life. Your dream has to be a reflection of you, what makes you tick, and your ideas for the life you wish to lead. The beauty of a dream is that you are never too old to construct one and decide to follow its path. Your dream may make you change practice areas or fields. It's up to you to follow it. The road to success begins with a dream, a desire, a vision in your mind that you can see. It's your dream! But a dream will not turn into reality on its own.

Second, have a vision of the dream you want to achieve and how you want it to look. That isn't to say that once you are there it will look the way you envisioned it, but you will at least be in the place of which you once dreamed. Your vision should be an image you can see coming together when you close your eyes. Once that vision is in your head, you have to see it over and over again so that you have a tangible plan to work toward in your life.

Third, have an actual plan. Your plan should include markers and targets that you will hit once you get to a certain point. It should be a road map that guides you along your way. Your plan should be so deliberate that it includes the events you will attend to network and make an impact, and the types of jobs you will take to get you to the next level. Your plan should be flexible and fluid enough to adapt to life's curves. But no matter what happens, your plan should always be somewhere in the execution stage. There shouldn't be a moment when your plan stands still or is stale. Plans should always be in motion.

A plan is the road map that will take you to personal success, so treat it like one. Seriously, don't be too lazy to create a plan. Put in the effort required, and do not stop until it is complete. Purpose and desire get you started; a plan keeps you going on the right path. If you do not currently have a plan to accomplish your goal, then sit down and write one. Look at it daily. Do not set it aside and forget about the plan. Most of all, it should be thoughtfully designed to ensure personal growth and to make your dream become a reality.

Remember that your plans should be flexible enough to allow for changes along the way but rigid enough to help you weather the storms life throws at you. When you change your plan in your mind, change it in your document, and start working the revised plan. Most important, see the plan through to its end. When you get to the end, if you have planned diligently, chances are good that your dream will be a reality.

I have two adult children who are millennials. I am amused that millennials are often referred to as floaters or wistful thinking loafers. My children have found happiness in careers I would not have thought of, and they aren't as tied to "forever" as my generation was, but they too, and likely their entire generation, do have plans. It's just that their plans don't look like the plans of previous generations. And that's okay. Even if people in their generation don't plan on working for nine years at the same firm before they make partner, it doesn't mean they won't one day be the partner they plan to become. We can all learn from their ingenuity in making short-term plans for a long-term goal. Consider adding this ingenuity in your own planning.

Most important, I am a spiritual person, and I know I wouldn't be where I am without God's purpose for my life. But I also know that God didn't put me here just to take up space. My life is the single biggest gift I've ever gotten, and I know it is incumbent upon me to do my best with what I've been given. That's what I urge you to keep in mind as you make your plans. Plan on being the best at whatever you choose. I do, because ultimately when my life ends I want to stand before God and echo Erma Bombeck saying, "I used everything you gave me." See? I even have a plan on what to tell God.

Developing Goals That Matter, Both Professionally and Personally

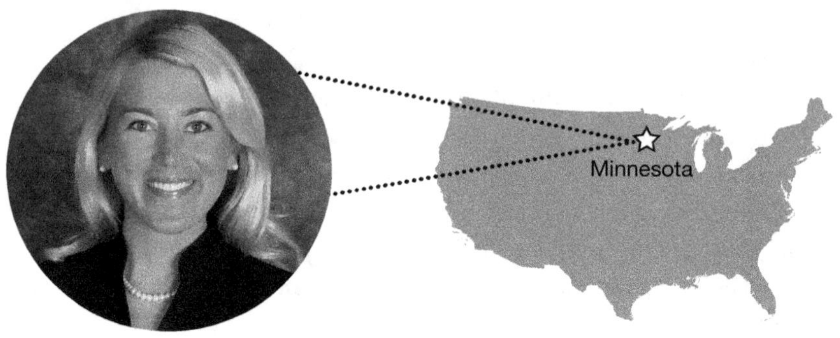

Her Story

Amber N. Garry

Career

Shareholder at Lind, Jensen, Sullivan & Peterson, representing health care providers in a variety of matters.

Education

University of Wisconsin-River Falls, BA; Hamline University School of Law, JD, *summa cum laude.*

Best Advice

Realize that there is no such thing as perfect balance. There will be times when your work requires your focus and you may miss out on personal activities. There will also be times when personal matters need your full devotion and your work will not come first.

Personal

Married (six years) with three-year-old twin girls.

For more information about Amber

www.lindjensen.com/attorney/amber-nicolle-garry

> *"There is no such thing as work-life balance. Everything worth fighting for imbalances your life."*
>
> —Alain de Botton

> *"It is a mistake to look too far ahead. Only one link in the chain of destiny can be grasped at a time."*
>
> —Sir Winston Churchill

Much about our professional lives as lawyers can feel out of our control: court schedules, the demands of the workplace, and the constant grind of networking and professional development. It is easy to lose sight of what matters in both the little and big pictures. Personal and professional goals can pile up without receiving the necessary attention, leaving one feeling rather lackluster about one's ability to prioritize. It is possible to make time for personal and professional goals, but making that time can be challenging. It is time worth making—the sense of accomplishment, the building of skills, and the occasional reprieve for oneself make it all worthwhile.

As the mother of three-year-old twins and a lawyer with a litigation practice, sometimes the treadmill of life seems just like that—a conveyor belt of "to-dos." I find it important to focus on goals that truly matter both personally and professionally in order to give maximum effort when and where it is needed. I am a list maker, but being a juggler of multiple and sometimes competing priorities does not come so naturally to me.

Focusing on the task or goal ahead can be a great way to combat the feeling that you are drowning in a sea of never-ending tasks, expectations, and poorly defined goals. Here are some general tips and thoughts that I have found helpful. Perhaps you will too. I urge you to take what is helpful and leave what is not.

Be Present and Be Focused

Select personal and professional goals that are important to you, and identify why they are important. After my girls were born, I decided to stay committed to a career in litigation. I also decided to continue my personal hobby of running marathons. It would have been easy to put either or both of these on the back shelf for a few years, but why? There may be days or weeks or moments when I have felt overwhelmed and certainly stressed out, but I have gained purpose, confidence, and so much more from both aspects of my life. This has meant many early mornings and regular self-reflection as to what I am doing and why, but I have not regretted a single moment of pursuing personal or professional endeavors. Look at your calendar, decide what you need to focus your efforts on, and go for it.

Choose Carefully

I find it best to realize that I cannot possibly do everything, so it is important to choose goals with care. I know some lawyers who aim to attend one (or more) networking event(s) each week. For me, this just is not possible without leaving my family in the lurch, so I have chosen to aim for two each month. Likewise, as many runners know, signing up for another marathon is often a side effect of running your first (or second, or third, or tenth) marathon. Because my personal and professional schedule would probably burst if I did a spring and fall marathon, I limit myself to one in the spring or one in the fall.

Accept Imbalance

Although I do think a general level of work-life balance can be achieved through constant effort, it is probably best to accept that there will be times of imbalance, and that is okay. As Alain de Botton noted, "There is no such thing as work-life balance. Everything worth fighting for imbalances your life." Growth comes from being out of your comfort zone. There will be times when work takes the front seat. There will be times when personal commitments take the front seat. It's okay. I try to do my best to notify my husband in advance if I have a busy period on the horizon at work so he can hunker down and take over more household responsibilities. Likewise, if you have an important personal commitment that is going to make you less available at work, keep those who need to know in the loop.

Don't Underestimate the Impact That Achieving a Goal in One Area of Your Life May Have on Another

If you have overcome something or accomplished something in your personal life, it can have a huge impact on your confidence and abilities in the professional arena. Although I have sarcastically stated that the law is a profession where no one listens until you are a male or you have at least half a head of gray hair, I remind myself when I walk into a courtroom or room—"Hey, I manage twins every day, I can manage this." or "Hey, I've run two marathons in six days, I have the stamina to do this." Of course I'm just trying to build up my confidence, but it can be helpful. Likewise, when you're chasing your significant other or children around, don't forget the importance of the work you do. We are not our work, but our work does matter a lot to who we are.

Remember Why It Matters

In my life, one of the reasons I have chosen to pursue a career and to continue running is because I have little girls. I want to do my very best while I have the time and capacity to show them they can do whatever they want to do. My own mother was recently diagnosed with Alzheimer's disease at age sixty-five, and I have felt more compelled to do what I can while I can do it. This won't be the same for everyone. Your circumstances may lead you to a different conclusion, but reflecting on the "why" of your goals can make a difference in moments of doubt.

Self-Defined Success

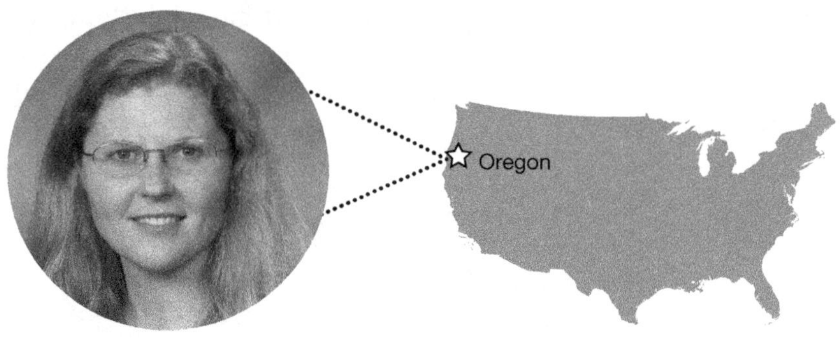

Her Story

Heather J. Van Meter

Career

Senior assistant attorney general, Oregon Department of Justice, civil litigation defense (civil rights, torts, employment, contracts, statutory claims), and adjunct professor at Willamette University.

Education

University of California, San Diego, BA; Willamette University, JD, MBA; University of Oxford, MS; University of Birmingham, PhD (candidate).

Best Advice

My recipe for success in all endeavors: work hard, do good work, be good to all people, be honest with everyone including yourself.

Personal

Happily divorced with two children just starting school.

For more information about Heather

www.linkedin.com/in/heather-j-van-meter-59179027

Women born around the 1970s will remember the jingle, "I can bring home the bacon, fry it up in a pan, and never let you forget you're a man." This was the era I was born into. Women's liberation from the home was a given, and expectations were high for the first postliberation generation of women. College was a must; postgraduate education and professional success were mainstream middle-class goals. Once at work, we were simultaneously expected to be likeable but tough as nails, be a bulldog but gentle, be smart but not too smart, look strong but not manly, and be aggressive but pleasant. We were to be just as pitch perfect at home. In short, the expectations were to bring home the bacon, fry it up, and keep "your man" happy. Many of us adopted these expectations as our own set of goals, falling over ourselves to simultaneously accomplish polar opposites—like trying to freeze fire. In hindsight, of course, these were impossible demands.

As a female lawyer and civil trial attorney, I spent the early years of my career vacillating between confidence and despair: a layoff here, a trial victory there, a promotion here, a verbally abusive partner there. One male partner was an amazing mentor and another groped my leg during a law firm dinner. One female partner was a terrific role model and another punished the women attorneys around her thinking it would make them stronger, better lawyers. I often walked into courtrooms as the only female except the court reporter and was asked more times than I can count if I was the court reporter. All the while, I tried to meet everyone else's expectations and make everyone else happy. But this was not always making me particularly happy. On more than one occasion, I vowed to quit law entirely.

But I stuck with it, I was not raised to be a quitter; after all, how could the first Title IX generation be quitters? We were to be superwomen, nothing less. Too many women left the ranks of trial lawyers; we needed some to break through the glass ceilings. The challenges of being a female trial attorney were just that—challenges to be conquered. I powered through, working late hours, marketing around the country, volunteering for various organizations, working toward becoming partner, and attempting to have a happy social and family life. Seventy- and eighty-hour weeks were not uncommon, just as they were not uncommon for my working mother and my small-business-owning grandmothers before me. I enjoyed the hard work; it gave me a sense of purpose and accomplishment.

Several years into my career, I finally seemed to grow up and hit my stride. I knew a lot about what I was doing and was on track to become partner. More important, I embraced being a successful lawyer as *my own personal goal*, not a goal imposed on me by my family, society, or the era in which I was born. I finally realized that I remained a lawyer not because it was expected but because I loved the law itself. I did not always love the people working in the law, and I learned to steer clear of or work around difficult people. I did not always love my cases, but I kept a positive attitude most of the time and looked for the bright side of the mundane or difficult cases. I did love learning new things: facts about cases or clients during site visits, details about people and personality types in depositions, and the variations of the law itself. As I became comfortable in the areas of law in which I worked, I loved the law and learning so much that I sought out education in new areas of law completely unrelated to my work. It took several years, but I was finally "comfortable in my own skin" as a lawyer and embraced the confidence that came with that comfort. I became a partner in my law firm, but more important, I was a "successful" lawyer in my own mind because I was happily a lawyer and chose the profession for myself.

Naturally, around the same time my career was solidly on track, my home life fell apart. I had two beautiful, long-awaited children but a train wreck of a marriage. I was bringing home the bacon and frying it up, but it wasn't enough. Although I was not raised to be a quitter, divorce was the best, really the only, option. Once again, I needed to redefine success *for myself*, not define success in the manner of my family or society. I considered what was truly important to me—being a good lawyer and a good mother—and realized that I could not do those things within my marriage. So began yet another new chapter of life. Many of the same self-doubts I felt as a young lawyer crept into my new role as a single mother. But by now I knew I could overcome these self-doubts and rise to the occasion on my own terms based on what was important to me. Years of hard work as a female trial lawyer taught me that

I could accomplish difficult tasks and gave me the confidence to take them on.

Today, I no longer impose on myself the need to bring home the bacon, fry it up, and keep a Stepford-style home life. Success to me now means simply doing the very best work I can as a trial lawyer during the day, then being the very best mother I can be in the evenings and nights. It is not always easy, but it is always fulfilling to me. I learned from my children that living in the moment makes the best moments in life. I learned for myself that setting my own goals and defining success my own way are the keys to my own happiness. Not coincidentally, I am now a happy working trial lawyer mom.

Defining what success means *to you* is the key. The postliberation era did not produce quitters. If you attend law school and do not become a practicing lawyer, it's okay to do something else with your law degree. If you are a lawyer but don't like what you are doing, it's okay to find a different job. If you are a lawyer but want to stay home and raise children, it's definitely okay to do that too. And if you are a woman trial attorney and you take a few knocks but stick with it, that's definitely okay, and there are more than a few of us here to cheer you on. Do not feel pressured into career choices by external forces. As long as you are defining success for yourself, on your own terms, it's okay. And your definition of personal success may very well change over the years. At twenty, I wanted to save the earth and the world. I still want to help save the earth and promote world peace, but "success" is much more tangible and personal. I just want to be the best lawyer and mother I can be, and that makes me happy.

The Joy of Success and Accomplishment

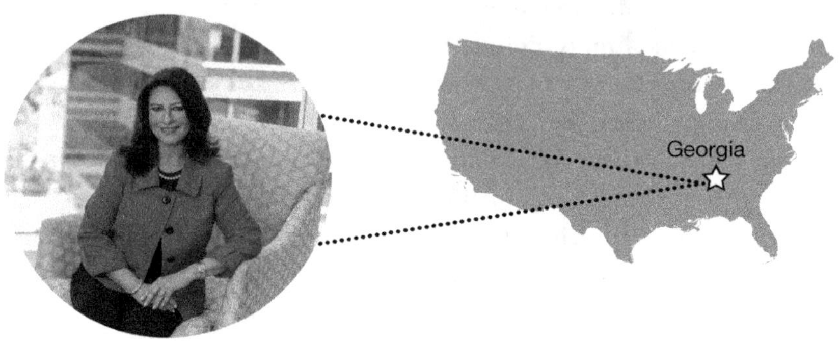

Her Story

Z. Ileana Martinez

Career

Partner at Thompson Hine LLP, where I practice Business Litigation, Product Liability, and Life Sciences.

Education

Florida International University, BS, High Honors; University of Miami School of Law, JD.

Best Advice

There is no "secret" to success; it requires hard work, meaningful relationships, proper perspective, and service to others. Although success does not ensure happiness, happiness is a necessary element of success.

Personal

Married (thirty-eight years), three grown children (a doctor, a business consultant, and a lawyer), three grandchildren.

For more information about Ileana

www.thompsonhine.com

"Success" is defined by the Merriam-Webster dictionary as "getting or achieving wealth, respect, or fame." From my perspective, this is a very narrow view of success. Many people are wealthy, respected, or famous who I believe are not successful because they are not living happy, fulfilled lives. What makes each of us happy and satisfied can vary greatly, and thus there is no one-size-fits-all when it comes to success. Moreover, at different stages and at different moments in our own lives, success may look different. In my younger days, there were small successes (arriving at work with two matching shoes after staying up most of the night with a sick child) and large successes (wining that big case or becoming an equity partner in my law firm). Achieving success in life is a journey requiring perseverance, meaningful relationships, hard work, proper perspective, and trying to make a positive difference in the lives of others. Here is a small glimpse into my journey along with some of the keys to my success.

Perseverance

I was born in the beautiful island nation of Cuba at a time when the sounds of salsa music and the roar of the ocean waves in Havana still drowned out the cries of revolution that were being echoed in the mountainside by Fidel Castro and his rebels. As my mother and father doted over their newborn baby girl, little did they know that in a few months their entire world would change; they would have to leave everything they knew and loved behind (even me at first) and flee to a strange country, with nothing but a $100 bill sewn into the lining of my father's suit jacket and the dream of a life without Communist tyranny. A few months later, just as the U.S. Embassy in Havana was shutting down, my grandmother left Cuba with me (then a baby) in her arms on a flight that was supposed to land on another Caribbean island where we would seek asylum and wait while my mother and father made arrangements to bring us to the United States. Instead, a day or so later my parents, who were now sick with worry as they had not heard from us, received a call from Madrid, Spain, where my grandmother and I had been sent. With just a few dollars in her purse, no warm clothing for either of us to fend off the cold Spanish winter, and no American visa or passport, things looked very grim for all of us. Every day for a few months, my grandmother would park herself with me at the U.S. Embassy and passport office in Madrid, pleading for entry into the United States. Whether it was my grandmother's tenacity, my relentless colicky cries, or divine intervention from the prayers of the nuns who provided shelter and clothing to my grandmother and me, we were finally granted entry into the United States and joined my parents in Miami.

Hard Work

As my husband tried to navigate his career path, relocations were necessary. This required me to live in three different states and to take three separate bar exams, each time having to leave family and friends and the law firms and communities where I had already planted roots. Doing this in our late twenties with a small child, a toddler, and a baby on the way was a particularly trying time in my life. Hard work is necessary in achieving success in life; there simply is no substitute. As a child, I witnessed my parents and family working very hard to make ends meet for me and my sister. They took whatever jobs were available (often more than one) and walked several miles to work because they did not have the money to buy even a used car. Throughout my career, my work ethic has distinguished me from more naturally talented people. I always go above and beyond what is expected and I am never satisfied with just doing the minimum to get by. Everything I do, whether in my personal or professional life, I do with my whole heart; it is one of the keys to my success.

Meaningful Relationships

True life success cannot be accomplished without the presence of loving, meaningful, and lasting relationships. My parents and grandparents were my earliest examples of this, and they set the bar high when it came to my later relationships. Choosing the right life partner is probably the most important decision anyone can make, and for me, this moment came very early in my life, when I was fifteen years old. It was then that I met and fell in love with a young man while attending a summer camp; we married three years later when we turned eighteen. This year, we are celebrating forty-one years together, and thirty-eight years of marriage. During this time, we have created a beautiful life and family built on respect, admiration, patience, humor, and deep love. We are each other's biggest champion, and together we function with the precision of gears in a Swiss timepiece, supporting and pushing each other along at just the right moments, never one ahead of the other, but in complete unison. Undoubtedly, in very large part, I owe my success in life to my husband.

My three wonderful, amazing, talented children (now grown adults, and one with children of her own) are also primary reasons for my success in life; I am truly blessed to be their mother. I am thankful that despite their sometimes being caught in the chaos of my trying to simultaneously be a good mother, a good wife, and a good lawyer, they turned out to be successful, well-balanced, productive members of society, and all-around great people. My husband and I take credit only to the extent that our children are the product of the loving, supportive, respectful, and encouraging environment in which we raised them; genetics and luck deserve the rest of the credit.

Proper Perspective

Often, we need to get out of our own head to gain perspective. No matter what difficulty or problem I may be experiencing in my own life at any given moment, I think about so many people going through unimaginable pain and suffering, and naturally my issues seem relatively trivial. Would I rather be the parent watching her child battle cancer, the mother who has no food or shelter for her kids, or simply the lawyer who has to work for the fifth weekend in a row with no end in sight? The answer is always obvious. Keeping a proper perspective, a strong and positive mental attitude, and a glass half-full view of the world have been keys to my success.

Making a Difference

Like Dr. Martin Luther King, Jr., I believe that "life's most urgent and persistent question is what we are doing for others." Whether it is mentoring someone, volunteering with a nonprofit, doing a good deed, or simply having a kind word for someone, everything we do (or don't do) has an effect on others. Trying always to have a positive effect on others has had a positive effect on me. My strong religious faith has always guided my actions and remains a cornerstone of my life.

Success Today

For me, success is having achieved a sense of overall and sustained happiness and satisfaction in my personal and professional life. Success is being able to live free in the greatest country in the world. It is being able to practice law with talented colleagues, and being a trusted advisor to great clients. It is being married to the most amazing man, father, and friend who possesses a great mind and a kind heart. It is seeing my children thrive in their own careers (doctor, business consultant, and lawyer) and watching them select their own wonderful life partners. It is having my mom by my side in her golden years and being able to seek her wise counsel over a cup of coffee on Sunday mornings. It is reading a book to my three beautiful grandchildren or watching them play by the ocean. But mostly, I feel successful and accomplished because I love and I am loved.

REFLECTIONS

1. Are you a good "manager" of your life? Do you have a support system or a team to help manage the demands of your personal life and your career? Is your employer part of that team?
2. What are your dreams? If you are dreaming as big as you can dream, what do you imagine for yourself?
3. How do you define success? What does it mean to you?
4. Has your definition of success changed over time?
5. What is most important to you?
6. Did your vision of success ever change because your priorities changed?
7. Do you have both personal goals and professional goals? Did you ever find that accomplishing a goal in one area of your life affected another area? Why are these goals important to you?
8. What are you doing now to accomplish these goals?
9. Do you have a plan? What is it? Is your plan fluid enough to adapt to life's curve balls?
10. How does having a proper perspective help you stay true to your goals and your plan?

3

GAINING MOMENTUM

Particular Strategies for Success

Introduction

To maintain a pipeline of female talent, women lawyers must stay in the profession. Yet staying in the profession can, at times, require a great deal of mental and physical stamina, which tests our endurance. Best known for her novel *Little Women*, Louisa May Alcott once said, "I am not afraid of storms for I am learning how to sail my ship." For women to remain in the practice of law, we must strengthen our ability to weather the inevitable storms. This chapter highlights stories addressing the many ways we can build momentum for a successful career, including negotiating worth to law firm management, dealing with bias so that it does not rob us of our spirit, learning to manage business development activities and our workload early in our career, developing a strong growth mindset to view challenges as opportunities, and using sponsors to advance. The stories here provide practical advice to build endurance in your career, which will help you sail through the storms that inevitably test us all. With these skills, we can maintain a pipeline of female talent prepared to manage the next generation of law firms and government agencies and to become corporate counsel.

Be Your Own Advocate by Negotiating Fair Compensation

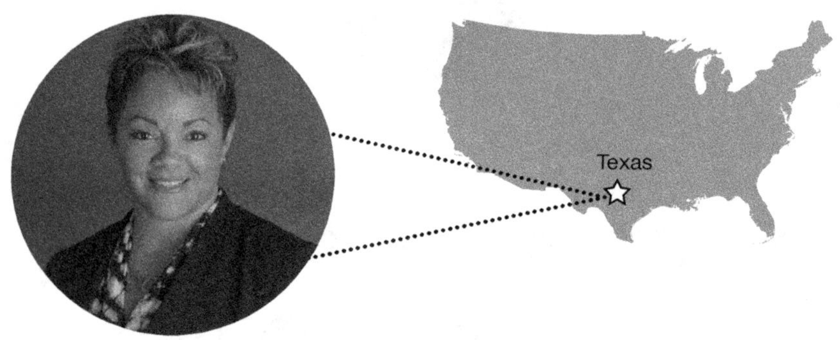

Her Story

Amy M. Stewart

Career

Partner at Estes Okon Thorne & Carr, where I specialize in Labor, Employment, and Commercial Litigation and Arbitration.

Education

Wake Forest University, BA Speech Communication, Captain of Women's Basketball Team; University of Missouri-Columbia, JD, Law Review Associate Editor.

Best Advice

Dedicate yourself to putting in the hard work and time it takes to learn your craft. Always be your authentic self. The goal of networking is building relationships that pass the test of time, not business development. Have a spiritual foundation in place when life's inevitable storms come your way.

Personal

Proud wife, mother, daughter, and sister.

For more information about Amy

www.estesokon.com

> *"I've learned that people will forget what you said, people will forget what you did, but people will never forget how you made them feel."*
>
> —Maya Angelou

As litigators, clients hire us to zealously advocate on their behalf. Yet when it is time to fight for ourselves (for example, to negotiate for fair compensation), we are not as tenacious. We second-guess ourselves. We diminish our own worth in various ways, through our own words, our facial expressions, and other nonverbal cues.

This is a challenge for many professional women. Indeed, if you conduct an Internet search using the words "woman," "negotiate," and "money," you will see a long list of self-help books, articles, websites, and blogs that advise how to negotiate "like a man." In 0.6 seconds, the web browser will locate materials titled "Why Women Don't Ask for More Money"; "Lean Out: The Dangers for Women Who Negotiate"; and "Are Women Lousy Salary Negotiators?" Honestly, reading these titles alone makes me even more anxious about negotiating.

No matter how prepared you are, negotiating for compensation is a stressful endeavor. It can be a rewarding experience if we use the nervousness we all feel as a motivating force, not a debilitating one. A pregame pep talk from my college coach continues to help me resolve anxiety issues I face in my career. Twenty years ago and before our first collegiate basketball game of the season, Coach F. told us that if we did not have butterflies in our stomachs before a game something was wrong. After peering into a locker room of confused faces, she went further and explained that the nervousness and anxiety we felt in the pit of our stomach was a physical manifestation that the upcoming game *mattered*. It was an important event in our lives that would have definite future consequences. Coach F. closed out the pregame talk and explained that we had two choices—we could use that feeling as fuel to focus on winning the game *or* second-guess ourselves and ultimately not meet the personal and team goals we all had worked so hard to accomplish.

I remember this discussion after all these years, and it has helped me to overcome the normal anxiety related to practicing law, dealing with work-life management, and negotiating for compensation. To help you negotiate your next blockbuster compensation package, here are some of my experiences and the lessons I learned over the years. In addition to the normal advice regarding negotiating (that is right, you *always* make a counteroffer), here are some keys to use when you next negotiate the salary you deserve.

I Am Smart, *I* Am Beautiful, and *I* Am Important

If you watched the movie *The Help*, you probably remember a maid repeating a similar statement to a young girl who was not growing up in the most supportive environment. These three affirmations are a confidence-building mantra that I believe all women should remember and internalize before starting the interview process or seeking to renegotiate a salary. Because the process can be stressful, to say the least, it is important to remind yourself that you are worthy and that you possess special attributes and skills *before* you attempt to explain to someone else why you deserve a compensation package or a raise.

I learned this lesson when I negotiated for my first associate position at a law firm. When my family unexpectedly moved to Dallas, Texas, for my husband's new job, we did not know anyone who lived in Dallas or who worked in the legal community. It was 2006, the legal market was on a downturn, and the country's financial collapse was imminent. When we moved, our beautiful *and teething* daughter, Ava, was two years old. As soon as we arrived, my husband was immersed with his new work responsibilities, including travel. For the first few months, we rented a small apartment while we looked for a house and dependable day care for Ava. If that was not enough, I had to start studying for the Texas bar exam. Can you imagine my mind-set during this time of transition? I can tell you that I did not feel smart or beautiful, and definitely not important. Today, I believe strongly that my attitude negatively affected the first interviews I had. I came across as too anxious, impatient, and did not do an effective job of focusing on the goal—why I was the best candidate for the position because of the unique skills I would bring to the position.

At one point, I shared my frustrations with one of my girlfriends. As a good friend does, she waved off my litany of reasons why I thought I was not getting hired. She reminded me that the challenges I was currently facing, including that the legal profession was a second (or fourth but who is counting) career for me, was a huge advantage and selling point that I had failed to discuss in my early interviews. This slight alteration of my perspective had a profound effect on my approach to the interview process. I entered my next interviews with quiet confidence, knowing that if I could embark on a new career at thirty-one years of age while dealing with a teething two-year-old in a new metropolitan city where I had no friends while my husband was traveling for his new position, all while studying for the bar exam, I could handle a first-year position at a law firm.

State Your Worth, Then Stop Talking

I do not know about you, but I cannot gracefully accept a compliment or respond gratefully, for example, when a colleague grabs the bill for a round of happy hour drinks. When I receive a compliment, I get flustered and recite all the reasons their eyes must be deceiving them. If someone buys me a drink, I reach in my wallet for loose dollars while yelling that I must pay the tip. Why do I do that? Why can I not just say "thank you," smile, or say nothing? The same holds true when we are negotiating our worth. One of the most rewarding negotiating experiences I have ever had was the result of me doing one simple thing—I stopped talking.

I was at the end of a prolonged interview process with one of these "bet the business" type litigation boutiques fueled by testosterone, caffeine, and sweat. After some small talk, the hiring partner closed the door to his office, and it was clear it was now time to get to the nitty-gritty—talking about money. Remember, I am a former college athlete and women's basketball coach, but my heart rate hit the roof. The numerous times I had practiced how I was going to ask for this seemingly insane amount of money flashed before my eyes. Then he asked me the simple question, "What is the salary range you are seeking?" This question cued that same sinking feeling in the pit in my stomach that I experienced in that dark locker room in 1990.

After stating three reasons the firm should hire me, I looked him directly in his eyes, took a deep breath, and claimed my worth. Then, I simply stopped talking. There was an awkward silence that seemed to last for at least two minutes. I did not say a word, and I never looked away from this intimidating man, even when he looked down and started shuffling documents. I could feel the sweat rolling down my back and was glad I had kept my suit jacket on so he could not see the stains forming on my silk blouse. I felt like I had stopped breathing, but I stayed silent. He finally looked back at me and said "Okay." I wanted to jump out of the chair with a fist pump! Instead I stated, "Great, so let's talk about the additional benefits the firm offers." He smirked, and we began to hash out the other benefits.

In the past, the awkward silence would have led me to say something to fill the void, as if I had uttered something wrong or was asking for a salary I did not deserve. This time I was prepared mentally and emotionally and I was armed with information. I had done my research and knew the salary range this firm was paying attorneys with my level of experience. Expecting that there would be some back and forth in the negotiations, I started high; however, *he* did not counter. I will never forget calling my recruiter and telling her about the compensation package and hearing her scream in my ear about how proud she was of me. Frankly, it was not the amount of money I was going to earn that was the win. The true victory was that I pushed through the anxiety and *asked for what I was worth.* This is still one of the most rewarding experiences I have had so far in my career.

It's Not Always *All* about the Money

Sometimes we become too focused on the monetary compensation when pursuing a new opportunity. Do not misunderstand, salary is important. As women, it is crucial that we know the magic number we need to live comfortably. Early in my twenties, I remember being ecstatic regarding the salary I negotiated for my first "real" job. That euphoric feeling quickly dissipated in thirty days when I received my first check, sans taxes, fees, and other deductions. I quickly understood the phrase "The tax man cometh!"

Salary is but one component of the entire compensation package. As innately creative thinkers, we need to consider other benefits that could affect our long-term goals, including earning power. For example, early in my sixth year of practice at a small law firm and during my yearly evaluation, I asked about becoming a partner. After affirming that I was "doing the things to become partner," the evaluator told me that the firm would make the decision *in around* six months. I shared that I was not concerned with a change in the compensation package or a deduction in billable hours. Indeed, I believed that by getting a promotion from senior associate to partner I would be able to leverage my networking activities and contacts to create additional business not only for me but for the firm. Even though there were probably more important issues the firm was dealing with during that six-month period, I became frustrated with the lack of nimbleness of such a small firm and looked for another opportunity to join a firm that recognized my hard work, accomplishments, and would support me while I continued to build my practice. I was terrified, but I decided to remain true to myself. I did not want to settle.

Accordingly, I leveraged my contacts for an introduction to a fast-growing, energetic, minority-owned law firm in Dallas. Within three weeks, I accepted a partner position at this fierce, female-owned firm on the terms I had with the firm I was leaving. As anticipated, because I earned the partner "tag," I quickly developed more business for myself and for my new firm.

Do Not Be a Girl

Most girls are raised to be overly accommodating, to "play nice," and to follow the rules. The ability to get along with others and put them at ease is a reliable weapon female litigators normally have in their arsenal. Remaining conciliatory, despite being in an adversarial position, is an asset. Yet it can also sabotage your ability to negotiate a more lucrative compensation package and remain steadfast in your salary demands to earn your worth.

Several times in my life, I have almost talked myself out of what I deserved because I did not want to come off as combative, greedy, or adversarial. Other times self-doubt crept in, and I was convinced that I would forsake a wonderful opportunity if I did not immediately accept less than my counteroffer. As a protective mechanism, I learned that it was prudent to reach out to my mentors for advice during those times. In one instance, I was grappling with requesting a title change, and I called my "no-nonsense" mentor, who is prone to set me straight when necessary. After hearing me hem and haw, she responded, "Do not be a girl." I immediately knew what she meant. Over the years, in terms of negotiating my worth, my no-nonsense mentor has never been interested in hearing that I had "made nice," agreed to a title I had outgrown, or failed to require that I get paid the same as my colleagues.

My other mentor, my "cheerleader" mentor, has no patience to hear my negative self-talk or my rationalizations. As my cheerleader mentor tells me, "You go in there and be you, because *you* are the prize." They are both right. As a professional woman negotiating my worth, I needed to exude confidence and put my demands on the table for consideration. If you do not have a no-nonsense mentor and a cheerleader mentor yet, I advise you to go find them. When those two people agree, that is a clear sign that you are moving in the right direction.

In conclusion, sometimes we can be our own worst advocate. The good news is that I am living proof that this weakness can be easily overcome by making a commitment to use your anxiety as fuel to reach your goals, clearly understanding what your market sector will bear in respect to salary, unabashedly negotiating your compensation range, relying on your mentors for guidance, and confidently exuding the traits of the deserving woman you are. When you are willing to commit to doing those things, you are ready to negotiate your own worth.

Dealing with Bias: Exit, Voice, or Loyalty

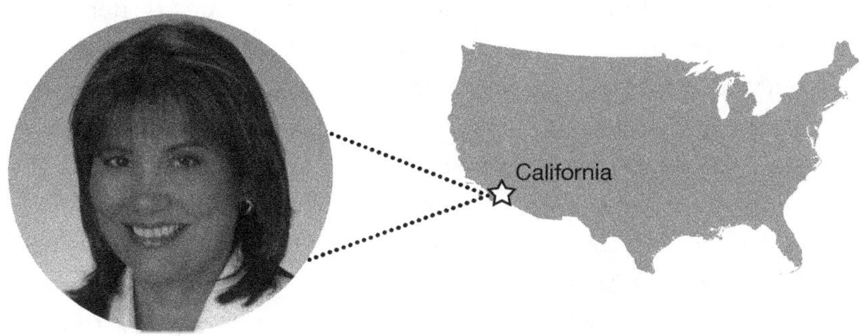

Her Story

Lucia E. Coyoca

Career

Litigation partner at Mitchell Silberberg & Knupp LLP. Specializing in entertainment and intellectual property, insurance coverage, and employment-related disputes. Extensive trial, appellate, arbitration, and mediation experience.

Education

UCLA, BA in Political Science, 1983; UC Davis School of Law, JD, 1986.

Best Advice

Try not to react too quickly to negative setbacks or downturns in your career; use them as a springboard to a new direction. Keep things in perspective.

Personal

Married thirty years and mother of two adult children, Olivia and Andrew.

For more information about Lucia

www.msk.com

I grew up in the beach cities of southern California in the 1970s; half Filipina/half Caucasian. As naïve as it may sound, I truly did not think I would have any gender or ethnicity issues to deal with when I began practicing law in 1986. The legal world was a very different place back then. It was a time before the Anita Hill/Clarence Thomas hearings, before society and the media had coined terms like "sexual harassment," "diversity," or "mommy track." We, the women in the class of 1986, thought it was perfectly doable to have full-time legal careers and also families and fulfilling relationships, without losing our health or our sanity. Also, I graduated from law school in California. My classmates and I were mostly going to work for law firms in Los Angeles, San Francisco, and San Diego. We congratulated ourselves that California law firms did not have the white-shoe cultural biases that existed in more traditional East Coast or Midwest law firms, or so we thought. We could have it all, and we told ourselves we were so much better off than our counterparts in other parts of the country. After all, California was the land of Hollywood and the laid back southern California beach lifestyle. The hippie movement of Haight-Ashbury had sprung up in San Francisco less than a generation earlier. I simply could not conceive of working in a profession where my gender, race, or background would even be a factor.

I had an early wake-up call. During one of my summers in law school, I worked for a midsize insurance defense firm in downtown Los Angeles. I went to court to observe a hearing with a young woman associate who was perhaps five or six years older than me. There were ten or twelve corporate defendants, all insured by different companies, and each had separate counsel. And, of course, all other counsel were male. The hearing did not go well for the defense. Counsel gathered in the hall afterward to regroup and discuss strategy. I hung back, listening and thinking about what I would say or how I would interject if I were participating, but my colleague from the firm did not say anything at all. The group continued to talk but began to drift down the hall, and the discussion continued—right into the men's room.

My colleague and I just stood outside waiting. Eventually the group started exiting and everyone began to disperse. My colleague made a comment to one of the group saying that our client would probably be willing to go along with what was being discussed prior to the *en masse* bathroom break. One of the men looked at her and said—"oh, that's not even on the table anymore; we've worked something out, and your client is not included." My colleague and I took the escalator down one floor, and when we were well clear of everyone in the group, she went into the ladies' room and burst into tears. I was completely taken aback. She explained to me that this was not the first time, and that she was constantly being excluded from discussions or meetings. She was afraid to tell the partner on the case about it, for fear that he would think she was at fault. My reaction? That situation was an anomaly. She was partly at fault—she should have insisted on participating in the conversation from the start. Again, so naïve.

After I graduated, I went to work for the Beverly Hills office of a national law firm. The firm handled complex cases and had a lot of different types of interesting, challenging legal work. Culturally, however, it was not a great fit for me. I was recently married. We had several senior partners in the office who were divorced, and a few who were not, who liked to socialize with the younger female associates. One in particular had quite a reputation. He also had one of the best books of business in the office, with lucrative clients and interesting, sophisticated work. The associates used to congregate in the law library (we still had such things back then), particularly on Friday afternoons when we were trying to finish up projects and get out for the weekend. This particular partner would make it his practice to call the library every Friday afternoon and ask by name for one or another female associate to come to his office, ostensibly to discuss work or a new project. Everyone knew what was coming next—the cajoling to join him for a drink at a popular Beverly Hills or Hollywood hot spot, with assurances that it would be a great opportunity to meet connected people, but which invariably turned into a grab fest by the partner and his friends that would join us. We all had a pact that we would not go to partner X's office alone; there was safety in numbers. But again, I did not think too much of the shenanigans. We just developed ways to maneuver around the situation so that partner X would not be angry if the invitation was declined. After all, everyone knew that the best way to get the plum assignments was to be on good personal terms with the partner who had the client relationships.

That firm dissolved before the end of my first year, and I went to work for another national firm, this time Chicago-based, that had a stellar reputation but was very "white-shoe." I traveled to Chicago with the rest of the associates for a firm retreat during one summer in the late 1980s. We did the obligatory day of golf and tennis at a very posh north suburb country club. I remember standing in the back of the cocktail reception and looking around the room, mentally counting the number of women (seven or eight), Asian American or Hispanic lawyers (about six), and African American lawyers (one) in the room of about two hundred. It felt odd, but I did not necessarily feel unwelcome, just different. One of the senior litigation partners from the Chicago office came up to me, and we started talking. A few cocktails in he asked me point blank if I had gotten into law school on affirmative action because "a cute girl like you could not have studied that hard in college." (I am pretty sure I am quoting him verbatim, even twenty-five plus years later.)

I was angry. I tried very hard not to let it show, instead laughing it off and then making it a point to make sure that all of my subsequent successes were well reported and news of them made their way back to the Chicago office. But I left that firm after only one year. Near the end of my tenure there, I was taken off all of my cases and assigned to sit at counsel table during a six-week trial in a voters' rights gerrymandering case that had been filed against a central California municipality. I had not been involved in the case and knew nothing about the facts or the law, but the client had been promised that an African American, Hispanic, and Asian lawyer would be present at counsel table. I was upset because I felt the firm was using my ethnicity in a rather transparent attempt to curry favor with the trier of fact, and I also thought it likely would backfire. I left the firm before the trial began, not solely because of that incident, but because it was a final tipping point for me, and I think my discomfort with the culture of the firm had a lot to do with it.

I then went to work for a midsize (about 100 plus) West Side Los Angeles law firm that does a lot of entertainment-related work for film and television studios and music labels. I am still with that firm today, although I did leave for a few years in the early 2000s. One of the reasons I went with my firm in the first place, and why I returned after my sojourn to the talent side of the entertainment practice in the early 2000s, is because it is a place that is a good cultural fit for me. What do I mean by "cultural fit"? The firm certainly is not perfect; when I joined, it did not have substantially above the norm numbers for either women or minority lawyers. But what it does have is a system that values hard work, intelligence, judgment, and integrity above all else. Through the years, the most important thing has been to be a good, ethical lawyer. My success in the firm did not depend on what I looked like, where I came from, or whether I intended to have children (I did, and have two adult children today—a twenty-three-year-old daughter and a twenty-year-old son—who grew up perfectly content with a full-time litigator mom). The firm did not insist that only one particular style of lawyering could be effective: being aggressive, employing scorched earth discovery tactics, speaking loudly and rudely to opposing counsel. They recognized that individual lawyering styles could differ and still be effective.

How do you know if a firm is going to be a good fit with your own cultural values? When I first joined my firm many years ago, it certainly was not clear to me that it was a model of progressive law practice management. The firm did not have a stellar maternity leave policy, or a Women's Initiative or a Diversity Initiative or any formal programs designed to help women and minorities succeed in the profession. They were just one of many firms in those days trying to figure out how to make things work as more women and more minorities began practicing law. Situations often developed that had to be handled on an ad hoc basis. It was in those situations that I grew to appreciate the culture of the firm. For example, in one of my early court appearances in federal court in the Central District, the judge reprimanded the woman lawyer ahead of me on the calendar, telling her that she was being disrespectful to the court by wearing a suit with trousers instead of a skirt. The male partner that I was accompanying leaned over to me and told me what a jerk the judge was, and went through each of the judge's shortcomings in detail, and then also gave me a catalog description of the various ways to respond to a situation like that, which would not damage the client's position or my reputation. I appreciated the practical, level-headed advice and response rather than some well-meaning rhetoric that would have left me clueless as to how to deal with this particular judge.

On another occasion, a client responsible for a significant portion of billings came to one of the partners and told him that he simply was not comfortable having a woman corporate associate on his matters, and he wanted her replaced. He made it clear that he had no problem with her or her work, he was just not comfortable with having a woman on his matters. The partner quietly removed her from the client's matters, apologizing to the associate, explaining it was not her fault and it was wrong, but he had no choice. As word slowly got out as to why she had been replaced, a revolt developed among the associates. A group of us went to the partner and engaged him in a dialogue about the issue. None of us was particularly business savvy at the time, and we certainly did not think about the financial impact to the firm or to him if he lost the client. We just wanted him to do "the right thing." In hindsight, I realize now what a significant thing his response to our visit was. He went back to the client, insisted that the woman associate stay on the engagement, and went through some tough months when it appeared this significant client would leave the firm. In the end, the client did not leave, and the partner's book of business remained intact.

It has not always been easy. As a young partner, I had an opportunity to prepare a third-party witness for deposition. The senior partner I was working with told me it would be a good opportunity for me to try to develop business from this witness, because he had a lucrative and well-connected insurance brokerage firm that did a lot of entertainment work. I took the witness out for lunch on the day I was preparing him for his deposition. I kept attempting to engage him in discussions about the work his firm did, and how we could be of assistance. He did not want to talk about that though. Instead, he wanted to talk about my ethnic background. Upon learning that I was part Filipina, he told me he thought it was a shame that Filipinos had no sense of cultural identity. Historically he said they were always so willing to be subsumed into whatever cultural group was taking over the islands. He then recounted to me his fond memories of being stationed near Subic Bay in the 1960s, where prostitution was rampant. *That* particular discussion was a novel one, even for me at that time. I was completely flabbergasted and sought to end the lunch and get back to work as quickly as possible. In the days that followed, I reviewed the conversation in my mind many times, trying to figure out if I had said anything at all that would have sparked such disclosures on his part. Of course, I had not. His inappropriate comments had nothing whatsoever to do with me—they revealed only his own prejudices, lack of cultural understanding, and, frankly, ignorance.

In my thirty years of law practice, I have been fortunate to have encountered very few instances of bias directed at me in the courtroom. I cannot know for sure, but I think that is due in part to the demeanor I have tried to cultivate in the courtroom over the years. I simply refuse to be overlooked or not heard. I am never disrespectful, but I do my best each time I am in the courtroom to portray confidence and authority. I will not countenance being interrupted by opposing counsel. If they begin speaking when I am still speaking, I will not be quiet—I will continue speaking and not cede the floor. I do not complain or raise my voice at such interruptions but make a concerted effort to remain calm, and I speak even more slowly when a situation becomes heated or antagonistic. I argue facts and law and stay away from emotional rhetoric, using it in only the very rarest of situations, such as closing argument with a jury, when there is no possibility that the emotion can be attributed to my gender or ethnicity or to me personally. I believe that a woman litigator needs to be even more in control in the courtroom than a man to be persuasive and command respect.

What is the meaning of these various stories and bits and pieces of advice? As you probably have noted by now, there is no common theme in terms of my reactions to instances of bias or prejudice. I did not always speak up or protest when confronted with inappropriate behavior. At times, I even reacted inappropriately or at least with less than full sympathy or empathy for the situations my female colleagues faced. I had to figure out on my own each time what I was personally willing to put up with in order to further my career and those times when I simply could not be silent or laugh off an inappropriate comment. A good friend of mine told me once there were really only three reactions to a troubling situation: exit, voice, or loyalty. He was referring to the work of prominent economist Albert Hirschman, who argued that people have three different ways of responding to disappointment. They can vote with their feet (exit), stay and try to effect change (voice), or remain silent (loyalty). Over the years I have employed all three, sometimes choosing voice when perhaps loyalty might have been a better personal option, other times choosing loyalty when my conscience strongly urged voice or exit. But it is in the balancing of the three options that I have tried to make my way in the legal profession, to build a successful career in keeping with my own values and ethics.

Five Strategies for Managing Advancement Early On

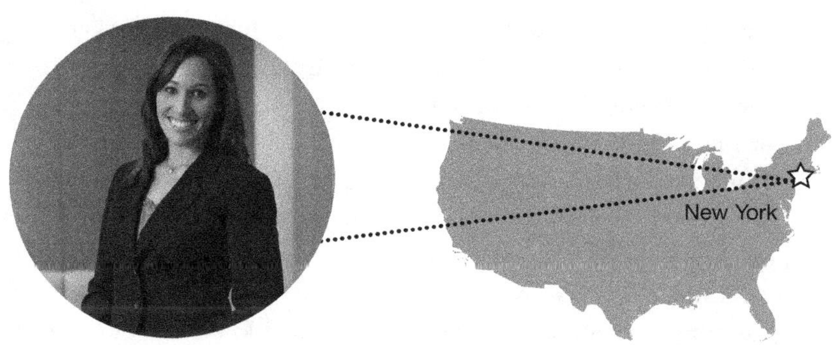

Her Story

Jacqueline Mecchella Bushwack

Career

Partner at Rivkin Radler LLP, where I practice Civil Litigation Defense, particularly in the areas of Construction (Labor Law § 240(1), § 241(6), and § 200), Product Liability, Toxic Torts, Premises Liability, and Medical/Dental Malpractice.

Education

Syracuse University, BA, *magna cum laude*; Albany Law School of Union University, JD.

Best Advice

Take a look beyond your desk and start developing your career early on. Learning to juggle your workload along with professional and business development activities is a skill that takes time to master. Start preparing now for the opportunities that await you.

Personal

Married for nine years to an incredibly supportive husband with two daughters (a toddler and an infant).

For more information about Jacqueline

www.rivkin.com

As lawyers, we prepare. Proper preparation may not guarantee a specific outcome, but it maximizes your ability to handle a given situation, boosts confidence, and increases your likelihood of success. Developing strategies to master the art of managing your life and your career should be no different. Just like everything else we do, it requires constant work, energy, and focus—it requires preparation. My advice is to start early.

For me, I could not be more thankful that I heeded the advice of others and started networking and developing business from the beginning of my legal career. My ability to manage a full caseload while also juggling professional and business development activities has opened more doors than I could ever have imagined. When starting out, my goal was simple—generate business. Little did I know the number of opportunities that awaited me and the types of skills I would develop. Participation in all of these additional activities not only prepared me for partnership but slowly and steadily improved my abilities to be efficient, handle stress, and multitask in a way that even amazes me sometimes. What I found is that by slowly adding more and more to your plate, you can handle a lot more than you ever thought possible. All the while (and while you are probably unaware of it), you are developing time management skills that will help you in all aspects of your life.

It was a Wednesday night in December when I received the call advising me that I had just made partner. Less than twenty-four hours later, my husband and I welcomed our first child, a precious baby girl. Twelve weeks later, I returned to work. With more on my plate than ever before, I was prepared, *in the best way possible*, to handle it all. This is not to say that the transition back was easy, but my efforts early on provided me with valuable time management skills and the mind-set needed to overcome the particularly tough moments. Whether it is a new child, a new job, young children, family, illness, environmental disaster, or something else, we are all confronted with challenges that require us to maintain focus in the office while also managing the demands of a full life. Developing strategies early on will help you more than you can imagine.

For years, I have been mentoring junior associates at my firm. Until becoming involved with this book project, I did not realize how heavily my advice focused on the successful integration of career management for overall well-being and happiness. Having my first child further underscored the importance of these concepts. I offer the following five strategies, which have helped me build endurance, find balance, and maintain happiness both at home and at work while advancing my career and achieving my goals.

1. *Make Time to Develop Your Career.* Managing your workload on a day-to-day basis versus developing your career are two separate issues. It is so easy to become fully consumed with billable hours, client demands, and court deadlines that your days are spent playing catch-up to a never-ending to-do list. Even when this is the case, I believe it is important to carve out time to develop your career from the very beginning. Whether joining a professional organization or a bar association, take a look beyond your desk. The earlier you dive in, the better. It takes a great deal of time to navigate professional associations and to find the perfect fit within the organization. Once involved, participate. Join a committee, volunteer to work on a project, and make an effort to attend the events. Like everything else, your contacts will grow, your network will expand, and you will be exposed to inspiring individuals from whom you can learn so much.
2. *Do Not Underestimate the Importance of Business Development Efforts.* Cultivating contacts and the skills to pursue those contacts takes time. For even the extrovert, networking is an art that takes a great deal of practice to master. A few hours a month add up. From day one as an attorney, I seized every networking opportunity my firm had to offer in addition to those I discovered on my own. Although the benefits may not seem immediately apparent, you never know what opportunities may be available down the road. If you are starting from square one, consider volunteering at the business level for a local organization. Not only will you meet corporate contacts in your area, but you will be spending your time in a worthwhile way. Seize opportunities to attend luncheons or conferences and then be sure to follow up with the contacts you meet at these events. Get involved with your college or law school alumni organizations. Keep in mind that continuous follow-up is critical to developing and maintaining contacts.

Even if you are dealing with a demanding caseload, find time to do these things periodically and consistently. As life becomes more complicated, your availability both after and before work will diminish . . . so start now.

3. *Learn Your Limits.* The struggle to find your balance when working in a high-intensity job with lofty goals begins early in your career and requires pushing yourself to your limits (and beyond), establishing yourself as dependable and hard-working, and may even include burning out from a wildly disproportional work-life balance. Throughout it all, the most important part is being in tune with your body and mind so you realize when you have hit that limit or are dangerously close to it. It is up to you at that point to get your mind right, take a step back to decompress and recalibrate. You are a more valuable employee and will naturally feel more motivated to excel when you are not experiencing symptoms of burnout or irritability from a lack of work-life balance. It might be time for a vacation. A vacation does wonders for your psyche, giving you time to reflect, reset your goals, and realign your priorities. There is never a good time to get away, but that makes it all that much more important.

   When I was a third-year associate, I proudly told my supervising partner that I lost close to twenty days of employee allotted vacation time because I had barely taken any days off that year. Without skipping a beat, he looked at me and said, "Don't ever let that happen again." At first I was surprised by his response, but he then reiterated that the road ahead was long and it is up to the individual not to burn out too soon. This advice echoes in my head every year, and I am thankful to have received it so early in my career.

4. *Smile.* At the heart of my advice is a positive attitude. I strongly believe this is a critical element to successfully managing the demands of your career, your workload, and your personal life. Growing up, my siblings and I were discouraged from complaining. Any complaint would get turned into a positive, and if it could not be, then we were told to simply deal with it. Thanks to my parents, I am now one of the most optimistic people you will find. And what naturally flows

from optimism? Resilience. No one ever said this path would be easy. Being able to adapt, remain positive, and not dwell on life's small stressors will help you roll with the punches. An optimistic attitude will not only help you endure the long days, the setbacks, and the increasing demands of the profession, but it will make you the kind of person that others want to work with. Optimism will help keep you fulfilled and happy while juggling assignments, extracurricular activities, business development commitments, and a busy personal life.

5. *Learn from Others.* Having mentors who successfully manage their careers while demonstrating an overall happiness with their own work-life balance is critical. One of the benefits of becoming involved with other professional organizations is that you meet so many other attorneys who are similarly motivated to succeed and face the same struggles. Listen to the advice of others who have achieved the goals you are working toward, and take note of the strategies utilized by those who have managed (or are managing) the work-life balance you desire. There is no need to reinvent the wheel. Plenty of other attorneys are facing the same struggles. I have the benefit of working with and for a number of mentoring attorneys (both men and women) from whom I learned a great deal and whose advice I've put to use in my own career. I also have the benefit of working for attorneys who generally care about my overall well-being and understand the importance of a vacation or a day off.

The ideal work-life balance is an ever-changing vision, which is incredibly personal and completely dependent on both your current situation and your goals. Deeply rooted in this struggle is the knowledge that persistence, endurance, and hard work are required every step of the way. At the end of the day, you need to focus on doing an excellent job on your everyday assignments so you can establish yourself as a dedicated asset who is dependable, intelligent, and motivated to succeed. But you also need to find time to develop your career. The grander your goals, the harder you are going to have to work, and the tougher it is to manage your time. But *this* is when it is most important. As you move further into your legal career, you will have more work to do and more life to balance! Start now, and you'll be prepared for what's to come.

Lessons from the Farm: Networking, Building Key Relationships, and Rainmaking

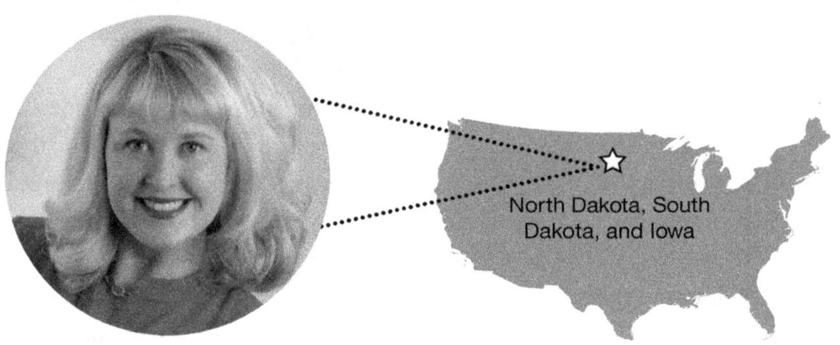

Her Story

Jeana L. Goosmann

Career

Attorney, CEO, founder, and managing partner of the Goosmann Law Firm, PLC, providing sought-after legal advice to the region's most successful CEOs.

Education

Creighton University School of Law, JD, *summa cum laude*.

Best Advice

The clearer your vision, the quicker those who do not buy into it will leave. Capture opportunity, focus on your strengths, and surround yourself with people whose strengths fit your vision.

Personal

Married with two children; lake home in Okoboji.

For more information about Jeana

www.goosmannlaw.com

Networking, rainmaking, and building key relationships are the foundation on which I built my firm. In 2009, I decided to take a leap from a well-established law firm to launch my own law firm, which provides strategic legal advice with big city style and hometown service. Being a farmer's daughter from the Midwest, I understand the importance of growing a business that believes in strong relationships with clients as well as our community. My experiences growing up surrounded by hard-working farm operations taught me the values on which farmers build their business. I used the same fundamental values to build my own firm through networking, building key relationships, and rainmaking. As I watch my firm grow, I've seen how to develop and succeed based on these same core values. I want to share with you my experiences in taking values from the farm to the courtroom.

Networking

In many small Midwest towns, the local farmers meet for morning coffee. They gather around a couple of booths at the local gas station or diner to talk about the weather, their families, and crop predictions. We can take away a valuable lesson from the farmers chatting in the booths—networking.

Networking is a key ingredient in growing my firm. I'm hardly ever simply sitting in my office. A good practice is to never eat alone. I prioritize time to meet people in our area communities, and I strongly encourage my team to do so as well. Whether it's a lunch, coffee, or event, networking opportunities give us easy avenues to meet people with whom we may not have had a prior connection. Networking also helps us maintain relationships with those individuals we've grown closer to through business or personal connections. As an attorney, it's important to jump at opportunities to present, speak, or network with individuals. Look into your town or city's leadership and growth organizations. These are great places to start networking with individuals who are driven and passionate about business growth. Many organizations routinely look for inspirational speakers to talk about their experience and give advice on various matters. Become involved in organizations that match your areas of practice. This focused involvement will lead you to find additional routes to your next business opportunity.

Don't overwhelm yourself by attempting too many opportunities at once. Set realistic goals for meaningful networking and successful follow-up. View networking as a giant web. This web is filled with many connecting points of people who know other individuals throughout the web. The web is endless. As you connect with more people, it creates more connecting points for both you and the people you know. Networking word of mouth travels fast; your network web will expand quickly. This provides opportunity to grow your business by capturing more referral sources as well as direct clients.

A great example of a giant networking web is LinkedIn. You have direct connections as well as second- and third-degree connections. Do you remember the "six degrees" of Kevin Bacon? The concept of "six degrees of separation" states that two people anywhere in the world are six or fewer acquaintances apart from one another. People know people, who know other people, who know even more people. To connect personally, share your interests and goals with those around you because you never know where the conversation may lead you—to your next big client or maybe even to Kevin Bacon.

Now you may be thinking, "How on earth does someone have time for networking?" The farmers networking over coffee would tell you that they *make* time. Obviously, we all know that you can't "make time." We all have the same twenty-four hours a day to utilize. However, you can prioritize those twenty-four hours to your advantage. Some folks are eating alone, skipping a ribbon cutting, and heading home early for the day; but others are maximizing their time to take advantage of opportunities, and those people continually grow and succeed.

Prioritizing your time to create opportunities to grow your practice takes practice. Use your expertise and connections to advance by building key relationships and ultimately become a rainmaker.

Building Key Relationships

Farmers are skilled at many things, such as knowing the intimate details about their land, crops, and animals. You might think all farm fields in June look similar—all green fields—but to the farmer each is a field with individual characteristics, not quite ready for harvest, with promising potential, and a target calculated estimate yield. Attorneys should use a similar approach when building key relationships with their clients and potential clients. It's important that an attorney knows her client beyond his or her legal needs and understands that the individual is not only a client but also a parent who loves to go boating with his kids, takes his coffee black, and is passionate about his small business and family.

Building key relationships with people through meaningful connections without using a sales pitch up front will set you above the rest. People notice when you know their name, profession, family, hobbies, and passions. Have you ever heard that people love to talk about themselves? Well, it's true! Give people an excuse to talk about themselves, and listen and learn about them as individuals. Impress referral sources and clients by remembering details about each person. Individualize your connections to grow successful professional relationships.

Growing up in the Midwest, it was easy to see farmers' passion for working hard on the farm. Much of a farm operation's success is based on strong relationships with others. Building and maintaining strong relationships requires genuine passion. Whether it's in a time of need or when you're looking to increase your client base, having key relationships is essential to the success of your practice. One way I impress referral sources and clients is by creating moments I call "WOW" moments. Putting yourself in situations to "WOW" a client or potential client will show that you went above and beyond for them.

I had a "WOW" experience while making a pitch to a client for a flat fee engagement. We were at lunch when the CFO of the company began telling me about his daughter wanting one of his grandma's collector Barbies, but there were conflicts in the family that wouldn't allow his daughter to keep one of them. I actively listened to this story, and I remembered how important it was to him. In preparing for the flat fee pitch, I bought a Barbie, wrapped it in brightly colored tissue paper, put it in a big princess bag, and gave it to our client as a gift for his daughter. My pitch went from great to "WOW!" After the pitch, our client gave us a handwritten thank-you message from both him and his daughter. A little attention to detail can go a long way to show clients you care about them as individuals. Listen to everything clients tell you about what matters to them.

Another "WOW" experience happened while I was working on a pitch to a bank. I introduced the bank leadership to a potential board member. This individual became one of the bank's key board members. "WOW" can be information and an introduction. Connecting people with one another may turn an experience into "WOW." Not only are you building meaningful strong relationships to grow your firm, you are also helping others build key relationships to succeed.

You can also add "WOW" to a relationship by doing something over the top using your network connections. For example, if you have a potential client taking a vacation trip to Napa and you know a vintner through your wine club, line up a private tour for your client during the trip. After you engage the client to provide services, have a bottle of the same vineyard's wine delivered as a thank-you note. Or maybe you know a potential client enjoys a particular type of music or a specific band. Snag them firm tickets to a concert. Whether the gesture is big or small, find opportunities to bring "WOW" to your relationship.

Rainmaking

Farmers wish they could make it rain, literally; we seek to make rain in business by making a lot of deals happen. Rainmakers progress from networking to building key relationships to finally making the deals happen. Though it may seem like magic to those who don't understand the work involved, a rainmaker knows these deals don't happen with the wave of a wand. Rainmakers know how to close the deal through strategic steps. Becoming a rainmaker takes time. I've found two key characteristics that every rainmaker possesses: (1) confidence and (2) the ability to identify the true needs of others.

Have you ever asked a farmer how are the crops and the farmer came back with a negative comment? Probably not. Have you ever wondered why? Farmers are optimistic and confident in their work and their ability to surround themselves with tools for success. They always have hope for a great crop season regardless of the meteorologist or economist forecast for the season because they're confident. Confidence through the ups and downs is a must-have strength for a rainmaker.

We all go through struggles in our lives when we wonder if the sun will ever shine, or in a farmer's case, if the rain will ever come. People notice a confident person and steer clear of pessimistic people. People are drawn to rainmakers because they are making things happen! To become a rainmaker, you must stand out from the crowd by radiating your confidence.

When I attended the International Telecoms week in Chicago for the first time, I strategically packed my summer blazers. Although slightly uncomfortable at first, my bright tangerine blazer definitely stood out in the crowd of gray and black suits. Don't be afraid to switch things up and stand out. Take what makes you different and embrace it. As a female firm leader, I am often the only woman in the room of business owners. Don't hide the fact that you are female; show confidence, stand out, and be memorable.

Many women today struggle with their confidence and self-esteem. Do not neglect yourself. Take care of your appearance and health as it will make a significant difference in your self-confidence. As busy attorneys who also may be parents, we need to prioritize personal time to take care of ourselves. Our personal health affects how well we perform as attorneys. Women may feel guilty about spending time on themselves; however, we should consider it an investment in our long-term personal and career health.

The second must-have strength of a rainmaker that stands out to me is identifying the true needs of others. Jumping back to my farm days, my parents always knew the true needs of others in the community. Similarly, a rainmaker identifies the needs of clients and potential clients. Anticipating the business advice and legal services clients will need shows the effort you are putting into listening and understanding the client. Show people more than the black and white print of the law by raising issues and counseling your clients to meet their underlying needs. Doing so will build long-term professional relationships that produce more than a one-time client engagement. All of these factors play a role in closing the deal and growing your book of business.

Conclusion

Growing up a farmer's daughter, I learned first-hand the concept of "you reap what you sow." The hard work put into networking, building key relationships, and rainmaking will pay off more than you expect and in ways you do not expect. In a relatively short amount of time, my firm has grown to a team of more than twenty people across locations in two states. Despite this growth, networking, building key relationships, and rainmaking remain as important as ever to my success. I love to share these seeds of success; now the key is whether or not you use them to grow your business. I hope you will!

"Failures" Are Inevitable Opportunities for Growth: Reflections on the Importance of Grit and a Growth Mind-Set

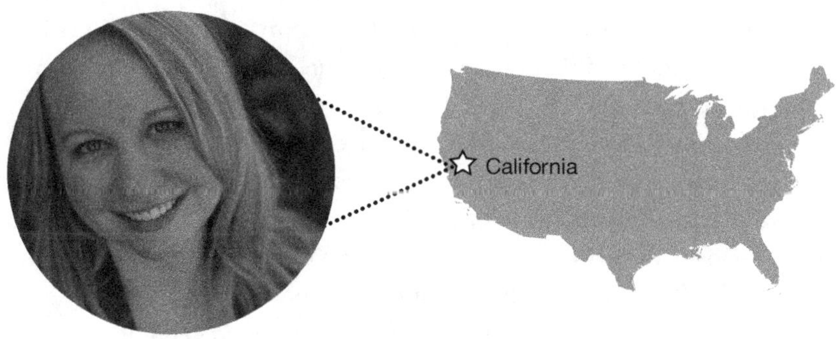

Her Story

Katherine M. Larkin-Wong

Career

Litigation and trial associate at Latham & Watkins LLP in the Antitrust and White Collar Practice Groups.

Education

Claremont McKenna College, *cum laude*, BA; Northwestern University School of Law, JD.

Best Advice

In law, you must get comfortable with being uncomfortable. That's where you grow!

Personal

Originally from Montana, married to a Kiwi with a pup named Wes, former president of Ms. JD.

For more information about Katherine

www.lw.com; www.ms-jd.org

I did not love law school. When I graduated, I was desperate to start practice. Having always been an applied learner, I could not wait to get out of the "theory" of law school classes and start applying what I had learned. I also thought I was ahead of the game. Having been a paralegal before law school, I thought I would be more prepared for starting my legal career. How *woefully* wrong I was. My first year was like a wet blanket on all my aspirations. The learning curve was exponential. I cried (in my office and at home with my husband), questioned my decision to go to law school (was it the right decision), questioned my choice of law firm (today, I truly love working with our team), and, perhaps most desperately, worried about how I would ever pay off my crushing student debt when my supervisor determined I was not "good enough" and I was inevitably fired (still working on that one at times!).

I did all of this worrying, agonizing, and emotional venting *silently* and, as a result, felt very alone. It seemed that everyone around me knew exactly what to do and never made a single mistake. Then one day a friend and fellow associate came into my office, closed the door, and collapsed into my guest chair, saying "I'm certain that I will be fired. I just made a massive mistake." I finally realized I was not alone.[1] Today I recognize that law is a career built on many, many years of exponential learning. If you are not uncomfortable, at least sometimes, then you are not pushing yourself, and you are not growing. So the question for me became, "How do I get comfortable with being uncomfortable?"

Early in my career, I met and started working with Milana Hogan. Milana is the professional development and recruiting director at Sullivan & Cromwell in New York. At the time, she was completing her PhD. She was examining how two psychological concepts—grit and growth mind-set—apply to women lawyers, specifically women partners in the AmLaw 200.

Milana explained that "grit" entails perseverance, dedication, and a strong drive and commitment to achieve one's goals. As opposed to being Type A, people who have grit ascribe to Malcolm

1. Note to all first years: Your job is important, but no one is under the impression that you have it all down. You will make mistakes, but it is very hard as a first year to make a mistake that cannot be fixed. The biggest mistake you can make is *not* reporting your mistakes to others.

Gladwell's idea that it takes 10,000 hours of practice to master any task. Thus, they are distinguished by their persistence even in the face of challenges to their goal. "Growth mind-set" is the belief that our abilities are flexible and adaptable and can be improved through sustained, conscientious effort. People with a strong growth mind-set believe the mind is a muscle that can be trained and that there is no ceiling to our intellect if we apply ourselves to learning.

Milana's research showed that women partners had grit in spades and at a higher rate than the general populace. Women partners also had higher than average scores on the growth mind-set test, although these showed room for improvement. Significantly, studies have shown that grit and growth mind-set are monotonic, which means that we can build and improve our grit or growth mind-set. In other words, these traits can be taught, and we have nowhere to go but up.

After talking to Milana, grit and growth mind-set became an integral part of how I viewed my career development. Suddenly, every memo or brief that was bleeding from track changes was an opportunity for me to learn that particular attorney's unique preferences and do better next time. My growth mind-set told me that I could improve, and my grit told me that a successful legal career would require persistence in the face of my "failure." For me, grit and growth mind-set gave me a framework that I could use to deal with the exponential learning curve of a legal career.

Since those early conversations, I have spent several years actively thinking and writing about grit and growth mind-set.[2] To be clear, expanding your grit and growth mind-set does not mean that you do not have bad days or moments when you are still certain that you have failed. We all have those failure voices, the inner monologue that tells us we are imposters and should not be lawyers or that we will be fired and be unable to pay our bills, and that we will end up homeless. Grit and growth mind-set do not shut down those inner monologues.

2. Milana Hogan, Carrie Hightman, and I cochaired the production of a toolkit designed to teach lawyers about the application of grit and growth mind-set. To learn more, see Ms. Hogan's dissertation research, and see other articles we have written on the topic at www.americanbar.org/groups/women/initiatives_awards/grit.html.

Instead, grit and growth mind-set govern what you do next. Your grit helps you reaffirm your commitment to becoming a successful lawyer. Your inner "gritty" woman can stand up to your failure monologue by helping you recognize that we do not become good at this job overnight. Law is about judgment, and judgment requires being in many situations to help you improve your intuition. So grit stops the failure spiral. Then, growth mind-set kicks in. Growth mind-set helps you take a step back from the "failure" to ask, "What is the growth opportunity in this moment?" It ensures that you view your career over the long term, shrug off the fear, and recognize that if you are going to get good at the practice of law, you are going to have to get comfortable with being uncomfortable.

Developing your "gritty" woman with a growth mind-set will not happen overnight. It takes sustained practice. For better or worse, being a lawyer gives us plenty of opportunities for practice. If you want to develop these traits, consider doing the following:

1. ***Get Your Baseline.*** The grit and growth mind-set tests are just a few dozen questions together. Completing them takes less than twenty minutes. You can find copies on the ABA Commission on Women in the profession's website at www.americanbar.org/groups/women/initiatives_awards/grit.html.
2. ***Read Up on Grit and Growth Mind-Set.*** On the Grit Project website, you will also find a number of additional articles describing why grit and growth mind-set are important and ways that you can leverage them for your success. Do some reading so that you get more comfortable with the concepts.
3. ***Try on a Gritty Woman or Growth Mind-Set Attitude.*** I like to say "fake it 'til you make it." Even if you do not think you are particularly gritty or, at the moment, do not see yourself as someone who can grow as much as a growth mind-set would suggest, try the attitude on for size. The next time you have a failure moment, think about what you can learn from it. I applied this by considering how a friend from law school who had a very strong growth mind-set would react to a situation. It helped me adjust my perceptions.
4. ***Seek Feedback Using the Growth Mind-Set Model.*** Ask, "What are my opportunities for growth in the next quarter?" When I changed my feedback requests from the negative "Tell me

> what I've done wrong" or even "How can I do better?" to a positive request that sought help in my professional growth, my supervisors were much more willing to give me constructive feedback.

In a long legal career, you are going to lose motions, cases, and pitches. You will have briefs and motions that do not live up to everyone's expectations. There will be bad days at home, days you struggle to be the partner, mother, sister, or daughter you imagine you would be on your best days. The truth is, that is life. You would have those issues (or similar ones!) even if you were not a lawyer. Grit and growth mind-set are traits that can help us put those moments into perspective and view ourselves as malleable individuals who can grow to achieve our long-term goals together.

Sponsorship: The Key to Shattering Glass Ceilings

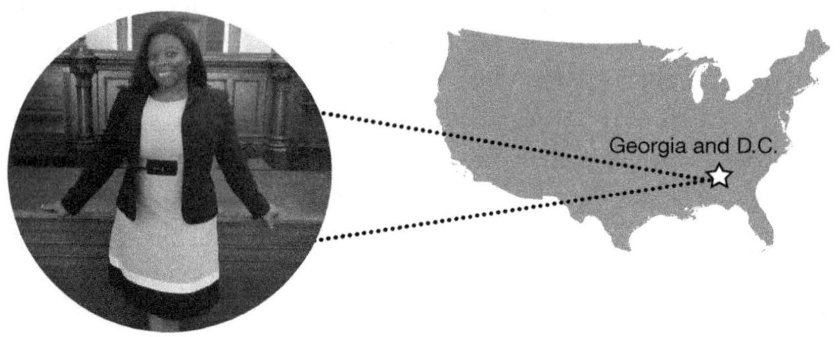

Her Story

LaKeisha R. Randall

Career

In-house trial attorney for State Farm, Corporate Law & Insurance Defense.

Education

Georgia State University, BA in Sociology with honors; Universidad de Costa Rica, studied comparative biotechnology, bioethics, and pharmaceutical law while in law school; North Carolina Central University School of Law, JD.

Best Advice

Life isn't a dress rehearsal—live boldly, challenge your comfort zones, and enjoy it!

Personal

I attribute my balance to prayer, yoga, and boxing.

"If you want to go fast, go alone. If you want to go far, go together."

—African Proverb

Brand development, sponsorship, and philanthropy—these concepts are generally associated with business, but it is critical to know how they interconnect and differ in professional advancement. As CEOs of our careers, we must strategically plan, execute with precision, and critically evaluate our progress to achieve optimum success.

Shattering glass ceilings is a difficult task for all women, but the additional intersectionality of race makes this arduous task further from reach. Sponsorship is a proven way to increase the odds of success and level the playing field for women and people of color. Though I have had a personal board of directors for years, I have achieved particular success by morphing some of those relationships into sponsorships. This has broadened my awareness of their utility and opened doors to rooms that I may not have otherwise accessed.

I truly hope you will reap the same benefits I have, or more, as you create your own board of sponsors. Let's begin!

Sponsorships Propel Careers Forward

In business, sponsors enhance a company's or a brand's image, increase visibility, broaden exposure, aid in the development of new relationships, and strengthen existing relationships. The mere alliance instills trust in a product or service that may not have been garnered absent the partnership.

Similarly, a professional or career sponsor is a business ally who invests in his or her pupil and expects a return. Although the nuances of each relationship vary, sponsors generally invest their time, talents, resources, and contacts with their pupils. Sponsors give advice and guidance similar to that of mentors, but they also believe in your value or potential enough to link reputations, go out on limbs on your behalf, and have the requisite clout to be your champion. A sponsor is your advocate, supporter, coach, and cosigner.

Forming sponsorship relationships is critical to the success of all professionals, but research by the Center for Talent Innovation (CTI) showed women and minorities are particularly vulnerable if they do not have sponsors. According to research by CTI, men are 46 percent more likely than women to have sponsors, and Caucasians are sixty-three percent more likely than professionals of color to have sponsorship relationships.[1] The leading author on this subject, Columbia University professor Sylvia Hewlett, attributed these differences to myriad reasons but largely suggested that the difference is a quirk of human nature: people in power tend to invest in those most similar to themselves.[2] Or, as it plays out in the legal profession, white men tend to sponsor other white men.

Although there is probably some truth to this notion, ending the discussion there would disserve women, minorities, and minority women. It is no secret that the legal profession lags behind other industries in the recruitment, development, and retention of women of color. In fact, the American Bar Association's *Visible Invisibility Report* concluded that "female attorneys of color are more likely than other groups to be sidetracked by obstacles which limit their opportunities early on in their careers."[3]

Also according to the *Visible Invisibility Report,* female attorneys of color have the highest attrition rate of any group of attorneys; are more likely than any other group to experience exclusion from other employees based on racial and gender stereotyping; are most likely to feel the need to make adjustments to fit into the workplace; and are more likely to cite dissatisfaction with current levels of work and access to high-profile client assignments relative to experience.

Sponsorship relationships will not eradicate all of the barriers identified in this report, but sponsorship relationships will certainly contribute to solutions for several reasons.

---

1. *See* http://www.talentinnovation.org.
2. Sylvia Ann Hewlett, *Forget a Mentor, Find a Sponsor: The New Way to Fast-Track Your Career* (Harvard Business Review Press 2013).
3. *Visible Invisibility Report* (ABA 2013), *available at* http://www.americanbar.org/content/dam/aba/administrative/diversity/Convocation_2013/CWP/visible_invisibility_fortune500_executive_summary.authcheckdam.pdf.

How Sponsorships Work

Sponsors are not simply altruistic; they also gain from the relationship. A sponsor sees furthering your career as an investment in his or her own career too. Like mentors, sponsors offer advice and guidance but they also:

- Are in positions of authority or respect;
- Believe in your potential or see your value enough to link reputations;
- Are prepared to convince others that you deserve the job, increased level of responsibility, or pay raise; and
- Willingly protect you if you make a mistake.

Resembling corporate sponsorships, sponsor/apprentice relationships are reciprocal. Over time, the pupil should enhance the sponsor's image and visibility; the relationship should add differential value and help the sponsor develop closer relationships with current and prospective clients or contacts and highlight the strengths of both the sponsor and the pupil.

Sponsors provide career traction and put pupils on the path to power and influence by affecting three areas: pay raises, high-profile assignment distribution, and promotions. Building sponsorship relationships is critical to the success of all professionals. But research by CTI showed women and minorities are particularly vulnerable if they do not have sponsors.

According to CTI's research, which was reported by the Harvard Business Review Research Project:

- When it comes to asking for a pay raise, the majority of men, 67%, and women, 70%, are hesitant to directly approach their boss. With a sponsor in their corner, however, nearly half of men and 38% of women will make the request—and focus group research suggests those asking often will succeed in getting the raise.
- Regarding assignment distribution, in getting assigned to a high-visibility team or coveted project, some 43% of male employees and 36% of females will approach their manager and make the request. With a sponsor, the numbers increase to 56% and 44%, respectively.

- Individuals who are most satisfied with their rate of advancement are individuals with sponsors. 70% of sponsored men and 68% of sponsored women feel they are progressing through the ranks at a satisfactory pace, compared to 57% of their unsponsored peers.[4]

Other research shows minorities tend to leave organizations when they do not feel they have someone to advocate for them for advancement opportunities. Often left out of relationships with members of an organization's power structure, the National Black Chamber of Commerce reported thirty-four percent of people of color said they would have stayed at their job if their employer had managers who recognized their talent.[5]

In fact, women of color make up seventeen percent of associates who left their firms in their third year. "Aside from not feeling valued and appreciated, women of color leave law firms because they do not feel supported (22%), they are unable to establish mentorship relationships (21%), they feel isolated and marginalized (16%), and they are subjected to stereotypes and discrimination (11%)."[6]

Corporate law departments have been able to capitalize on this dissatisfaction and have successfully lured away record numbers of women of color who are looking for opportunities to advance their careers in more welcoming environments than law firms have been able to offer. Recognizing the exorbitant cost of training associates, this is a business case that should not be ignored.

These statistics remind us that we must work to bridge the pay gap between genders, attract and retain talented employees, and begin honest conversations about the complexities of career advancement. Sponsorship relationships will not eradicate all of the challenges to advance as an attorney, but they are certainly a strong start. Whether implicitly or explicitly, organic or structured, sponsors are the first step to shattering glass ceilings.

---

4. "The Sponsor Effect," *Harvard Business Review Research Report* (Dec. 2010).
5. *See* http://www.letstalkaboutwork.tv/work-sponsor.
6. American Bar Association Commission on the Status of Women in the Profession, *Visible Invisibility Report* (ABA 2012).

Mentoring is necessary, but insufficient, for advancement. Mentors are unquestionably valuable, but they are more akin to donors than to sponsors. In an organic mentor/mentee relationship, mentors generally take interest in mentees because they like them or the mentee may remind them of themselves. But, as some researchers have highlighted, the contributions of mentors are typically psychosocial. Mentors explain the unwritten rules and informal culture of the firm or organization, offer a sympathetic ear, help you recognize your strengths and areas of development, or serve as an indispensable sounding board as you identify your career goals. But who's putting your hat in the ring? A sponsor.

Although a sponsor and a mentor may be the same person, it is important to understand the differences between the relationships. Some make the fatal mistake of assuming a mentor is also advocating as a sponsor—the success of your career is too important to leave anything to chance.

Finding a Sponsor—Let's Begin!

Start by determining your goals. Don't lose sight of the big picture—always plan with *your* goals in mind. Then make a list of potential sponsors and determine what you're seeking from each, both in the short and long term. Remember that sponsorship is not just about salary increase—think of board service opportunities, speaking engagements, client referrals, and article publications. Finally, don't forget an often overlooked step—assess what you are offering to the relationship.

Develop your brand. Start by knowing your brand! What can you bring to a sponsorship relationship? What qualities or characteristics make you distinctive from your competitors or colleagues? What is your greatest strength? What are your noteworthy personal or professional traits? Remember that sponsorship is a two-way street. The sponsor helps develop the pupil and accentuates his or her strengths for promotions, board service, awards, high-visibility assignments, and increased responsibility. In return, the pupil must display impressive availability, work ethic, and brag-worthy results. The sponsor's profile is also enhanced because he or she will be recognized as a leader who can identify indispensable talent.

Stand out from your peers. Show initiative! Get outside of your comfort zone. Volunteer for projects that are above and beyond your role. Or request a difficult assignment that others are shying away from. This will show senior leaders that you are committed and ambitious.

Advertise your brand. Without being obnoxious, make sure potential sponsors know about your accomplishments. Strategically connect your achievements with business goals, client satisfaction, skill development, or general increased value to your firm or organization. Although e-mails are fine, take it a step further! Break up the monotony of the day by scheduling a five- to ten-minute call, inviting potential sponsors to lunch or coffee (*your treat*), or sending a handwritten note or letter.

Target sponsors. If you were asked to sponsor an event, what key things would you like to know? Likely, you would want to know the reputation of the organization making the request; the potential effectiveness of the partnership; clarification of everyone's expectations; and plans to measure return on investment. A career sponsorship is very similar. Your sponsor will want to know your brand or reputation, the reciprocal expectations, and potential return, short-term and long-term.

Who are the senior leaders best positioned to get you your dream job? Seek out thought leaders positioned to improve your career or connect you with those who can. Here are some tips:

- Look beyond your immediate circle of mentors and managers. Who can be a valuable connection to potential sponsors?
- Diversify your portfolio—build alliances across intergenerational lines, racial lines, gender lines, or other great divides.
- Inside your firm or organization: (1) choose someone within your division or group; (2) select another person outside of your group, but within the firm or organization; and (3) choose an equity partner or key decision leader. A properly targeted sponsor will help make sure your goals are aligned with the firm or organization's strategy. A sponsor will be able to garner support (and overcome resistance) from other senior leaders and provide ongoing direction as your efforts unfold.

- Outside your firm or organization target bar and community leaders or stakeholders. Also select someone whose career you admire, even if that person is in a different area of law. For example, though you may be a transactional attorney, if you would like to become a trial attorney or strengthen your trial skills, seek a sponsor who is a renowned trial attorney.

Be proactive and reliable. Trust is key! Earn it by producing quality work within deadlines reliably. Sponsors want to see that you have integrity and credibility. They may test you to see if you do what you say. When you talk to potential sponsors, ask about their goals and expectations so you can customize your strengths to their needs. Then get them their information on time and arrive early to appointments. Keep in mind that you need to pass their unspoken tests to see if you can handle their brand image. Take initiative. Be deliberate.

Foster the relationship. Get to know each other outside of assignments. That said, not all sponsors want a friendship—remember, the goal is to create a strategic alliance for career advancement. Do not expect a personal relationship too. If that develops, take it as a nice bonus.

Final Thoughts

Sponsorships can be a powerful means for skyrocketing your business. When climbing the ladder of success in any competitive field, you'll need support from senior people of influence. Sponsorship is the route to career mobility for people entering the workforce and for those who have plateaued. Mentors may give, but sponsors invest!

Good luck finding your sponsors!

REFLECTIONS

1. When was the last time you negotiated your salary? What steps can you take to prepare for salary negotiations? Consider downloading the Closethegap app.
2. Do you incorporate business development and networking activities into your calendar on a monthly basis? How can you improve your efforts at networking? Which suggestions can you implement?
3. Are you working on developing your career beyond billable hours? Are you involved in any alumni organizations, bar associations, local organizations, or nonprofits? If not, how can you get involved? If so, what benefits have you gained from participation in these activities?
4. Have you analyzed where your best cases are coming from in order to develop more cases from those sources? What are they? How can you further develop those sources?
5. Have you dealt with bias? Share your experiences with people you trust. Think about posting your experience anonymously on Ms. JD's website with the subheading "Walk a Mile in My Heels" at http://ms-jd.org/search/results/search&keywords=walk+a+mile+in+my+heels/.
6. Assess your grit and growth mind-set at www.americanbar.org/groups/women/initiatives_awards/grit.html.
7. What can you do to improve your grittiness? In what situations do you struggle with needing grit? What changes can you make to improve?
8. Do you have a growth mind-set? How does your mind-set affect you in the practice of law?
9. Do you have a sponsor? Do you need a new or another sponsor?
10. What can you do to ensure that your sponsor relationships are serving you and your sponsor(s)?

4

BEING "IT ALL"

Keeping Values Straight and Valuing Your Strengths

Introduction

Stephen Covey, in *The 7 Habits of Highly Effective People: Powerful Lessons in Personal Change*, stated that "[p]ersonal leadership . . . is the process of keeping your vision and values before you and aligning your life to be congruent with those most important things."[1] Long before Covey entered the picture with his "7 Habits" series, Roy Disney had noted that "it's not hard to make decisions if you know what your values are" (*see, e.g.*, Maxwell, John, *The 360° Leader, Developing Your Influence from Anywhere in the Organization*). Aristotle also grappled with these concepts and developed a theory of ethics. As lawyers, we view ethics as required continuing education credits, but there is a values component as well in how we live our life and how we approach our work. In this chapter, the authors focus on concepts such as justice, courage, friendship, pleasure, honor, charity, and wealth. These lawyers struggle to

1. Stephen R. Covey, *The 7 Habits of Highly Effective People: Powerful Lessons in Personal Change*, 132 (2004).

align their values with their daily lives. The stories include tips such as not needing to see the entire museum in order to have a great day—enjoy the parts you see before everyone gets too cranky. Other stories describe learning to accept a little chaos and rising together to welcome love into your heart. You will also read essays about lawyers facing issues surrounding infertility, returning to work after being home raising children, and adjusting to the competing goals of being a mom and simultaneously excelling as an attorney. In all of these stories, the authors share their struggles to align their values with their lives.

People Plan and God Laughs: Follow Your Heart and Go with It

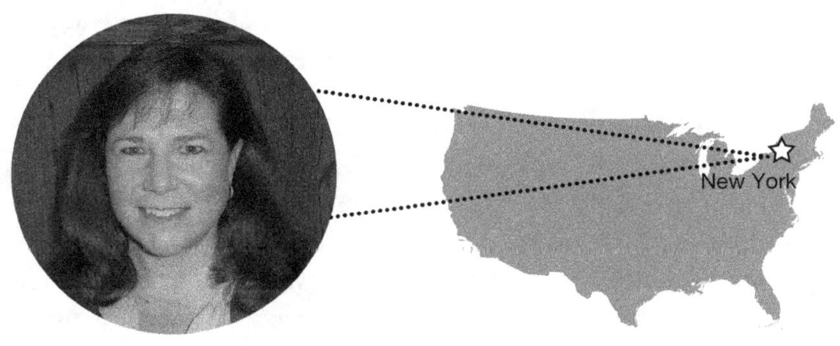

Her Story

Maureen McCormick

Career

Executive Assistant District Attorney, Major Case Division, Community Affairs and Intergovernmental Relations. I practice criminal prosecution with an expertise in Vehicular Crimes.

Education

Siena College, BA; St. Johns University School of Law, JD.

Best Advice

Set your priorities and then be true to yourself. Be realistic. Seek partners, employers, and friends who will support you and give you the flexibility everyone in a demanding career needs to be successful.

Personal

Married twenty-six years with three children. All have graduated college. (Thank God!)

For more information about Maureen

Maureen.McCormick@nassauda.org

It's hard to keep all of the balls in the air, but it is critical to know which of them are glass and will shatter if they fall.

—Coca-Cola CEO Brian Dyson, 172nd commencement of the Georgia Institute of Technology, September 6, 1991

For me, it begins and ends with passion. I believe in the work we do as prosecutors, and it drives everything. I wish I could report that it was my lifelong dream to be an attorney, but it wasn't. I didn't know what I was going to be, and I was envious of the kids who knew. I thought it was a blessing to have a specific goal. After law school, I was envious of the young attorneys with specific plans for their careers. I vaguely thought I would pursue a career in corporate law—something neat and clean.

My story begins with being open to possibilities and opportunities. It continues with finding ways to make it work. I was blessed with a dad who defined unconditional support and a strong mom who encouraged her daughters to believe in themselves. I strongly believe that women should mentor each other, but I have to acknowledge that my path was assisted by some extraordinary men: my uncle who persuaded me to go to law school and several bosses along the way. I worked for a small general practice firm in Manhattan during law school. The partners had both been assistant district attorneys (ADAs) and convinced me that I belonged in a courtroom doing trials. Both men insisted that I apply to the Brooklyn District Attorney's office to gain trial experience.

Plans and Reality

It was my "plan" to stay at the DA's office for three years. In metropolitan New York, most offices require a three-year commitment to staff all of the divisions. I thought I'd get enough trial experience to get a job as a trial attorney in a litigation firm. All I can say is, "wrong again."

Starting at the DA's office felt like being "home" except that the offices were disgusting: a cramped and dingy space on the second floor of the courthouse that had been subdivided into "offices" with old, mismatched furniture. There were seventy-six young attorneys in my incoming "class" of ADAs, and five of us shared a 10 × 10 office and two phones. I know I am dating myself, but there was only one computer for fifty ADAs, and it was used for the case tracking system. We had to submit written papers to the "typing pool." The work (not the typing) was fast-paced and collegial. The surroundings have gotten a little better in some DA's offices, but the volume of misdemeanor cases for incoming attorneys is still unworkable. It is still a "sink or swim" formula. My officemate tried a case seven days after we started. He was our hero. I still look upon those first two years as the most exciting of my career. The camaraderie and support among colleagues on everything from legal arguments to apartment hunting was a big part of the sense of home. But then there was the work.

Finding a Profession to Be Passionate About

Professionally, I was hooked. The first time I spoke with a victim, the first time a person looked to me to get justice, I felt a sense of purpose and belonging. Almost thirty years later, I still feel it. There is no denying that being a prosecutor is an essential part of my identity. In the course of writing this, though, I wonder if it wouldn't be better if that identity weren't so strong. For me, being a prosecutor comes with enormous responsibilities: providing justice to victims while protecting the rights of defendants, managing the urgency of cases that deeply affect people's lives, handling the frustration of a system that often works against itself, and coping with the desire to change it for the better where you can.

Coping with Change

I was assigned to the felony Transit and Auto Crimes Bureau after a year in the office. I didn't want to go. I wanted to be a "regular" prosecutor, trying "regular" cases. Nobody in the administration cared that I didn't want to go. The needs of the office always drive movement and placement of lawyers. We called ourselves "deals on wheels." We handled an odd array of disparate crimes in the transit system: auto thefts and felony DWIs, assaults, and homicides. They grouped the cases together because of their numbers. The bureau shared five court parts with Sex Crimes. There was no connection. It was about the numbers. I indicted and tried subway and bus robberies and assaults, carjackings, and chop shops. But it was a vehicular manslaughter case that broke my heart and shifted my career path for the next twenty-five years.

An older man was crossing the street to go home after work. It was six o'clock in the evening. Neither he nor his family had any reason to suspect that would be his last day on earth. A reckless, speeding driver snaked through traffic, accelerated through a red light, and struck and killed the man. His leg was found on the roof of a building almost a block away. His death was violent and brutal.

It is the common thread in most vehicular crimes: completely innocent victims in the wrong place at the wrong time, subjected to unspeakable violence. None of my intentional homicides had this same character. The truth is that most intentional homicides involve people in high-risk lifestyles: gang members, drug dealers, terrible domestic violence, and so forth. "Stranger homicides" are thankfully rare. Vehicular crimes, though, are indiscriminate.

The defense had high-paid, well-trained collision reconstruction experts. The police accident investigators' training was seriously deficient. I did my best to educate myself before trial, but I felt like I was at the mercy of the experts—mine and theirs. How was it possible to interpret a crime scene so differently? My gut told me (and the jury) to reject as ridiculous the defense position that the victim's age, and not the car's speed, was responsible for his leg winding up on the roof. It didn't change the fact that neither I nor the police had a strong enough grasp of the concepts. It was my first "expert nullification" trial, in which the conflicting experts cancel each other out.

We fought to have the police department collision reconstructionist retrained and continually educated. I received the training too, along with training in crash data retrieval and standardized field sobriety tests. I never wanted to be at the mercy of the experts again. My office allowed me to start the first vehicular crimes bureau in New York City. I supervised every vehicular crime in the office to ensure consistency and to assist the trial ADA with the technical issues. I continued trying cases. Eventually, an attorney who I had supervised became the first woman district attorney on Long Island, where I lived with my family. Ten years ago she asked me to change offices and start the first vehicular crimes bureau there. I did, and I proudly maintain that we have the best bureau in the office and the best vehicular crimes bureau anywhere. The dedication, intelligence, and skill of the ADAs and staff are unmatched. As an example of our success, the office ascended in rank to fourth from forty-first out of sixty-two counties for top-count DWI convictions, as well as first in counties with more than a million people and first in counties with more than five hundred DWIs. We have achieved legislative and regulatory changes. It isn't nearly enough to effect all of the changes needed, but we continue to fight.

I now train across the country on prosecuting vehicular crimes. I also still try high-profile cases, including a controversial depraved murder case that I also argued on appeal before our highest court. And I have been humbled by recognitions on the state and national levels as prosecutor of the year and with other awards. I never thought that the "fights" would result in awards.

The Family Side of the Equation

But at what cost? A young ADA is required to work schedules around the clock. I recall my future husband meeting me at central booking one New Year's Eve so we could "celebrate" together. Even now, I am on call to respond to crash scenes. Obviously, you can't plan for the crimes other people commit. I tried three intentional homicides while I was pregnant with my first child. When my child arrived two and a half weeks early, I had a case file with me at the hospital. It was the vehicular homicide case I referred to earlier. I had to finish the transfer memo. The office sent an investigator to pick it up. I shouldn't have bothered. The case was waiting for me when I returned from maternity leave. It was the first case I tried when I returned to work after my leave.

I would love to tell you that it has been easy to balance work and family, but I can't. I have found it to be really challenging. My mother's voice rings loud and clear in my head: "you can't do everything and do everything well." But there is something lacking in that statement. It is a simple fact that there are only twenty-four hours in a day. You could dedicate all of your time to work, believing the focus and effort are necessary. (I realized long ago that I could work twenty-four hours a day, seven days a week and still *not accomplish everything* I wanted to do.) Or you could forgo your career and dedicate all of your time to family. Which is better? In my experience, neither. It's all about balance and even that shifts back and forth.

I do not pretend to have the answers, but I have seen that my work benefits from my experiences as an involved mother, wife, and daughter. I have seen that my parenting has been informed by my work. None of it is possible without support systems and delegation. I'm not very good at the delegation. It is hard to let go of any aspect of things you are passionate about, and my life begins and ends with passion—passion for prosecution and an even deeper passion for my children, my marriage, and my family.

Support Systems

The people in our lives make all the difference. One of my first bosses was a man named Joe Petrosino. Joe was better to his staff than he was to himself. He took responsibility when things went wrong and used the events to teach, not to blame. He always had your back. When I wanted to get training in reconstruction, he went to the administration to get the necessary approval. When I suggested that we had to "persuade" the police department to get the detectives better training, he supported me at the meeting while I fought with the hierarchy. I completely trusted Joe's judgment and relied on it. He was a friend in the truest sense. I wish I were the kind of empowering boss that Joe was to me. It is something to strive for.

Joe and I tried publicity cases together. His kids were older. He would make me go home to arrive at school concerts and other events on time. He told me again and again, it's a marathon, not a sprint. If you don't pace yourself, you won't be able to sustain it. He was right, of course. Joe had the gift of perspective, and without his encouragement and understanding, I don't know if I could have managed the intensity of criminal trial work with a young family. Without his guidance, I would have stopped working or found something less challenging for the "benefit" of my family. Everything would have been different and, I believe, worse.

The Only Thing That Stays the Same Is Change

When I thought it was time to have a second child, I was involved in some major projects as a deputy bureau chief in the investigations bureau. I delayed trying to get pregnant for six months and then stupidly, arrogantly, was annoyed when it didn't happen the first month. In retrospect, I realize that if I had been pregnant when I originally planned, the projects would have worked out. I still have to argue with myself about my own perspective on short-term urgency versus issues of real importance. In the moment, it all seems important. Developing real perspective might be one of the most important things a woman attorney can do. Either way, you have to know yourself and learn coping techniques for your own personality.

Finding the Opportunities

Maybe I have gotten things done by recognizing the "windows of opportunity" and seizing them. In my experience, waiting for the perfect moment almost always results in the opportunity being lost. I have observed that some "steady" ADAs, living well-ordered lives, don't necessarily get the job done. When it comes right down to it, though, very few projects are worth pushing forward at all costs. Joe is no longer my boss, and now I have to rely on my own perspective. Joe was better at it.

My second child turned out to be twins. I didn't find out they were twins until six and a half months into the pregnancy. It was ironic that I had finally planned out everything: how long I would work, how long I would take maternity leave, I saved all of my vacation time—everything. The doctor told me the pregnancy was "high risk" and I had to stop commuting and working immediately. That thwarted all of my plans. If I left right away, I would use up my maternity leave before the girls were born. My original decision to stay in the DA's office brought with it the financial reality that I couldn't afford to be out of work for very long. My husband owns a small business, and among other things my employment provided the health benefits for my family.

After receiving the news, I went back to work the next day to try and tie up loose ends and gather projects to finish at home. I was panicked. How could I make this work? Another male boss provided the answer. I went to see Chief Assistant DA Al Teichman to report on the status of my projects and to tell him I was leaving things, unhappily, unfinished. He literally took the file I was holding out of my hands and told me to relax. He told me to go home. He arranged something extraordinary for the 1994 DA's office: he arranged for a computer link from my house and allowed me to keep working from home so I wouldn't have to use my maternity leave. Once again, the decency and flexibility of my bosses and my employer allowed me to stay in the legal workforce. My daughters were born six weeks early. When I came back to work, Al Teichman made arrangements for me to work part time while I set up the vehicular crimes bureau. Joe Petrosino was once again my immediate boss. Both men were ahead of their time.

Support Systems at Home

At home, my husband was also ahead of his time. Now I see things are changing for my young women colleagues. Generally there is a better understanding that home and family responsibilities really have to be shared—all of it. There has to be flexibility between professional parents about whose work life has to take a backseat to travel to the soccer tournament or the science fair. But twenty years ago traditional roles still had the potential to make a woman's work life impossible. I am so impressed with the young dads in my bureau. They really seem to "get it." Their parents should be congratulated for producing such men. For us, it made a big difference that my husband's business was close to home. He became the "class dad." After he'd open at 8 a.m. and give instructions to his staff, he could leave for the birthday parties and field trips. I'd bake the dinosaur cupcakes, and he'd deliver them.

I am also blessed with a local family. I had an arrangement with my sister to provide child care. I cannot overstate the relief that comes with knowing your children are in loving, safe hands while you are at work. Every working mother knows she is only as reliable as her child care. I don't know how moms do it without this support network. (The only downside is that my sister is inherently so much nicer than I am and my kids thought I was the "mean one.") As a society, I think we still have a long way to go in providing affordable, safe, and happy child care.

After thirty years, it is still a challenge. There is nothing more important to me than raising smart, healthy kids with good character who live up to their potential. I recognize the importance of instilling in my daughters a sense of their own strength and self-sufficiency. But it matters just as much to me to raise a son who will be a good man and a good partner.

Finding the Sweet Spot

On any given day, I have felt as though some aspect of my life is getting the short end of the stick. We were watching home movies recently in which one of my daughters was about eighteen months old and wouldn't look at me while I was filming. She was mad at me because I hadn't been home much during the week. I was on trial. Even now, that tugs at my heart. But recently her twin sister wrote an essay about me and my influence on her life for her "Women in Literature" college class. She read it to her class and told me how proud she was of me. I can't express how that makes me feel. My son has now graduated and is working. He laughed as he told me that he found himself employing one of my "annoying life-work lessons" at his job. He is happy and doing well. I am proud of them all.

The Bottom Line

Looking back, it seems to me that self-discipline and organization can be very helpful. On the other hand, I think it is just as important to be flexible and open. Too much of either position can make your life unworkable. Remember to seek employers who will reward your hard work with flexibility when you need it. And don't be too proud to take the help and advice of those you trust when you need it.

Family Unplanning: One Lawyer's Journey to a Family

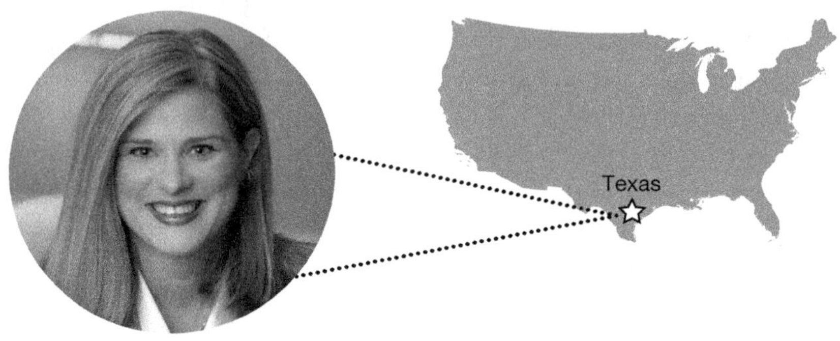

Her Story

Gindi E. Vincent

Career

Author, speaker, and counsel at ExxonMobil.

Education

Ouachita Baptist University, BA, *magna cum laude;* abroad at Oxford University, Magdalen College, and Moscow State University; Vanderbilt University, JD.

Best Advice

Roll with it. Closed doors and changed circumstances lead to opportunities you would never have found otherwise.

Personal

Married (ten years) with six-year-old triplets.

For more information about Gindi

www.gindivincent.com

I'd wanted to be a mother longer than I'd wanted to be a lawyer. Actually, in my adolescent mind, I would have a whole team of children after finishing my medical residency. *Like everything in life, it didn't work out quite like I had envisioned.*

After a career shift in college, I landed at Vanderbilt Law School. I loved law school and was determined to stay focused on finding a job—a critical focus given the law school debt I incurred—and I avoided serious relationships I thought would take me off course. (This is incredibly amusing to me now given that my entire life has been a series of events taking me "off course.")

As I pursued success as an associate in a regional law firm, I continued my laser focus on my career. I never stopped believing I would have a family, but I thought it would happen "one day." After four years of building a reputation in a specialty area, I found a development opportunity in a major metropolitan region. A new firm, a new city, a thirtieth birthday celebration, and a two-week excursion to Italy with a fellow single friend left me in my fifth year of practice happy and fulfilled. The week I returned from Italy I met the love of my life.

I won't detail the completely un-Hallmark nature of our two-and-a-half-year courtship, which ended with a completely Hallmark walk down the aisle one Saturday morning, but there we were: two career thirty-somethings, ready for a family. I hadn't thought much about there being challenges with getting pregnant, and I certainly didn't think through how trying to start a family would change my career. When I married, I was eight years into my career, growing a reputation at a national law firm, and sitting on six community and professional boards. I was busy and traveling and loving it.

Then, right before our first wedding anniversary, we received a doctor's verdict: we had a three to five percent chance of conceiving a child. One of the most unifying goals of our marriage was our desire to raise a family together. My husband came from a big family and wanted one of his own, and I was raised with divorced parents with only one sibling and wanted a big, happy family. This prognosis shook us and our future plans.

We took long walks through our family-friendly neighborhood talking and praying about what to do and ultimately decided to start with less invasive fertility treatments. I began a time-consuming and emotionally exhausting process of charting my body temperature and taking medicines that resulted in weight gain. After those failed, we tried three rounds of intrauterine insemination (IUI), each of which required me to undergo numerous doctor's visits and blood work, all while working and volunteering full time without telling anyone at my firm what we were up against. Rising female leaders in law firms typically don't advertise their efforts to get pregnant, and they certainly don't broadcast their fertility woes. I kept a brave face, bought bigger suits, and tried to move forward with both my professional and personal goals.

When we realized IUI treatments were not working, we had another series of long talks and soul searching. First, infertility not only takes a toll on a woman's personal physical and emotional health but also a toll on her career, marriage, and other relationships. Second, we knew more invasive treatments and time with me out of the office would challenge our efforts to keep our struggles private.

After extensive consideration, we decided to move forward with in vitro fertilization (IVF). This required me to juggle client demands and a heavy workload with every-other-day doctor appointments to monitor my blood levels and time off for the egg extraction and embryo transfer. Our doctor also recommended I stay in bed for days after the procedure to improve our chances, which required me to take additional time off and monitor work e-mails from bed. After two failed IVF treatments, we decided to stop trying. We had no next steps in place but knew we couldn't continue.

At our closing meeting with our specialist, he noted one possible medical option to rule out any remaining causes. When we agreed, the outpatient procedure turned major when he had to open me up to cut a tumor out of my uterus. Fortunately, it was benign. Finally, I shared with my law firm all I had been going through as the unexpected procedure now required me to take a brief medical leave.

You don't ever expect any of this. I was in my peak career performance season, and these three years were incredibly challenging. I spent days trying to achieve my billable hours requirement and engaging in business development and volunteerism, all while juggling the toll of infertility without sharing our struggles at work.

As a result of the discovery and removal of the tumor, we decided to try IVF one last time. Ten days after the procedure, I received a call at work from the doctor's office. My blood results came back with sky high HCG levels, indicating the likelihood of multiples. I stepped back into the conference room for my meeting, trying to mask the whirlwind of emotions going on in my head.

At six weeks, our ultrasound technician found three heartbeats. Three teeny tiny heartbeats (which caused extreme panic in my husband and more joy than anything else in me). *If you don't plan for years of infertility, then you also do not plan for a high-risk pregnancy with multiples. I am a planner of the highest order.* Everything you've ever thought about what you would do with your employer when it comes to pregnancy, maternity leave, and reentry to work, goes out the window with an unpredictable pregnancy.

To begin with, most of my friends waited to share the news of their pregnancy at work until after their first trimester. With triplets, you begin to show almost immediately, and colleagues close to me started to ask questions. So I shared the exciting news with our section leader at ten weeks. Then I resigned from all of my nonprofit leadership roles during my pregnancy, including vice president of one organization I was set to lead as president in the upcoming year. I had individual conversations with each of my clients and formed transition teams to integrate into all my matters so representation would continue without a hitch in my absence. I held in-person meetings with internal and external team members early on in my pregnancy because I had no idea when I would be placed on bed rest with triplets. The order came twenty-six weeks into my pregnancy.

From twenty-six weeks to thirty-one weeks, I worked full time from a hospital bed at home. I, like many career women, needed to stay busy and focused, and work enabled me to remain productive and minimize worrying. Weeks thirty-one and thirty-two meant working part time from the hospital. With the regular doctor and nurse visits, conference calls became harder, but managing case statuses remained possible.

One day shy of thirty-three weeks, on a Friday afternoon, we welcomed two boys and a girl into our family in the span of two minutes. Then my career mode turned off.

For the next fifteen weeks, I was a new mom and a new mom only. I spent all day every day of the first month in the NICU with the babies with my phone turned off. Once they were released, I spent the next two and a half months figuring out what life at home with three babies looked like while also celebrating our first expanded family Thanksgiving and Christmas.

Life was radically different in the best and worst of ways. As planned and scheduled as I was, I felt completely overwhelmed and exhausted. We were thrilled to have the big family we'd always dreamt of, but it put a tremendous toll on all our resources: marriage, money, work, health, family, and friends. After visiting with advisors and my law firm team, I returned to work when the babies were fifteen weeks old with a revised salary and a seventy-five percent modified hours' requirement. We hired two nannies during the day for the first year because of the needs of the babies and household needs as well. I tried to learn a new work schedule and adapt to an "ambition hiatus" by refusing extracurricular commitments.

It was a brand new experience for me as I'd spent over a decade networking, developing, volunteering, working, and leading. I was now surviving. *The first two years are survival.* This is true for any new mother returning to her job, whether she's had one baby or four. I love my work and always planned to return, but the new schedule limitations and the competing demands of a two-career household take time to navigate (not balance, navigate). The first year, I tried to work full days Monday through Thursday and only monitor e-mail on Friday. It failed because my clients needed Friday access. The second year, I worked five days a week with modified hours, which worked far better because I was available every day but usually left work by 4:00 p.m.

I also modestly put a toe back in the volunteering waters near the end of year two. I had lost touch with most of my friends, at least in person, and I hoped reengaging would reignite my passions, help jump-start fresh business development, and help me connect with other working women, especially moms. I volunteered for a women's energy organization and also started a quarterly downtown lunch for working moms of multiples.

Although things grew slightly more predictable, I realized I would likely need a different job. I loved my work and the mentors who had developed me over the eight years at my firm, but the constant stress over my originating and billing credits along with an ever-losing battle of billable hour requirements led me to consider a move in-house. I interviewed with three companies the year the triplets were two. One option would require significant travel (something I couldn't wrap my head around at that stage). One option would place me in an environment where I wasn't sure my values aligned with the company's. And the final option was just right. I felt a little like Goldilocks!

I started the new position right after the children turned three, and the decision ended up as the exact right one for me at my crossroads. The role provided me with continued room to grow and develop, opportunity for promotion, exciting work, colleagues who became dear friends, as well as the chance to expand my leadership opportunity outside the company's four walls. Within my first year at the company, I kept a busy docket while working predictable hours, published a book on leadership, and became president-elect of an industry organization.

I regularly get the question, "How do you do it?" I regularly reply, "With peanut butter on my pants." Truthfully, it is one day at a time. You make sure you are doing what is most important to you, and if that means your goal post moves every few years, then *let it move*.

Life is unpredictable. It is often during the failures or the hard times or the unforeseen circumstances that you find a new passion or draw a new road map or develop life skills that equip you for roles you would never have imagined.

For me, going the distance means resiliency and adaptability—even for those of us Type A, uber-planner types (maybe especially for us!). There is no equation for living your life. What worked for me might not work for you in your individual circumstances. However, if you're wondering about growing your family and your career, you might consider asking yourself these questions:

- *Do I really want to be a mom?* For some women, the answer is no. One of my best friends decided it wasn't for her. For some women, there is no bigger life dream than to become a mom. Give yourself the freedom to set your own goalposts of success for your career and your personal life.
- *Do I have support? Can I get support?* I was fortunate that I had a husband who had the same priorities I had, and he was very much committed to raising kids together. A good friend of mine decided to go through the IVF process while single, and she has a deep network of friends in the community she can rely on as well as a mother who comes in to help periodically. A support network to help you juggle all that will come is tremendously helpful.
- *What will it look like?* You can never really know what life looks like after having kids, but you probably know what you'd like to happen. Do you want to continue to travel every week? If so, think about the external support you will need to hire and understand the budgetary impact. Would you like to go part time for a period? If so, you need to know if your current employer will allow for that option and how you should adjust your finances.
- *What just happened?* Inevitably, life throws a curve ball. You get pregnant unexpectedly. You can't get pregnant. You lose a support system or an income stream. Adjust to the changes by looking at your life priorities and your personal values and deciding what step to take next. Enjoy the ride. You can expect to be confronted with another surprise just around the corner.

Returning to Legal Work after Time Away

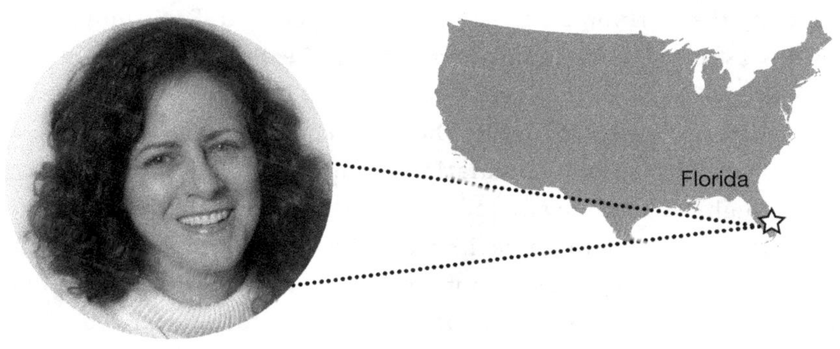

Her Story

Andrea Doneff

Career

Circuit mediator for the Kinnard Mediation Center at the U.S. Court of Appeals for the Eleventh Circuit. Commentary reflects solely my own views and does not reflect the views of the court. I was an associate professor at Atlanta's John Marshall Law School (AJMLS) teaching ADR, Legal Writing, Transactional Drafting, and Civil Procedure. I also served as the director of the Legal Skills and Professionalism Program. I practiced employment and commercial litigation.

Education

Emory University, BA and MA; Emory University School of Law, JD.

Best Advice

Try to learn something new every day.

Personal

Married with two daughters in college.

I waited until my biological clock ticked as loudly as the crocodile's to have children, so for me kids filled a very physical need. When we figured out I could stay home with them, I jumped at the chance. Leaving the workforce was not a difficult decision. Returning, however, was gut-wrenching and continues to be, even as my youngest prepares to leave for college.

I had all these conflicting thoughts about returning to work: I need more intellectual stimulation. Shouldn't playing with my kids be enough? If I stay away too long, I'll never be able to go back. Why would I want to go back? How about part time? Can I do it all—work, raise my kids, and more—or will I be doing everything poorly? I doubt I worried about having time for myself, but that should have been the third prong of my desire to "do it all." Yes, you can love your children with all your heart and still need an intellectual challenge. It's intellectually challenging to figure out just the right thing to do for your kids, but that is not the same thing as trying a case or negotiating a complex deal. You may feel guilty for wanting both, but it's normal.

I had just announced I was *thinking* of going back at least part time when my husband announced his company was going out of business and he would be unemployed in a couple of months. Decision made. It was time for me to go back to work, full time. I'd stayed home six years. I joked that he would stay home for six years and then it would be my turn again. I should have realized he wasn't sharing the joke. That was more than twelve years ago. He slowly built a business from home, and so it evolved that we are a two-earner family again.

Once you've decided to go back to work, you have a whole different set of worries: Can I still do this? What if my child gets sick? How much has changed since I left? Am I hurting my child by not being there all the time? Will I fit in? Can I fit into work clothes, get to work without spit-up on my suit, make it through the day with my usual four hours of sleep, get the grocery shopping done, and sleep? I can't possibly fit it all in! And you're right about that. You can't.

I was fortunate. I could return to work knowing the kids were safe. I still worried, though. Would they always get a well-rounded meal? Would they get picked up on time from school or activities?

Would they get everything I had so expertly provided over the past six years? First, of course, I had to admit, at least to myself, that I wasn't really any kind of expert. I'd made plenty of mistakes, fed them junk food, and been late getting them to school or activities. Then I had to understand that even though my husband's approach would be very different from mine everyone would be okay. We devised a phrase—*I've got the kids.* That meant back off and stop telling me what to do and how to do it. I've got this. And your way is not better; it's just different. He used it a lot over the years. It took a while for me to realize it was true.

It's scary to have to find a new job, knowing that you have people relying on you to eat. And when your choice turns out to be the wrong one, there's some sheer panic while looking for the right choice. Maintaining contacts by attending legal events while I was staying home had really helped. I didn't do that a lot, but fortunately I'd stayed in touch with some people, attended some events, and stayed connected. I made some calls, attended some meetings, talked to people, and told them I was looking. Yes, some of finding a job is luck, but putting yourself in the market so you can be in the right place at the right time makes a big difference. After a couple of short-term jobs at businesses that either couldn't provide a living or turned out not to be decent money or regular hours, as I'd hoped, I found contract litigation work in a law firm for a few projects. Fortunately, the firm needed more help, and I was asked to join full time.

One of the things you'll have to decide is how much you want or need to work and what kind of job will work for you. While working full time at the firm, I continued teaching as an adjunct and coaching competition teams (which I had started while staying home with the kids) until my family staged an intervention—you have to give up some activities so we get to see you once in a while, and it has to be the ones that don't put food on the table. No more teaching or coaching. A hard choice. I loved teaching but couldn't make a living as an adjunct. Still, even with one job, I worked all the time. I faced the pressure of having to work to pay the bills while still wanting to be home with my kids.

Since then I have changed jobs, gaining more flexibility but maintaining the intellectual challenge. I could drive my daughter to school and often pick her up. Sure, I worked after dinner and on weekends, but I had time to help with homework, cook dinner once in a while, and go to after-school events and sporting activities. Still, my daughters turned to their dad when they needed something. Understandable, but it still hurt. I'm still grappling with that one.

Over the years, my husband and I worked out what our roles with the kids were, which helped me find my place in the family again. I helped with reading, writing, organizing, and many of the social concerns. He helped with math and science, took them and their friends everywhere, and got more involved with their school than I could. He got to have much of the fun, but I didn't have the patience for all the driving and waiting, so it wouldn't have been fun for me. Also, he was much better at letting them do more and more on their own, so they learned independence (a bit younger than I would have let them, of course). He formed our social group of families with kids of similar ages. I planned get-togethers. We had some conversations about how to make the change in roles work before I went back, but we didn't really understand what it would be like, so it turned into an ongoing dialogue. The ability to evolve and talk as our lives changed really helped as we went from "I'll do diapers if you'll do throw up" through "I'll do writing if you'll do math" to "I'll help with college choices if you'll set up checking accounts and prepare them for financial independence."

Sometimes we stepped on toes. Other times I was grateful he had a completely different skill set. If you don't have a partner with the skills you lack, look around for a relative, a friend, or a tutor. When my daughter decided she wanted to learn to sew, she called her grandmother. It was a joy to watch them bent over a project together. And it turned out it was okay that I didn't know how to sew and a relief that I didn't have to get involved in figuring it out.

It's not easy to go back to work. At first, everyone just talks to you about your kids when you want to be treated like a professional. Remember, though, that the last time you talked with these people you were leaving the workforce to stay home with kids. That's their memory of you. Also, it gives them something to talk about that isn't just work. They probably have kids too and would love to be asked about them, and you'll realize that it's okay to talk about kids. You can still be professional, even with clients and opposing counsel, while telling a funny story about your kid's latest exploit before getting down to business. You realize that people really do take off Christmas week and spring break, and that you can too. It's okay that you won't be at work those weeks—no one expects you to be, and not much work gets done anyway.

The hard part is summer. There is a lot of guilt about putting the kids in summer camps or day care. And it's hard not getting to take all or really even a significant part of summer off. I tried to make sure we had at least a week of summer vacation. It didn't have to be fancy or far away; just time together. When you look up from your work, you'll see that people leave early in the evenings over the summer and take several three-day weekends. Take advantage of any time you can get. Go home and take a walk together. Make it a routine, something to look forward to, and not a chore. Or have a puzzle going so you can spend an hour a day together, even if you don't talk. One daughter and I started doing the Word Jumble and then the crossword together daily.

As you look for work or start a new job, you'll worry that you are too out of touch, regardless of how long you've been out of the workforce. You'll worry that you don't have anything to offer, or that your skills are stale. Instead, think about all the new skills you've learned—serious multitasking, getting things done on little sleep, figuring out what it takes to make everyone happy, accomplishing tasks with your hands already full, and understanding that we are all more effective when we're not hungry or thirsty. The most important thing that staying home with kids teaches you is that you can figure out all the stuff you don't know. Same goes for whatever is new in your chosen field. You may start out behind, but pretty soon you'll catch up.

Of course, you can't put all these newfound skills on a resume. But what you can add to the resume is the stuff that makes you a well-rounded person and makes you relatable (see, kids teach you a whole new vocabulary too). Active in the PTA? Put that under Community Service. Girl Scout Cookie chair? Shows that you're organized and not easily frustrated. Put it on the resume. Taught a "mommy and me" dance, piano, or acting class? Shows you're up for new and potentially difficult challenges. Think about the skills you learned from everything you did, and write the resume with the positive in mind. Of course, you don't want the whole resume to read like you've only done kid-related stuff. Pick the highlights that obviously demonstrate applicable skills. You don't have to explain the skills you learned on the resume—you'll be surprised at how many people did the same things and know how much work it took. Save the explanations for the job interviews if you are asked about those activities or to answer a question such as what skills you bring to the table.

The best thing I did when I went back to work was join a group of women lawyers who were also moms. I knew a few of the women in the group already and got to know the rest. We met once a month for lunch. Separate checks; about an hour and a half; no agenda. Way better than gobbling lunch at my desk. I can't emphasize enough how important this group was and still is to me. They laughed at my balancing kids and work stories and shared their own. They provided wisdom on how to manage things. One of the first and best things I learned was that I could go to important school events while working full time. I just had to say, "I can't do that; I have a meeting." And I did. No one questioned me. They did it too. Of course, I made up the time at night or on weekends.

When this group of friends wasn't sharing wisdom, they were sharing stories, tears, and laughter. We could talk about kids without worrying that it would harm our chances of success. We could talk about dressing for success while still fighting those extra pounds. And I had a network of people to refer business to, ask legal questions of, and look forward to seeing without feeling guilty that I wasn't at work or at home. Ask whether your women lawyer's group or your local bar association has any affinity groups. If not, start one. With a few e-mails, you can probably find any number of moms in full-time practice who would be thrilled to find like-minded friends. I was lucky that I didn't have to do the work of organizing, but if I'd known how helpful it was and not found a group, I'd have taken it on. All these years later, I still look forward to our now irregular lunches and holiday teas.

One of the hardest things about going back to work is getting it all done. It's really hard to have good quality family time when you have so much you need to get done. It will take time and effort, but you'll figure out what's important to you and your family. When I want to have real family time together, I have learned that it can't be in the house. I end up drifting away to work just a little, or turning on the TV for too long, or doing laundry, dishes, even cleaning the bathroom. Even if it's just a walk in the park, or running errands together, I have to make myself take the time with my family and not rush it. If I don't get it all done, that's okay (most of the time).

I realize now how much I learned from my toddlers that applies to my legal jobs too. You don't have to go see the whole museum. Enjoy the parts you see before they get tired or cranky. Make it fun; they'll last longer. Have a relaxed meal together. Take a nap. Make sure to give and get a hug. And say I love you. Enjoy the moment. That's what you'll remember. And that's how you can go back to work, without the nap or the hugs. You don't have to do it all, and you certainly can't do it all the time. Do what you can as well as you can. Enjoy every moment you can—at work and at home. If you're like me, you'll always worry about whether you made the right choices. Probably not always. But if your kids are okay and you're okay, maybe you did something right along the way.

Keeping Values Straight: Valuing Our Strengths

ANONYMOUS

One of the hardest parts of writing this essay has been choosing what to write. There are so many different values that are important in the context of being an attorney: values relating to what we can accomplish for our clients; how we can improve the profession and the experiences we create for our clients, ourselves, and our colleagues; and how we can manage the conflicts that sometimes arise between equally important values.

What ultimately motivated me to say yes to participating in this book project was the idea that by sharing a part of my own story another woman might feel more empowered to create a better life for herself. My path has been a progression of discovering what I needed to be happy in our profession (some learned through regret), how my values changed over time and came into conflict, and how I managed to lessen that conflict through change. For me, this has meant *learning to take responsibility for my experience of life and the profession, finding balance, and creating paths to progress.*

Discovering Values

Perhaps like many of you, I picked up different values along the way, and they have certainly changed over time. If there is one value I wish I had focused on earlier in my career it would be the importance of *perspective* applied to my *own* life.

One of my greatest assets as an attorney has been the ability to apply perspective to representing my clients. Clients usually present with a problem they are having, or something they want but don't yet have. They tell you (or you sometimes ferret out) their side of the story. But being a good lawyer means being able to see the other side too. To get our clients the results they want, we need to be able to see all the different facets of an issue, to recognize the interests and wants of the other side, and to leverage that to our client's benefit. We need to be able to view a case from the adversary's perspective to better prepare for the fight, to identify possibilities a client hasn't considered before, and to find ways around what appear to be showstoppers. The most common example of where I see attorneys learning this skill is in the context of reviewing case law or contracts. When an attorney comes to me saying that what the client wants is not possible under the law or contract, I always have the same response: keep looking.

That's what being a lawyer means to me—how not to say "no" and instead say "yes, and here's how." It requires perspective and *persistence* too. Before law school, I lived these values. After, I was able to use them right away to the benefit of clients. Yet it took me years to develop the courage to learn to apply these values to my own career and life, and I'm learning still. No matter where we start, we have opportunities to pause and look around, and ask a few questions of ourselves and others. Even if those answers don't lead directly to a life that reflects fulfillment of our values, it may help toward identifying them, and identifying steps we can take to achieve them.

Values at the Outset

Why be a lawyer? I chose my career path years before I had any real understanding of what it meant to be a lawyer. The earliest values I can remember adopting derived from growing up in poverty, and in an environment where *equality* and *empowerment* were given great significance. I was also fortunate to be raised in a family that valued *education*. Somewhere along the way, I got the idea that becoming an educated professional who could help people was a worthy goal, one reflecting great achievement that would lead to a comfortable life. If there were any other professions that qualified other than lawyer and doctor, I wasn't aware of them, and with an aversion to bodily matters, doctor was out. So I aspired at a very young age to achieving financial security, striving to meet my lofty goals, and helping others by becoming a lawyer.

A smooth ride it wasn't. I fell off track as a young teenager, having to overcome more than a few obstacles, personal circumstances well past the scope of this essay. Those circumstances led to my nearly flunking out of high school, marrying at nineteen, and almost choosing to skip college altogether. But after having a daughter at twenty, the need for financial security and the gnawing feeling that I was falling short of my potential helped push me back toward the goal of becoming a professional and building a life that would provide more security and opportunity for my daughter and for me.

With these motivations, and remnants of my romanticized notion of what lawyers do, I pushed forward. Through random jobs from housecleaner to deli clerk, I worked my way through community college, and then commuted from the Catskills to Albany to obtain a bachelor's degree with honors, as a double major in English and political science. As I progressed, more rational reasons for my career choice presented themselves: good income, interesting work, and it was a common progression for students with my collegiate majors.

So I decided to go to law school. My commute grew longer, each week traveling to Ithaca, New York, and back to the Catskills by the weekend. With a young child, there wasn't much time to think about what was happening, much less what my values were or whether I was adhering to them. My decision of what law school to attend was made at a time when hiring in the legal profession was in a lull, so I chose my school based almost entirely on hiring rates. This was one point in time that I look back and wish I had the ability to gain greater perspective by becoming more informed. The better hiring rate did get me a job, but it also left me with tremendous debt—debt that dictated my career choices for many years.

It was more than a little frustrating to later find out that I, with my large debt load, ended up working at the same firm as alumni of a school I could have attended for free. I can't say now that I would definitely have made a different choice, but I'm sure I would have taken more comfort in my decisions if I felt more fully informed and prepared for the impact substantial debt would have on my career and life choices after law school.

Entering the "Real" World

With large debt and a child in tow, there wasn't much to decide as far as the type of job I looked for after law school—I needed to be paid well, the kind of salary that demands a lot of hours in return.

From college and law school, my loftier and altruistic values suggested that working in the fields of Constitutional law or pro bono areas would be most satisfying. Yet positions in the former area were few and far between, and neither field was one that tended toward high-paying positions. I took the best paying job I could find, in a field that at least seemed similarly interesting, if not similarly inspiring.

In addition to the general challenges of starting a new job and a new career, I was confronting challenges with working in a new environment. With just a few legal internships prior to and during law school, I had very little experience working in an office environment long enough to learn to manage office politics. Being already geared toward student schedules, those few positions I held before starting to work full time were also much more user-friendly in terms of managing child care needs. In beginning a "real," full-time job in the New York City legal community, I was afraid. I wasn't sure what to expect, and more important, I did not know what I was entitled to expect. My sense of my market strength was virtually nonexistent. I had visions of being literally trapped at the office late into the evening, unable to leave to get home to my daughter. The first purchases I made after law school were a fax/printer/copy machine and a computer, everything I could buy that might make it easier to be at home when I needed to be.

My fear was not unwarranted either. Within the first few months of my employment, a senior attorney admonished that the salary I was earning meant I was never going to be too busy to take on a new assignment and was expected to be working 24/7, literally. And I did.

In my first year, every vacation I planned, even just the long weekend type of vacation, was canceled or interrupted. I had to cancel plans so routinely that I simply stopped making them. I pulled all-nighters on a regular basis; one month I recall in particular had four of them. I sacrificed time with family and friends, and sleep, constantly. I was always worried about losing my job. My interest in being a good lawyer for the sake of doing a good job vanished, replaced with being focused on doing good work to keep my job.

My personal situation either was or certainly seemed unique. None of my peers had children, nor do I recall any of the few women who were senior to me having any children. There were male attorneys who had kids, with wives who seemed to manage that aspect of their lives. There were no women's groups or structure within the firm that were identified as being a source of support or education. It wasn't until I was pushed into an untenable position of being forced to actually choose between my job and my daughter's well-being that I finally discovered a boundary I was able to set.

It was midevening, and I was home. My daughter had become sick, and my sitter was not going to be able to come the next day to stay with her. I called the senior associate on one of my cases, a woman, to let her know I would need to work at home the next day. Her response was a not-so-veiled threat to the effect that if I did not come to work I would be at risk of being fired. Hanging up the phone, I was in tears. At that most basic level, there was no question of where I would be the next day. I'd be fired before I'd leave my daughter.

Fortunately for me, by this time I had made an ally, a woman whose relationships at the firm were secure enough that she was able to speak up for me to our boss, to share what had occurred. After her intervening on my behalf, I was reassured that I did not have to choose whether to stay with my ill child or lose my job. Of course, I should never have had to even think about making such a decision.

Work Conflicts with Life—Values Change

Being asked to choose between my child and my work was the first real conscious recognition I had of the way that my employment goals conflicted with my personal values. It also contributed to my thinking more about the type of legal career I wanted to have altogether. Although I was getting more perspective about how my work life and personal life were coming into conflict, the idea of being able to do something about it more permanently still seemed far out of reach and unattainable. Perhaps because so many of the people around me also seemed "stuck" in their jobs, I did not see a clear pathway out. I wanted to prioritize my family, take care of myself physically, and have a good quality of life, but I was not yet able to recognize my own value professionally, which was exactly what I needed to do to be able to set more of the boundaries I needed to be setting.

One step I was able to take near that time was expanding the scope of my work experience. It seemed like the more I could become proficient in different areas of law, the more options I might have, especially developing more expertise in transactional areas versus litigation. Transactional work generally seemed to be more in demand and more predictable in terms of scheduling. Although it actually required me to work more than I would have otherwise, as it turned out, it was effective (my practice area was 100 percent litigation when I graduated and now has shifted to anywhere from fifty to seventy-five percent transactional).

Still, I had yet to fully recognize the value of my own work. For several years, fear of being unable to find a position that would allow me to place greater weight on taking care of my family and myself, along with my effort to be prepared for the possibility of a next position, kept me more in the mode of working too hard, suffering from a virtually constant lack of sleep, and worrying about financial stability concerns. It took a series of major firm upheavals—firms going under—and family and health strain to finally push me over the line to make the hard choices between work, family, and advancing my career.

Starting Over

After over a decade of working, and even though frightened about the process, I finally came to a tipping point. If I was going to find a comfortable balance, I was going to need to find it for myself. No one else was going to do it for me. I had also become secure enough in my own skills as an attorney to be confident that I could find a position that better suited my needs, and I was prepared to give up compensation to work in an environment that places equal value on its human resources, and encourages healthy and happy lifestyles.

With this job move, I spent many months considering potential options and obtaining the perspective I did not have the first time around. I considered different areas of law, different types of clients, working in-house versus in a firm, working in the profit versus nonprofit sectors. And I talked to people, and people, and more people. I met with and interviewed and spoke to as many people as I could. I developed, for the very first time, skills in networking, and I discovered how happy most people were to share their experiences, allowing me to make what felt like the first truly informed decision of my career.

I took two months off before starting at my new firm to try to recover from my burnout, and I spent almost the entirety of that time weeding my lawn and creating a household supply closet so clearly organized that it's held up for five years now. Of course, I also completely shifted my priorities around in terms of family. That's not to say I don't juggle, or that there aren't times when I still have to compromise, but in general I put so much more emphasis on family first that in those times when work takes over the forefront, it feels much less difficult and is felt less by my family.

Perhaps not surprisingly, the shift to a somewhat calmer work-life balance allowed the years of physical strain to catch up with me, leaving me unable to work for a couple of months. But the firm I signed up for proved to be as advertised, offering tremendous support during my difficult time.

Values as an Ongoing Project

No sooner had I recovered from my illness than I decided to take on a new career project and go back to school, while continuing to work, to obtain credits needed to sit for the patent bar. And with that, perhaps the most important value to me today became clear: *self-awareness*. I had to recognize my own role in perpetuating my professional and personal life experience. I had finally become comfortable that there would likely always be options for gainful employment, and I was doing well with identifying options and conscious paths of progress. But I had not realized that I needed to set my own limits, as no one else would do that for me.

In our ever-demanding profession, it's easy to give too much, to never say no. We want to be part of a team, to be viewed as valuable and helpful. But sometimes we have to say no; we have to set our own boundaries. No one else will do that for you, not out of malice, but simply because we're all working hard, and most of us want as much help with our work as we can get. It's up to each of us to identify what we hold most important—our values—and then take responsibility for identifying the right balance and creating our own path to get there. Unless I become stagnant, a place I'd never want to be, it is a process that I will continue to work through with each new turn of my career.

The Trials of Motherhood: My Experience at Trial as a New Mom

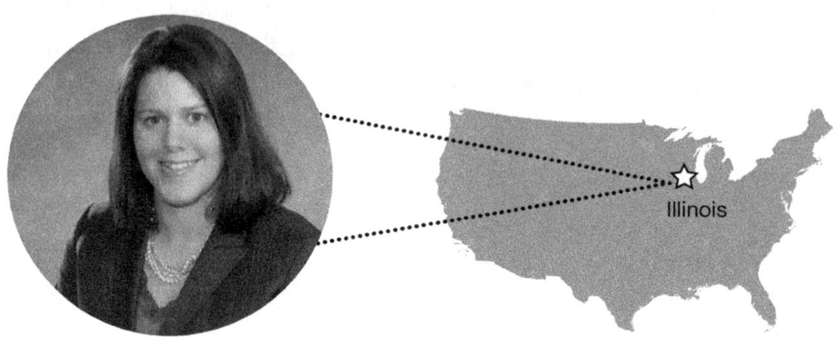

Her Story

Jenny A. Austin

Career

Partner at Baker & McKenzie LLP.

Education

Washington University in St. Louis, BSBA, BA, and JD; New York University, LLM.

Best Advice

Don't be afraid to ask questions or ask for help, and find a mentor (or two).

Personal

Married with a toddler daughter.

For more information about Jenny

www.bakermckenzie.com/en/people/a/austin-jenny-a

A few years ago, before my daughter was born, I was preparing to leave my house for three weeks for trial. At the time, we had two six-month-old kittens, and I turned to my husband and said, "What if they don't love me when I get home?" to which he replied, "Don't be silly." When I got home, sure enough, one of the kittens proceeded to sleep on my head, purring, for a week. Turns out, toddlers aren't that different.

In June 2013, my daughter "B" was born. I had been a partner for about six months and had actually told my partners that I was pregnant the day before they voted on me. I represent multinational companies and the occasional professional athlete in disputes against the Internal Revenue Service.

About a month after B was born, we received our first discovery request from the IRS in a large case before the U.S. Tax Court for a medical device company. Prior to going on maternity leave, I had been a key member of the defense team. Although I was out on maternity leave at the time, I had asked to be copied on any e-mails that I would have been copied on if I was not on leave. I wanted it to be my decision how involved or not involved to be while out on leave, and by reviewing the e-mails that came my way, it made my transition back easier. I participated in two calls about the discovery request while I was out, but it was my choice to do so.

Transitioning Back to Work

With the first discovery request served, the games had begun. At least I knew what to expect when I got back, although I have to admit I wasn't sure how I would handle it all: the long hours that come with discovery; making dinner; finding time for myself; finding time for my husband; finding time for B; waking up in the middle of the night; or even finding time just to do nothing. Instead of coming back 100 percent after my leave was over, I chose to transition back to full time slowly. So, around the end of August, I came back a few days a week for part of the day, gradually working my way up to four days a week in the office by the end of September, continuing to take Fridays off through the end of October. This allowed me to ease my way back into my projects and to slowly adjust to my new life as a working mom.

Part of what made my transition back to work successful was our amazing nanny, "MP." We hired MP early, and she joined our family when B was only a few weeks old. She works from 7:30 a.m. to 6:30 p.m. five days a week. In life before B, my husband and I would go to the gym around 6:00 a.m., get into the office early, and rarely leave before 6:30 p.m. My husband is a consultant, so he also works long hours. We managed to avoid rush hour traffic most of the time.

In life after B, at least one of us has to stay home until MP arrives. This, unfortunately, means we encounter rush hour traffic, making our commute last up to an hour (instead of twenty minutes). It also means that one of us has to leave the office by 5:30 p.m. to make it home by 6:30 p.m. for MP. This huge shift in my schedule required me to learn to work from home more effectively and to be much more efficient in the office. I am extremely fortunate that B is, and always has been, a good sleeper. B goes to bed around 7:00 p.m. and wakes up around 7:00 a.m. This makes it easy to have time to go back to work after she's gone to bed.

Before B was born, my husband and I had discussed who the "lead parent" would be—the parent who would take the lead on doctor appointments, getting home, staying home, even visiting preschools. Because he travels less and has more flexibility in his schedule than I do, he is our "lead parent." In return, as long as I'm in town, I treat my husband's biweekly "guys' night" as sacred on my calendar.

But I've had to experiment quite a bit since B was born to figure out how best to accomplish anything after she's gone to bed, when I, too, would rather just relax. I like to cook, but I've had to learn that I can't cook meals every night of the week. I've had to learn to rely on the slow cooker and to let my husband have a turn. I've had to learn how to plan meals ahead of time and to ask MP for help with prep work. We don't start cooking dinner until B's in bed.

As you can probably guess, I don't see B much during the week. We have a morning routine and a bedtime routine, and I try to be there for both as often as possible. If it's B-time, I'm not going to read your e-mails, and I'm not going to answer calls. Although there are always exceptions, these are my operating guidelines for my time with B. I don't turn on the television when B's awake.

Instead, you'll find me across the street at the park, playing with B, reading books to B, or whatever we decide to do that day during the time we spend together. Both my husband and I do this.

For me to get work done at home, I've had to learn that I can't eat dinner with my husband because I will struggle to go back to work. Instead, I've learned that I need to go into my home office as soon as I can after B goes to bed and eat in front of my computer, just like I would if I had stayed late at work. I hold my weekends sacred and do my best to minimize working while B is awake. It took a while for me to figure out what actually worked for me.

Finding some time for myself was also key to staying focused and happy at work and at home. Even after B was born, I had to find time to exercise. It was a struggle figuring out how to fit in working out after B was born. Before B, I never went to the gym on the weekend. My primary gym has a kid's club that will watch infants at twelve weeks old. At twelve weeks, B was a member, and we were at the gym every Saturday and Sunday for an hour. During the week, my husband and I negotiate who can work out each morning. I would wake up at 5:15 a.m. to go exercise for an hour and come home before going in. If I was staying late at the office, I would use the office gym toward the end of the day. Because it is important to me, I somehow found time to do it even if I had to have multiple gym memberships to make it happen.

Heading to Trial

At the time I came back from leave, we were at the beginning of a year-long discovery stage. Initially, our team was comprised of three partners and three associates. By the time the six-week trial began in February 2015, we had added a fourth associate, a small team for the size of the case. For pretrial matters, I was responsible for discovery, our extensive stipulations, and ultimately, making sure the train stayed on schedule. I had no idea how different and difficult it would be going through the trial process as a new mom.

In life before B, if I needed to stay late or go in on the weekend to get stuff done, I just did. I did whatever it took to get what I needed to get done, done. I didn't have to negotiate or discuss travel schedules with my husband to make sure one of us would be in town at all times. My husband and the cats could fend for themselves. Life after B wasn't so easy. One of the best pieces of advice I received was to treasure mornings with B. When I could make the time work, about once a week, I went into the office an hour or two hours later than usual. I'd ask MP to come a few hours late, and I'd spend the extra time in the morning playing with B. Spending the extra time with B in the morning made it so much easier for me to work late or go out of town.

Trial is brutal: It is all-consuming and demands almost every waking minute. By August 2014, I started traveling weekly. It wasn't uncommon for me to be gone for an entire week and to be home only on the weekend. Of course, by this point in time, I also had to work every weekend, as did everyone on the trial team. There was nothing easy about the months preceding trial. I learned to leave for the airport when B and MP were out or when B was sleeping. It was simply easier for me to leave her when she wasn't around. I committed to take B to swimming every Sunday afternoon, and we made it through December. It was our time together. When we were setting up a weekly Sunday team status call, B's swim class time was off-limits, and ultimately, because I spoke up about what worked best for me, we scheduled the call during her nap. My husband and MP stepped up and took care of everything at home. My husband still takes B to the grocery store every week; I think he likes the attention she brings him. I planned ahead as much as possible for everything. For example, we put together B's holiday gifts in October when I had time to help.

For most of the time leading up to trial, B was too young to FaceTime and definitely too young to talk on the phone. But MP sent me pictures and videos of B every day. B didn't walk until December, just shy of turning eighteen months old. I was in Puerto Rico between meetings when I received the video of her finally walking on her own at her music class. I was on cloud nine even though I wasn't there. But honestly, if I had been home, I wouldn't have been there either. The only thing that would have been different is that I would have been able to see her walk that same evening, instead of days later. Just a few months later, she now runs, skips, jumps, and falls down. And she doesn't know or care that I wasn't there that one day in December.

At home, we implemented a "No Complaining" rule. I'm exhausted; he's exhausted. We're both running ragged, and complaining wasn't going to make either of us feel better. For example, my husband can't put things away in our kitchen where I want them (and where they were). My complaining about his reorganizing my kitchen wasn't going to make him do it my way. Instead, I'd open the refrigerator door, take a deep breath, and remind myself that in April I could move everything back to where it belongs. Not complaining to each other really helped us get through the long months, and we both knew it would all be over by the end of March.

Trial was scheduled for seven weeks to begin on February 2, 2015, in Chicago. In the end, we had seventy witnesses, including twenty experts, but we were preparing for more than a hundred witnesses. As one of three partners on the team, I had significant responsibilities for witnesses and experts. I was also responsible for the day-to-day management of the trial team. Even though the trial was in Chicago, where most of the trial team was from, we all moved into the hotel next to our office for the duration of trial. I literally lived in the hotel ten miles from my house (and B's bedroom) for about eight weeks.

I know a lot of working moms have sworn that family help is what gets them through. Neither my husband nor I have parents who live near us, but one grandma is retired and willing to fly to Chicago to babysit occasionally. We only ask her to do so in cases of emergencies, for example, when my husband had to travel for a couple of days while I was away during trial. MP will also stay overnight with B if we need help. I don't know how often my husband had to ask MP to stay late or to come early while I was in trial, but I know she did, and I'm grateful that she was able to do so.

By the time trial began, B knew everyone on the trial team. Both my husband and MP brought B down to the office when I had time so we could have some time together. We had dinner together in a conference room. B colored in the conference room. B walked up and down our long hallways, and, thank goodness, stayed out of the pond on our conference room floor. I didn't see them often or for long, but I appreciated that they took the time to bring her down to see me before trial began.

So how do you stay in touch with a toddler who wakes up around 7:00 a.m. and goes to bed by 7:00 p.m. during the crazy long hours of trial? FaceTime at breakfast became the solution that worked for us. B was happy and not distracted. I was actually available. Until trial, we hadn't used FaceTime, so it was new and novel for us. Now we weren't having long conversations, but we were able to see each other, which was great. Apparently, every time B saw a phone until I returned home she pointed at it and said, "Mom Face."

How do you give your husband a break when he's taking care of the world while you're away in trial? Saturday mornings at the hotel gym. Although I tried to make it home one weekend night to sleep in my own bed, often I ended up just staying at the hotel. My husband would bring B down to the hotel to hang out with me one morning a weekend. B and I would hang out in the hotel room or go for a walk (yes, you can go for walks in Chicago in the winter), and he would go use the hotel gym.

After Trial and Beyond

While I was away in trial, I missed time with B. But we made it through, and I came home just in time for B to be in a "mommy mommy" stage. Despite my exhaustion, I appreciated "mommy mommy." In the few months since trial has been over, I've been taking advantage of more free time to spend with B. We took a family vacation. I've taken a lot of time off and have gone to B's music class and done other activities with her. There were times during the last year when I felt guilty for not being around and not being able to help out more at home, but I wouldn't want it any other way. B doesn't know any different. I love her, I love being a mom, but I also love my job and being an attorney. I'm glad my husband and I figured out how to make this trial—and everything that went with it—work for our family, but it took a lot of trial and error to do so. I realize that what worked for my family to survive through this long trial may not work for us next time. Next time, trial probably won't be in Chicago, and B will be older. But when I get home, B will still love me, and the cats will still sleep on my head.

All This Luscious Chaos: On Fostering, Adopting, and Doughnuts for Breakfast

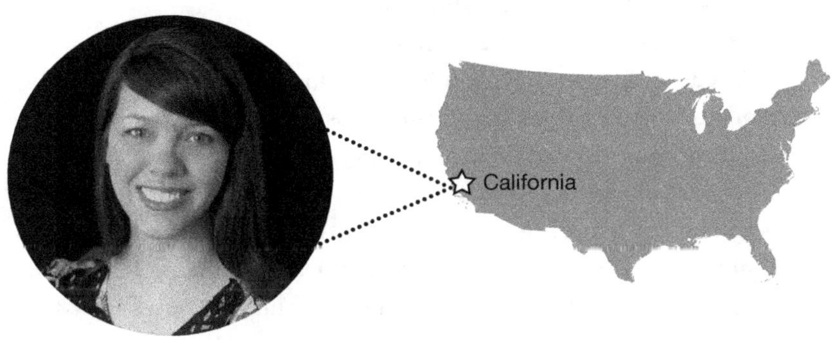

Her Story

Janet L. Wallace

Career

Attorney in Trusts and Estates.

Education

University of California, Santa Barbara, BA (2003); University of California, Davis, JD (2010).

Best Advice

We can go further, rise higher, be stronger, and accomplish greater things if we are in this *together*.

Personal

Married to William Wallace; one adopted son, Julian.

For more information about Janet

www.ms-jd.org/profile/Janet

"Oh, so you had your baby the easy way."

It's a statement I hear with some frequency. I'm a foster and adoptive mom, so there's a speck of truth to the statement. I didn't carry a child, birth a child, or breastfeed a child. Physically speaking, it has been a relative breeze.

But otherwise, it's not been so easy.

To become licensed foster-adoption parents, my husband and I attended tens of hours of in-person classes. We underwent exams of the physical and background variety. We filled out volumes of paperwork (the best use of my lawyerly talents, perhaps, but massive and time consuming nevertheless). My husband built a five-foot fence around a small backyard pond at the insistence of the Department of Social Services. We moved the Clorox Bleach to a higher cabinet, which we probably would have done *anyway* if a small child was present in our home, but we did so under the watchful eye of a social worker whose job it was to scrutinize every bottle in every cabinet, every smoke detector in every room, every pet, every bed.

In retrospect, this process of becoming licensed was not even the hard part, although at the time it seemed extraordinarily burdensome. Becoming licensed was just a really long checklist of sorts, provided to us by the county and overseen by an overworked social worker. Like most attorneys, I'm good at checklists. The checklists were long, but unambiguous: Fill out this, build that, sign here (and here and here).

Once all the checklist boxes were dutifully ticked off, and correspondingly approved by our social worker, we had the next hardest step in the litany of hard steps required to become parents to somebody: We waited. We waited for a child, which is, in itself, not all that extraordinary, except that we didn't have a tidy nine-month timeline to prepare for a newborn. The child (or children!) could have arrived the very night we received our licensing certificate, removed from a situation that most of us cannot truly imagine, cold and hungry and scared.

Well-meaning family members and friends (not to mention the occasional bold new acquaintance) often ask questions relating to the *why* of it. Why would we voluntarily open our home to these children? Why would we choose to build a family this way, especially considering we are not infertile? Why would we choose children who might have *problems*?

These are hard questions to answer, not because I don't know the answers but because the truth can sound cavalier and idealist, though I mean it to be neither. My husband and I foster-adopt because the world is not a good place for many children. Many children—millions, in fact—are cold and hungry and scared in ways that I cannot comprehend because I always had a warm bed, food on the table, and people who loved me. As a child, I didn't realize how immensely privileged I was for these simple realities, let alone the added extravagances of standing at the edge of the Grand Canyon, finding wrapped gifts under the Christmas tree, and choosing my favorite doughnut from the pink cardboard box on Saturday morning. But now I understand these indulgences, these advantages that I received only because I was lucky enough to be born to middle-class parents who could afford trips to the zoo and boxes of name-brand cereal.

My husband and I decided to love some kids who don't have enough. We decided to love children whose so-called problems were not any fault of their own, but the unjust result of somebody else's disastrous life choices or devastating addiction or pure unwillingness. Why, then? Because, love. We foster for the sake of love.

The issue, of course, is that love is not enough (despite the Beatles' advice to the contrary). Love is the reason, but love doesn't fold the laundry or chauffer the kids to day care or pick up the groceries. Love doesn't bill the hours or call the client or file the motion. The struggle to balance the personal and the professional is very real, even if it sometimes manifests in different ways for foster and adoptive parents.

We do the things parents with biological children do: mash sweet potatoes to be fed one tiny spoonful at a time, pour a cup of warm water over a head soapy with tearless shampoo, and fill stockings with tiny books and toys. We face the same struggles too: restaurant meltdowns, fevers, diaper rash, late night visits to the emergency room. Except that, while a child is still in the foster care system, this everydayness is imbued with a twinge of trepidation. The terrifying truth is, unless and until a judge says otherwise, all of these joys and all of these struggles could end in a snap with the child returned to his or her birth parents, extended family, or elsewhere. The potential temporariness nags. We signed up for it, understood the implications, comprehend the goals of the state to reunify families, but it still nags. Should we have Pottery Barn embroider the baby's name on the Christmas stocking when we lack assurance the stocking will hang on the fireplace next year?

In addition, the foster system presumes that one parent will not work. The sheer volume of appointments with social workers, early interventionists, physical therapists, speech therapists, and assessment professionals presupposes that I am available for upwards of five appointments a week, most of which are scheduled to occur midmorning or midafternoon. One pediatric services company *fired us* when we requested the first or last appointments of the day. My husband covers most of these appointments, but the foster system still assumes that the stay-at-home parent will be the mom. Even when I am not attending the meetings, I serve as the appointment scheduler. The system seems convinced that mom keeps the calendar, and no amount of carbon copying my husband seems to change the approach—the foster system has yet to embrace "reply all."

Worst still is the judgment. Not long ago, my husband tried to get an appointment with a pediatrician. She refused to see our sick child because she did not want to deal with any potential implications of the child's state-sponsored medical insurance plan, even though we offered to pay entirely out of pocket. The pediatric dentist granted an appointment, and told us they would accept the state-sponsored insurance only after our first appointment, and then in a hushed whisper (don't let word get out).

At the direction of my social worker, I've used food stamps to purchase baby formula, pulling the stamps from my Kate Spade handbag. "I'm a foster mom," I tell the cashier, loudly enough so the wide-eyed patrons in line behind me can hear. I hustle out of the store, juggling baby and groceries, so the people in line behind me won't judge as I load the bags into a shiny new vehicle. I let the state-issued farmers' market checks lapse because I am so tired of *explaining*.

So, no. It's not easy. It's pretty hard, actually—maybe not harder than parenting biological children, but at least equally as hard. Being an attorney affords me certain advantages. I can afford reliable child care, for which our county, at least, does not provide a stipend. I understand the legal lingo and the various foster and adoption timelines—the hearings, continuances, trials and appeals that leave many children, including mine, in limbo for years.

But being a lawyer also has certain disadvantages. How do you bill the required hours when you have five foster-related appointments per week? When you have to make half a dozen phone calls to find a doctor who will see your sick child? When you have stacks of adoption paperwork waiting at home *plus* a fence to build? There are ample articles and essays on how to maximize your time, your efficiency, your schedule. I'm not an expert, but I employ the following to maintain sanity:

- *Find Reliable Day Care.* Bottom line. Enough said.
- *Life-Hack Your Routines.* Amazon Prime delivers diapers to my front door every four weeks. When I am faced with buying a wedding gift, I always order champagne flutes. My husband and I divide the responsibility of getting our child ready for day care by day—my husband is the "morning captain" on Mondays, Wednesdays and Fridays, and I take on the captain role on Tuesdays and Thursdays. I only buy work clothes that match black shoes—and I exclusively wear black shoes (not as strict a uniform as the late Steve Jobs and his turtlenecks, but close). Simple life hacks such as these can radically streamline day-to-day living. Find your life hacks.
- *Protect Your Time.* When I first became a foster parent, the social workers, early interventionists, physical therapists, speech therapists, and assessment professionals did not take my time seriously. I would book the first appointment of the day, but I would often receive a call or text that the service provider was running late. Annoyed, I soon instituted a rule—it was fine if the provider was late, but we would not extend the appointment to accommodate the late arrival. I would usher the service provider out of my house at the originally scheduled end time. Interestingly, once we stopped

catering to late arrivals by extending the appointment, the providers started to show up timely—they, too, have hours to "bill."

Protecting my time has become central to achieving some semblance of so-called balance. Some of the ways I protect my time include booking appointments for the first slot of the day, choosing providers who are geographically close to my home or office to reduce travel time (my doctor and physical therapist are both within walking distance from my office), consolidating appointments when possible, declining certain invitations, and, of course, being straightforward about my time limitations.

- *Accept (a Little) Chaos.* The artist Brian Andres once quipped, "I'm beginning to think peace is something we made up to keep us from being satisfied with all this luscious chaos." Repeat after me: I accept this chaos. I accept this chaos. I accept this chaos. There is a corner of our living room that is pure chaos—piles of toys and stuffed animals that seem to multiply overnight. No amount of tidying can tame the toys. I've stopped fighting it. When people come over, I shove it all behind the couch. I accept this chaos—this luscious, luscious chaos.
- *Find Your Tribe.* Hillary Clinton had it right—it takes a village. I know the people who will watch my toddler if the nanny calls in sick, pick up my child if a meeting runs late, help me plan a baby shower, give me advice on negotiating my salary, suggest a good contractor or dentist, or show up with a bottle of wine when I've had a bad day. My village includes my husband, my sister, my parents, my friends, my housekeeper, the guy who delivers the Amazon packages, my day care provider, my paralegal, my mentors, my sponsors. It probably goes without saying, but I'll say it anyway: Express gratitude to these people and reciprocate.
- *Rise Together.* One thing I know for sure: Fostering/adopting is not the "easy way." I also know that most women in our profession have not chosen the easy way, whether they have biological children or foster children or adopted children or no children at all. It's just not always easy. The very best

> thing we can do is support each other, to look at one another and say, "I know it's not always easy, but you are doing it." Let's deliver lasagnas to each other when hard things happen. Let's open a bottle of wine and talk about it. Let's send each other texts that say, "You are doing a great job!" Let's tell the woman in the restaurant who is struggling with a crying baby that we get it—oh, do we ever get it. Let's tell each other we've been there. Let's send each other uplifting cards filled with confetti. Let's stop comparing our burdens, and let's look for ways to lift each other up so the burdens lessen. Let's rise together.

The most common thing people ask me is how I guard my heart because the child might not always be mine. That's the hardest emotional burden of all, but it's also the easy question to answer: I *don't* guard my heart, because children need love *today*. No child should have to wait one minute longer to be swooped up in love. The best women in my life support this mission—they pass down a crib, loan a swing, deliver birthday gifts, serve as sitters, help fold my laundry while we watch reality TV, pour glasses of wine, and tell me I'm doing a great job despite it all. I don't have it all figured out, not even remotely close, but I think I've figured out some things that matter most.

And, so, I buy doughnuts and have the stockings embroidered. *That's* the easy part.

REFLECTIONS

1. Is there a role for law firms in facilitating the competing issues faced by lawyers in the workplace between home and work?
2. What can be done by firms to facilitate these competing interests?
3. How does your firm stack up?
4. Do lawyers at your firm feel comfortable being honest about their current situation?
5. What policies could be shifted to facilitate honesty and comfort within your workplace?
6. What are your core values? Why?
7. How do you integrate those values into your daily life?
8. How do you integrate those values into your career?
9. How can you improve the integration of those values into your career?
10. Do you feel supported at work? Can you be supported better? How?

5

BUILDING ENDURANCE

Life Lessons and Big Picture Strategies for Achieving Long-Term Success

Introduction

It is a fact of life: there really are only twenty-four hours in a day, seven days in a week, and 365 days in a year for a total of 8,736 hours. Oprah Winfrey noted that "you can have it all, just not all at once." This chapter highlights women lawyers who have figured out how to maximize and manage their time, life, and careers with expertise, and they offer incredibly useful practical suggestions and advice. Each of these authors reflects on her own experiences to provide big picture strategies for success and maintaining perspective through it all. "Don't spend time beating on a wall, hoping to transform it into a door," Coco Channel famously said. These stories demonstrate the importance of tackling tasks at hand by placing one foot in front of another, with a plan in hand, and moving forward without regrets, one step at a time.

Living Life Deliberately along the Road to Success

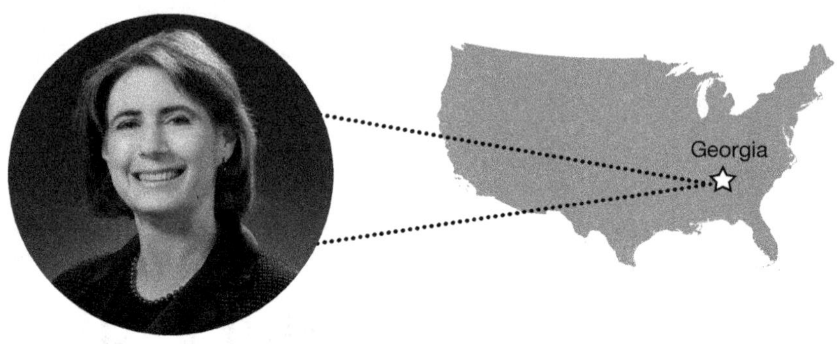

Her Story

Shayna M. Steinfeld

Career

President and CFO, Steinfeld & Steinfeld, PC, where I practice bankruptcy with my family lawyer husband.

Education

Emory University, BA, JD, and MBA; Board Certified Business and Consumer Bankruptcy Law, American Board of Certification.

Best Advice

Take control over your life and career, making choices deliberately with aforethought.

Personal

Spouse (twenty-six years) and three sons: a graduated mechanical engineer and two business students.

For more information about Shayna

www.steinfeldlaw.com

"Life is a journey, not a destination."

—Anon

"The good news is that the moment you decide that what you know is more important than what you have been taught to believe, you will have shifted gears in your quest for abundance. Success comes from within, not from without."

—Ralph Waldo Emerson

I am a bankruptcy lawyer practicing in Atlanta at Steinfeld & Steinfeld, PC. I have spent the past seventeen years running my own firm with my husband, Bruce, a family lawyer. My life is not where I thought it would be when I graduated from law school in 1990. Upon graduation from law school, I joined a bankruptcy boutique in Atlanta; I expected that I would become partner at that firm. Instead, I left the boutique firm when I became pregnant with our youngest child. I did not expect to be running my own firm with my husband, without staff. Because I have an MBA, I am the president and the chief financial officer. We have three sons: one is a mechanical engineer who has graduated college and moved back home and into the workforce, one is a business student in college about to graduate into the world of consulting, and our youngest just finished his second year of college.

Life presents us with many twists and turns. It is the journey that facilitates success and is a necessary component for the many hats we all wear. It is critically important to be involved in activities to grow as an individual, as an attorney, for client development, and for developing a reputation as a practitioner. One of my current "hats" is cochair of the Work-Life Management Subcommittee of the Woman Advocate Committee of the Litigation Section of the ABA. I previously served as chair of the Bankruptcy Committee of the Family Law Section of the ABA. Also, the ABA has published *The Family Lawyer's Guide to Bankruptcy*, a book I coauthored with my husband that is on the shelves of most law schools around the country and is used by many family lawyers and judges. The third edition was recently released. Of the numerous other "hats" I have worn, I am a past-president (one of only a half-dozen or so women) of the Atlanta Bar Association; a past-president of the Georgia Association for Women Lawyers; a past–board member of the National Conference of Women's Bar Associations; a past-chair of both the bankruptcy sections of the Atlanta Bar Association and the State Bar of Georgia; and a past-chair of the sole practitioner section of the Atlanta Bar. I am also a founding "mom" and past-president of the Georgia Network for the International Women's Insolvency & Restructuring Confederation. I have received various achievement awards and have been recognized as a top 100 lawyer in Georgia and as a top 50 woman lawyer in the state somewhat regularly. Does all of this make me "successful" in my career?

What is "success"? How does one define "success"? I graduated from Emory University with a law degree and a master's degree in business administration. As I understood it at graduation, the Emory Law School definition of "success" as an attorney was "partner," "big firm," "big money," "big law"—that's not my life. On the other hand, I am a leader, I am published, I have an amazing husband, and we have been married more than twenty-six years; all three of our sons are each, individually, incredible and are doing really well. My career is doing just fine, and thankfully, the health of all five of us is really good. Truthfully, life really doesn't get any better.

As a couple, we have had to adjust our situations as our lives took different directions when jobs with firms did not play out as expected: initially, when I was pregnant with our oldest, and my husband left his first firm; then, when I was pregnant with our youngest, and I left my firm; and then again when my husband left his second firm as a partner. We ultimately decided to take control of our destiny by becoming self-employed. "Control" is beautiful. Having absolute control over our lives, except for the number of in-coming clients, courts, and filing deadlines, has been one of the best aspects of being in our own two-person firm. Technology is a critical aspect of this control. It enables us, for better or worse, to practice 24/7 from anywhere in the world, on land and on sea (and we've done just that, at times checking and responding to e-mails from a ship or from the other side of the planet). We are available as much or as little as we want to be, away on vacation, in the office, or on the sports field. When we began practice in the late 1980s and early 1990s, technology was not what it is today. There was no e-mail; there was no Internet; there were no cell phones; there was no easy access to online research (we read headnotes in books in law libraries). There was no online electronic service and filing, enabling one to meet a filing deadline as late as 11:59 p.m. Life now is amazingly simple (or complicated) because of technology.

Choose Your Practice Area Deliberately

Doctors have an advantage. They are rotated through practice areas in medical school. We don't generally have the opportunity to do this in law school. Some practice areas are more conducive to working for yourself than others, and other practice areas absolutely require a large firm, large staff, or large city. I have seen instances when lawyers have stepped out of the practice of law to raise children or have left firms and unexpectedly needed to be self-employed. Practical considerations did not factor into my decision to practice bankruptcy; I took Dean David Epstein's bankruptcy class in law school and fell in love. Bankruptcy, as a practice area, is somewhat unique in that it is code-based. It changes relatively frequently (e.g., Congress overhauled the code in 2005). Cases older than 2005 are oftentimes no longer useful. It pulls in other practice areas because it is a combination of litigation and corporate work. On the other hand, it is not the most conducive to earning a living on your own—people are either broke, going broke, or trying to collect from people who are broke.

Appreciate the Life You Have

Take care of yourself. This is a key component of a balanced and deliberately led life. As my friends and I approach fifty and our children are graduating from college, some of our children's friends now have children. Life is a "Circle of Life." This includes death. We recently lost a very dear friend of ours who was a law school classmate. She died of leukemia. Another friend died a year earlier from lung cancer. She was in her forties. Both of these women left teenagers and husbands behind. Neither were smokers.

My uncle is in his sixties. He was diagnosed with Lou Gehrig's disease a few years ago. He recently lost his battle. Life is precious.

Your Health Is Really Important

Don't take your health for granted—exercise, eat well, and live life with gusto. It probably sounds cliché, but eating a healthy diet and exercising regularly is good for energy levels; it is also good for brain power, and it helps to keep stress levels in check when they start to max out during litigation. This isn't so easy for me because I don't really love eating healthy things, and I really don't love the gym. In our family, an intense health phase began when my middle son, now finishing college, entered middle school. Four of the five of us worked with a personal trainer, and three of us worked on losing weight. Three of us each lost forty pounds, the impetus for this being the tween wanting to get himself together. He went from five feet three inches and 170 pounds to five feet seven inches and 130 pounds, traded glasses for contacts, and lost his braces—a transformation! My oldest at the time needed to gain weight for baseball tryouts in high school. Through this process, the boys learned how to eat right and how to exercise properly. As twenty-somethings, my sons are all very athletic and health conscious; they regularly work out or play sports. My husband and I both hate exercising. Ultimately, we lost the personal trainer, and I joined a tennis team for professional women. I get out on the courts weekly. I like the group nature of this form of exercise. My husband and I take regular walks for a few miles at a time with the dog and, oftentimes, good friends, and I ride a stationary bike or use a treadmill regularly. I've recently added weekly yoga to the mix. It's not enough, but it's something. I am much more motivated when I have a ski trip on the horizon and I need to get my quads in shape. I really love to ski with my sons—it's something we do together each year.

Time Is a Valuable Commodity That Needs to Be Treasured and Balanced

Time is a key component of the deliberately led life. It took me years to fully appreciate that there really are only twenty-four hours in a day and 8,760 hours in a year. I can't extend the day, the week, or the year. I can't bill 2,500 hours a year for a firm and still have that same amount of time for kids or a spouse—and sleep, grocery shopping, meal preparation, and workout. If you were to sleep eight hours a day for 365 days, that's 3,920 hours, leaving 4,840 for other things. There just are not enough hours to go around. There are a finite number of hours, and you can't get them back (unless you have a "Harry Potter" time turner). You have to make choices, so make them deliberately. The kids will grow up, and they will not return to where they were. If you lose your relationship with your significant other or a parent, you may not be given time to reclaim it. Time only marches forward without that time turner. In that same vein, you only have your time to sell. We don't sell cameras or plastic household products like my parents do; we sell our legal skills and our advice, in increments of time. Know what it is you have to sell and at what price you are selling it. If you give away your time, do it deliberately, to a cause you choose.

Your Reputation Is Your Stock in Trade

It is awfully hard to clean up a damaged reputation. Guard it. Practice by playing by the rules and playing ethically. One client or one case is not worth your reputation for life or your license.

Do Not Assume Everything Goes According to Plan

I always thought I would wait to have children until I made partner at "the" firm. We also thought about waiting until we could "afford" it. I was then surrounded by a solid handful of women in my late twenties who were undergoing IVF for fertility issues. I received daily reports of their treatments. The end result of this was my husband and I forgoing my "make partner first" plan and going off birth control much sooner than we would have otherwise. Mother Nature was kind to us; becoming pregnant was not an issue for our family. The firm plans changed, but the family came together as we wished it would. As a younger lawyer, I assumed that I could have both on my own timeline and everything would fall into place. It is important to live deliberately and to also respect Mother Nature. Things do not necessarily work out, and there are additional risks involved with having kids later in life. Make informed decisions deliberately, and understand the decisions you are making on all of these fronts. Keep your priorities straight.

It Is Possible to Have a Thriving Law Career while Making Family Your Top Priority

My husband and I marvel at the incredible men our boys have become. We attribute this to a number of factors—perhaps you can apply some of them. I am grateful for good day care at the beginning. I stressed over day care when I returned to work at my firm, but I am now a huge fan. Do not have guilt over it. Our boys learned an inordinate number of life lessons and met some lifelong friends at day care.

Sleep away camp was also amazing. My sons bonded with, watched over, and protected each other while learning to live in a group environment without mom and dad to pick up the pieces for small things that go wrong.

I deliberately ensured that our boys learned resiliency. I wanted them on sports teams that kept score. I recognized early on that life has winners and losers. I could not control the prom date saying "yes"; I cannot control the Ivy League school, sports team, employer, or fraternity saying "yes." As much as I love control, there are many things in life that mom and dad cannot control, so I worked to ensure that my sons could cope with life's disappointments.

I also felt very strongly that my sons needed certain life skills: how to manage money, balance a check book, and handle a credit card. They learned to love and care for another life when we got our first dog and to mourn when he passed. They took martial arts for self-defense. We talk to them and have shared one-on-one activities with each of them—meals and trips. We communicate with them about tough issues such as sex, drugs, and politics. I want to make sure that my sons understand concepts such as informed consent and birth control. We share a clear understanding that they are not to drink and drive. They know they can call us and we will come, together, and pick them up, along with their car, at any time, and not ask questions or make any judgments in lieu of them taking risky behavior.

We do things as a family. Whether it's a yearly ski trip, a cruise, or an "extended field trip" to Europe, we treasure the time together. Two recent summers, my two older sons traveled together. The brothers are very close. Something really went right, and I am very grateful. You see, you can make time to raise your children in a meaningful way while also building a successful law practice and career. You must do this with effort and care and pay attention along the way. You are their role model too.

Life, as a working attorney, is really about living it to the fullest—smelling the flowers along the way; contributing to the community; doing pro bono work; getting involved in Bar work; being someone your grandmother would be proud of; doing good work; saving for retirement; and taking vacations (create and check off that "bucket list"). My friend who recently died from leukemia was short-changed—her life ended much too soon. But she did live her life to the fullest with her family, career, and friends. Sometimes the small plays add up to a big win, and sometimes the small mistakes result in a big loss. Sometimes we don't have control over things we desperately want to control. That's the way life works. But you can choose to live life deliberately so that you don't have regrets, or at least so that you minimize the regrets you do have.

Making Time for What Matters, Professionally and Personally

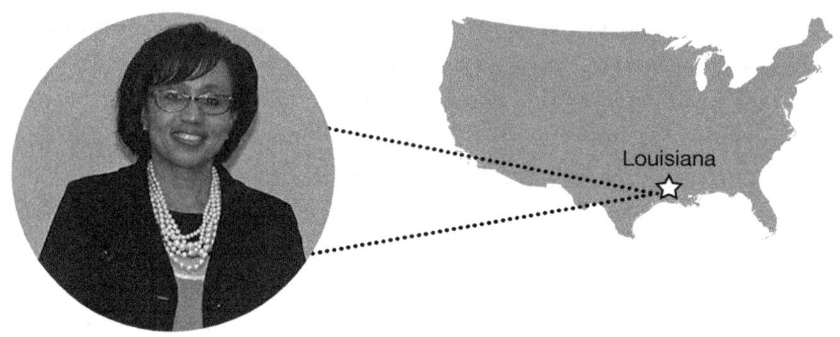

Her Story

Hon. Karen Wells Roby

Career

United States Magistrate Judge, Eastern District of Louisiana.

Education

Xavier University, BS, *cum laude*; Tulane University Law School, JD.

Best Advice

Keep track of your accomplishments because you are your best single advocate. Keep track of memoranda, projects, reviews, case results, and things that demonstrate your development as a lawyer.

Personal

Married (twenty-seven years) with two adult sons.

Making time for what matters is one of the most important skills a successful lawyer learns how to do well. We all struggle with multiple demands being placed on our time professionally and personally. We tend to make time for those things that are important to us, and the process of making time for both is not always easy.

It should not come as a surprise to us that our computer calendars, cell phone calendars, and Google reminders each say a lot about what we truly value in life. Although we may not realize it is happening, our calendars are mirrors into our perspective of our values placement. Our calendars from weeks or years earlier act like a mini time capsule, holding the treasures of our heart.

For me, the things that matter the most are my spirituality, family, career, professional friends, personal friends, and community. This list tends to be very demanding, but I learned to use certain techniques over the years that have proven beneficial. This essay addresses some personal and professional tips that have been helpful to me in making time for those things that matter.

Prioritizing my spiritual life has proven to be critically important in balancing and responding wisely to the many challenges that have occurred in the varying dimensions of life. To aid in spending time with God, I keep a prayer journal and write down those things that are weighing on my heart and the scriptural references that support my belief. Each morning around 5:30 a.m. it is important for me to spend quiet time with God, so I can focus on what he says about my problems. I have found that daily prayer is critical to my ability to function successfully despite the multiple demands on my time and to handle all things with grace. As my daily reminder of the importance of my time with God, I meditate on Matthew 6:33: Seek first His kingdom and righteousness [way of doing things] and all these things shall be added unto you.

Even when traveling on business, if at all possible, I arrange my return flight home so I can make church service. The ability to worship helps keep me focused on those things that are really important to me. It also has helped me face life challenges with hope that otherwise could be lost.

Prioritizing your spouse should also be included in the equation throughout the year. Periodic couple dinners, mini vacations, or adult group outings help you keep in focus the importance of your marriage. These events should be planned and placed on your calendar unless you have a standing date, whether lunch or dinner, or both. Always remember that *love* is an action word: saying it is one thing; spending time and prioritizing it is essential. These foundational principles will serve to help you meet the challenges and defeat the world's attempts to cause problems in your family structure and relationships.

Prioritizing your children is critically important for a successful personal life. For example, after my children reached school age, it became necessary for me to overlay my personal calendar on top of my professional calendar. Each May the school sent out the calendar for the upcoming school year. To plan to be available for sports events, school holidays, parent teacher conferences, and plays, I requested that my administrator place my two sons' school calendar dates in color (green for one and blue for the other) as reminders on my professional calendar. In prioritizing my availability for them, it was my way of noting that they did not ask to come into the world, so my world should adjust to them.

My calendar was set to send a reminder one week ahead of the event as notice that an event for a son was coming up. By color-coding my calendar and prioritizing the reminders, I was able to be very active during their elementary, middle, and high school years while managing my professional calendar as well.

Some would think that joining the bench would make balancing life easier. However, in my experience, the challenges remained the same. As a U.S. Magistrate Judge, my duties are most often tied to the scheduling orders of the twelve district judges I serve, so it is not easy to just block off time on the calendar. For example, generally I have two settlement conferences a day, and they are usually scheduled one month before the pretrial conference on the matter. I have found that scheduling the conferences after the discovery period closes is the best time to engage in most discussions because counsel for the parties know their case and are in the best position to engage in fruitful discussions. Securing the school calendars of my children in May of the preceding school year has really allowed me to see how to meet the court's demands and yet also be there for my sons' school events.

In addition to prioritizing their school life experience, it was important to plan a vacation for at least a week at some point during the year for our family. The term "vacation" for me means time off, preferably in the form of a trip, where the family can get away, relax, and focus on interacting away from the demands of the practice with no business-related purpose. Prioritizing time off helps by allowing the family to reconnect without the competing demands of the world.

In addition to managing all of these dimensions, it's important to prioritize your health. I have managed to incorporate the importance of my health by maintaining a workout schedule throughout my life. Whether it is running, walking, or a boot camp class, I found that the form of my workout depended on the time demands I was facing. Over the last three years, I have fallen in love with a boot camp class. The class is an intense form of exercise, and I really enjoy the diversity of women and men who participate. I have noticed the varying degrees of success from extreme weight loss to general fitness. It is a constant reminder and encouragement to me to continue to work to attain new fitness goals.

Another aspect of prioritizing my health is that I am completely fascinated by the power of raw foods and the degree to which our bodies need them to help us with an abundant life. If you are not familiar with raw foods, they are made up of fresh, whole, unrefined, living, plant-based foods—fruits, vegetables, leafy greens, nuts, and seeds—consumed in their natural state, without cooking or steaming. As a southerner, I was trained to cook all my foods, but I learned that cooked food did not provide the same amount of nutritional benefits for my body. As a result, in my spare time, I try to digest as much information and science as I can on raw foods. Although I continue to eat some cooked foods, my breakfast and lunch are always raw. The diversity and fun I have had in learning about different food combinations as well as the health benefits that I have received serve only to encourage me to continue to learn more.

I enjoy fresh raw juices, salads, and raw soups that I would never have dreamed of in the past. It is a completely different way of taking care of the body with which God has blessed me. The more I do, the better I feel. I also notice that I no longer get colds or the flu, so my immune system has been strengthened. It is empowering to naturally resolve health issues before they become major problems.

Professionally, it has always been important to me to be active in bar associations and nonprofits. These outlets have allowed me to meet like-minded people who deliver on their volunteer commitments. Volunteering professionally also allows me to engage in good deeds and fulfill a spiritual component of my life. Whether writing an article, coordinating a panel of subject matter experts, or serving as a subject matter expert, volunteering professionally helps me develop and maintain my knowledge in an area. It also helps me to expand my relationships. When I practiced law, it also helped me build my local brand for career or business development purposes.

Having a professional network of women is important. This network can provide professional support in addition to personal encouragement and advice. For example, over the years I have had a professional network of women of varying career experiences and ages. Each woman, however, was successful in her own professional environment. We all were also mothers and wives.

As a way of reminding each other that our lack of perfection in various areas of life was not unusual, we formed the "Mommy Malpractice Group." The MMG would get together twice a year and have dinner at Commanders Place, a five-star restaurant in New Orleans, while the children were with their fathers. We had a grand time sharing experiences over dinner and drinks, and we would remind each other that running late from a deposition to pick up a child, albeit not optimal, is not uncommon. We assured each other that the occasional mistake of forgetting about a half-day of school for pick-up purposes is not an indictment on one as a mother. Our MMG dinners permitted each woman an opportunity to feel better about her experience as a wife, a mother, and a lawyer. The MMG would have so much fun that the time would get away from us. Almost magically our cell phones would each begin to ring, and it was our husbands indicating that we had timed out and needed to get home as we could hear the kids in the background.

The MMG also served as career support and advisors. The MMG would remember its members for panel presentations, writing, or teaching opportunities. Over the years, having a network of successful women who were also lawyers served as a constant source of encouragement to stick with the profession even when the challenges seemed great.

In addition to the professional female network, it is important to have female friends who have no connection to the law. This group of friends may serve as a means of escape from the habit of always thinking, living, and speaking law. Over the years, this network of women has served to remind me of the importance of taking time off. Having time off, preferably in the form of a girls' trip, has allowed me to resume juggling the many balls I have been blessed to manage in life. An example of a rejuvenating girls' trip was a one-week detox spa trip to West Palm Beach, Florida. The spa's focus was spiritual, physical, and mental wholeness and health. Sometimes it may seem like there is not enough time. Remember, we make time for what is important to us, and we certainly should be important.

Finally, but not least, prioritizing and spending time blessing others generally brings a sense of purpose in life beyond the day job. Volunteering in church, the legal community, or the schools always gave me a sense of purpose disconnected from the law. For years I held brown bag lunches in chambers with younger female attorneys as a means of mentoring them through the law firm maze. It proved to help many survive and thrive in their law firms. When my kids were in elementary school, I volunteered on the PTA board, designed the school's website, worked to help bring computers to the school, and also served as chairperson of the board of directors of a golf program here in New Orleans.

So many things matter to me both professionally and personally. I have loved my professional journey as well as I love working to have an enriched family life. Contributing my gifts to my legal and local communities helps give me a sense of belonging that is invaluable. I often reflect on Mahatma Gandhi's statement that "we must be the change we wish to see in the world." Working hard to prioritize everything that is important to me—and as you can see, it's a lot—helps to advance positive change both in me and for my family, my profession, and my world. I invite you to check out your calendar and assess what it says about what is important to you. Make adjustments, if necessary, and be that change.

Strategies for Making Time for What Matters Most

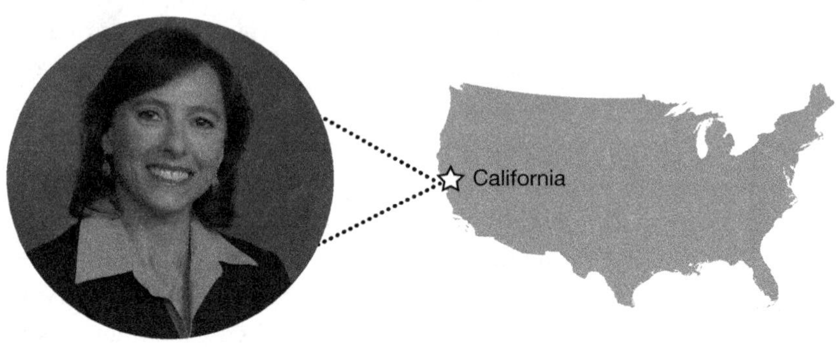

Her Story

Andrea S. Carlise

Career

Managing partner at Patton Wolan Carlise, LLP, where I practice employment litigation and provide advice and counseling to employers.

Education

University of California, Davis, BA, 1986; Santa Clara University School of Law, JD, 1990.

Best Advice

Find something you are passionate about, and infuse that in your law practice. Reevaluate your priorities regularly to ensure you are making time for what matters most to you.

Personal

Married twenty-four years, with two children in college, and lots of friends and extended family who keep me grounded and connected.

For more information about Andrea

www.pwc-law.com

In an ideal world, we learn from all of our experiences. If we don't figure out how to prioritize our time, we short-change ourselves and might not get to experience the things that are most important to us. The first step in this process is to figure out what actually matters most to each of us.

What matters most to me has morphed at each stage of my life. I am sure my priorities will continue to change as I move toward retirement. Making sense of what is important to me and focusing on those aspects of my life has been a moving target, but one worth pursuing nonetheless. My strategies for reaching that target have also varied over time. Perhaps you can learn from the following strategies and figure out how to attain the goal of spending your time on what is most important to *you* at each stage of your life.

Sunrise: Early Career Strategies

When I first began practicing law for a small firm in San Francisco, I was overwhelmed by the long hours and the sheer volume of work. I cried myself to sleep after an opposing counsel admonished me harshly when I asked for a discovery extension for the first time and was concerned about how it would affect the case. One of the partners told me that he had found working from 8:30 a.m. to 6:30 p.m. each weekday, at a minimum, and at least half a day on the weekend was required to get the job done. As I awkwardly navigated the world of civil litigation as a young associate, it began to dawn on me that I really didn't want to end up like this man. Though he was a good lawyer and, as far as I could tell, was a thoughtful and well-meaning person, it appeared that he had a limited personal life, was twice divorced, and didn't see his one child all that often. In my mind at the time, this partner was a micro-managing workaholic.

In retrospect, this partner was just doing what it took to manage a litigation firm the best way he knew how. What I learned from him, however, was what I didn't want to be "when I grew up." (I'm still waiting for that growing up thing to happen, by the way; but I digress.) I learned that having personal relationships outside of the office, getting married, having children, and being passionate about what I did every day were my priorities. My first strategy to reprioritize my time was to join a local women's bar association. I had always been passionate about gender equity and knew that meeting other like-minded women would help me find my passion as a lawyer while having fun along the way. It turns out that I have made many lifelong friends from women's bar activities, and after twenty-five years I remain passionate about gender equity and human rights.

Within the first five years after passing the bar, I got married and had a child. The next target to reach was to be able to spend quality time with my new family. The support I received from my women lawyer friends helped me figure out how to ask for parental leave. The firm I worked for was relatively new, and I was the first attorney to become pregnant while working there. The reproductive rights committee I was cochairing was drafting a model parental leave policy. Though my firm was not close to getting the "golden diaper award," I was able to take twelve weeks of unpaid leave—clearly not what we strive for, but I made it work. When I returned from leave, I second-chaired my first trial, and realized I was burning out from the sleep deprivation and trying to be all things to all people. After the trial concluded and I had been back at work for six months, I walked into a meeting with the firm's partners and told them I was quitting because I didn't have enough time to do anything right. They asked me if I meant I didn't have sufficient time at work or at home, and I responded "both." To my surprise, they suggested that I work part time instead of quitting. Wow, I didn't even realize that was an option!

After figuring out how to tell the partners what I could actually accomplish in three days each week, life threw me another bone. Another woman lawyer friend with whom I worked (are you seeing the trend here?) had interviewed for a part-time attorney position in a firm much closer to my home but had already accepted a position at another firm when she was offered the job. She suggested that the firm contact me. As it turned out, I have worked for this firm for the last nineteen years and am passionate about the employment litigation practice I have built here.

Full Daylight: Midcareer Strategies

The best thing about the new job I started in 1995 was that I was initially hired to work three days per week. This allowed me the time I craved to spend with my son and to get some much needed sleep. My strategy was to work during the three days a week that my son was at day care and to spend the other two days at home. I quickly learned that I had to be flexible about this timing, but fortunately I was able to have my husband pick up my son from day care when necessary and to make calls and answer e-mails from home. I continued with this strategy when my daughter was born two years later and avoided the burnout I had begun to suffer when I was working full time while my son was a newborn.

When my daughter and son were both in elementary school, I was able to switch my work hours so that I could pick up my kids from school each day. I worked from 9:00 a.m. to 2:00 p.m. five days a week. Again, flexibility and support from friends and my husband were key to executing this plan. Fostering relationships with other parents who had children at the same school allowed us to share pick-ups and after-school care when needed. Working six miles from home also permitted me to spend more time with my family, which is what mattered most to me at that time. Some would say I wasn't "leaning in" to my career during these years, but I was leaning in to living the life that I wanted—making time for what mattered most to me.

As my kids got older and seemed to need (and prefer) less time with me, I adjusted my schedule accordingly. I was able to devote more time to other activities that enriched my life, eventually becoming president of California Women Lawyers and later president of the PTA at my kids' school. Working part time for almost ten years was wonderful, and I am so grateful that I was able to make it work because so many people do not have this luxury.

As my kids headed toward middle school, honing my trial and other litigation skills became more important to me. I also had the opportunity to become a partner, due in no small part to the partner who had become first my mentor and then my sponsor—opening doors to increased client contact and greater responsibility. After observing my work as a part-time attorney, this partner wanted me to join the firm, but only if I was willing to work full time. I reevaluated what mattered most to me, determined that my priorities had changed, and decided it was the right time to lean in to my career.

Becoming a partner definitely made my work life more demanding. Fortunately, my husband changed careers around this time. We had met in law school, but he never really enjoyed practicing law. After working as in-house counsel for a title insurance company, he decided to quit the practice and open a restaurant about six blocks from our home. Being so close to home allowed him to be available for "kid duty" during the day, and it allowed me to spend longer hours at the office. Again, I was and am grateful for the luxury of having a life partner who supports my career. I am cognizant of the fact that single parents certainly find leaning in more difficult and prioritizing family time more challenging. I realize that the strategy of relying more on others to make more time for what matters worked for me, but it may not work in all circumstances.

Sunset: Late Career Strategies

All was chugging along relatively calmly after I became a partner, with the occasional bump in the road along the way. I became more adept at client relations and better at disciplining firm employees. Home life was pretty smooth, though worries about grades and later alcohol and marijuana use invaded my priorities and sucked up my time more often than I'd like to remember. As my family and I aged, so did my law partner. Eventually, he wanted to retire, and he wanted me to buy him out. I was conflicted about whether running a small law firm on my own was really how I wanted to spend the rest of my foreseeable working life. So I sought some outside, neutral guidance and hired a life coach.

My coach, a lawyer about ten years older than me, helped guide me through the process of evaluating my priorities and values once again. We looked into what mattered most to me at that time of my life. I was questioning whether to seek appointment to the bench or to move forward with purchasing this law practice. Support of like-minded women and furthering gender equity remained important. By this time, I was an officer with the National Conference of Women's Bar Associations. Again, the relationships I built through this organization have sustained me both personally and professionally. I now have friends and referral sources across the country.

My coaching sessions also helped me determine how to attain a healthy lifestyle and nurture my spiritual life while still attending to my home and work commitments. My coach's thoughtful probing prompted some soul searching. I ultimately decided that being a judge would prevent, or at least interfere with, my ability to continue advocating for gender equity and other civil rights. I also discovered that flexible work scheduling really is one of my priorities because it has allowed me to do what matters most to me. Ultimately, I decided to move forward with buying my partner out and running the firm on my own.

Just when the complicated buy-out was complete and I was feeling like things were falling into place, an unexpected health problem hit hard. My son, who by this time had just returned home for the summer after his freshman year at college, was diagnosed with stage four Hodgkin lymphoma. As you can imagine, what matters most came clearly into view at this time. My family focused on saving my son's life with all we had. I am so grateful for the outstanding oncology team at UCSF Benioff Children's Hospital in Oakland for the care they provided. My son went through six months of chemotherapy and radiation treatment and had normal PET scans as a result. He was able to go back to college in January and has just returned home for the summer. Our fingers are crossed for a complete and lasting recovery.

What I learned from this daunting experience is that personal relationships are indeed what matter most to me. My relationships with my friends and family deepened as a result of this health crisis, and we all learned valuable lessons from it. Although a few people were not as supportive as I would have hoped, others I didn't know as well really stepped up to allow me to spend time at the hospital instead of taking depositions. My daughter and my husband were and are amazing. My also-amazing son was a "model chemo survivor," according to his physician, and his patience and perseverance throughout treatment were truly incredible. My daughter is starting college in a few months, and in September my husband and I will be empty-nesters. I am sure that additional strategies for navigating the next stage of my life to ensure I make time for what matters most will be forthcoming. Stay tuned.

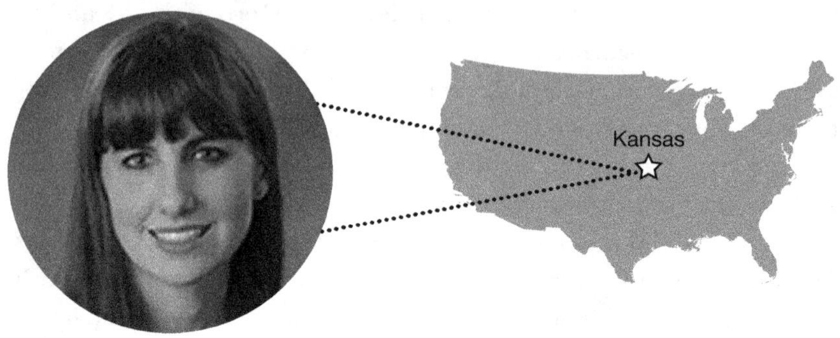

Her Story

Angel Zimmerman

Career

President and managing partner for Zimmerman & Zimmerman, PA, where I practice collection law.

Education

Emporia State University, BS in Public Administration; Washburn School of Law, JD.

Best Advice

Prepare the night before, wake up ready to go, and do good things enthusiastically. Be awesome.

Personal

Married (twenty-three years), four children (college and high school).

For more information about Angel

www.z2law.com

T—Team and Talent

I—Initiative and Impact

M—Moments and Momentum Matter

E—Energizing Enthusiasm Equals Exponential Effect

Time is a gift. At the twentieth anniversary of the death of my mother, the most influential person in my life, I dedicate this article to the one who created me—literally and figuratively—and who taught me there is always time for "one more thing."

My most vivid, lingering memory of my mom was sitting with her in my car after a mother-daughter lunch date. I was feeling that life was rather tough; I was taking twenty-one hours toward my undergraduate degree, working two jobs, and serving as a counselor to our children's organization at church. She responded bluntly, "It must be nice to have so much free time." Shocked and hurt, I spitefully thought, "I'll show you!" and I promptly packed my schedule even more.

I never asked what she meant. For years, I assumed she was trying to tell me that a "mother's schedule" is twenty-four hours a day, seven days a week. But now I believe that she was expressing awe at the immense privilege of living in a time and place that allows us the opportunity to fill our time as we choose.

My life is an exploration of my mother's lessons. Packing my schedule is now a source of real joy and satisfaction. I married my high school debate rival, and we are raising four kids (ages fourteen to twenty). My husband and I both went through law school full time with kids, with jobs, no day care, while anxiously engaged in church and community. If an organization shares my passions, then I join up, show up, and roll up my sleeves. My husband and I practice together with all four kids on the payroll. For the last sixteen years, I have started each school day at 5:50 a.m., teaching a room full of high school students the scriptures. I finally understand my mom's passion for time.

My mother's time management lessons, which I am still incorporating into my life, are especially applicable in the practice of law. Her lessons were these:

1. You are never able to do anything within a vacuum (Team).
2. Use what you've got, even if you don't believe it is very much (Talent).
3. Show up (Initiative).
4. How you do things matters more than what you have done (Impact).
5. Pay attention, keep your head up, and watch so you can serve (Moments Matter).
6. Keep at it, don't give up, and put one foot before the other; you will become impressed with what you have been able to do (Momentum Matters).
7. Passion is contagious; if you share yours with others, you will be amply rewarded (Energizing Enthusiasm Equals Exponential Effect).

T—Team and Talent

You have talent! You did not make it through law school and into this demanding profession without it. These words are true: "Your playing small does not serve the world. There is nothing enlightened about shrinking so that other people won't feel insecure around you. . . . And as we let our own light shine, we unconsciously give other people permission to do the same."[1] Your talents are yours to develop and share, but you have agreed to be a lawyer with the responsibility to defend and preserve justice. How will you in small and simple ways defend justice more effectively? You must be prepared to lead the charge in preserving society in large, often uncomfortable ways as well. Fulfillment occurs when we make life better for others and when we realize that we have been rejuvenated by someone who spent their precious allotted time on our behalf.

Team is vital—even for the sometimes solitary practice of law. Your team includes those you surround yourself with who have the

---

1. Marianne Williamson, A Return to Love: Reflections on the Principles of a Course in Miracles (Harper Collins 1992).

ability to be seen and speak on your behalf. To maximize your productivity within time's limitations, assemble an incredible team from the people around you.

We need our sisters on our team. We are women, and sisterhood is empowering. I am often asked, "Is there still a need for women's organizations?" Yes. No qualifiers or explanations needed. Women's organizations will become essential rather than meaningless as women truly gain choice. We have won many permanent victories, but we must reject the illusion that what our great-grandmothers, grandmothers, and mothers fought for is no longer a fight today. Regression happens; it is real. We need to be inclusive and to avoid being the "token" female.

Abigail Adams told us, "Remember the ladies"; now we must not forget the role men will play. I believe that working with men, we can crush the devastating salary discrepancies, entrepreneurial and C-suite leadership dearth, and lack of educational opportunities for women around the globe. I am a firm advocate for mothers like my mother-in-law who raised men who are ready to be equals. Whatever your opinions may be on marriage, the synergy of two people aligned both in home life and work life produces well beyond the capabilities of just two individuals. I have a husband who is an equal partner in parenting, household chores, and office commitments, which allows me additional time to serve. For those who choose this path, I believe it is our duty to marry men like this, to raise sons like this, and to encourage them to speak up and change our culture from the top down.

Next, seriously consider putting your children on your team. We often list ourselves as being part of our children's team, but not vice versa. I have been blessed with four children who were always part of my team. They helped me study, took business trips with me, and even helped me run conferences. Although we didn't have the typical Kansas family *farm*, where the kids learned to milk cows and collect eggs, we did have our Kansas family *firm*, where they learned to file, image, track statistics, and speak on industry topics. Office successes were their successes, and mom and dad's awards were also theirs. Most don't have a family farm/firm, but simple things like having clothes picked out the night before, bags by the door, and helping mommy find her keys are amazing ways for children to feel that they are part of mom's success team and the family team. Involving kids in our life creates the opportunity for our kids to see and learn from us how we handle difficulties in our strongest light. Raising children who have always felt like contributing members of their family's success will go a long way toward global camaraderie.

Look for staff that can be extensions not only of your work product but of your philosophy and demeanor. Delegation is a time extender: it is not only empowering to you but to those you have trusted. For those who tend to be control freaks (myself included), we need to learn to be time freaks and maximize our reach and impact, not our control. To have and feel a balanced life there must be more than work and home; make sure your team expands to your community. Find a way to have city, state, national, and international causes—feeling connected locally and globally is incredibly balancing.

I—Initiative and Impact

An age-old object lesson deserves repeating here. Take a pot and pour in water, then sand, then pebbles, and then several large stones. You will find that not all the stones will fit in the pot. Pour it all out and start again by putting in all the stones first, then the pebbles, then the sand, and last the water. Magically, it all fits. Mom would explain: the water and sand events are important (possibly vital) but are not necessarily fulfilling, so you must find the stones of impact and make sure they are in your daily pot of time first. This leads to a life without regrets. You must take the initiative to categorize the events in your life as sand, water, pebbles, and stones because it is different for each of us. And, contrary to the suggestions of many work-life balance discussions, who we are does not have to be relegated to a separate pot from what we do. Work is part of my life, and I love all my worlds most when they interconnect and meld together. My greatest feelings of success come when a single event affects multiple areas of my life (e.g., business trips *with* my kids; one project that can serve the needs of two or three of my organizations; improving my thinking and speaking skills by teaching seminary).

Initiative is showing up, being present in the moment, and responding, supporting, and bringing needed change. I had an "aha" moment when a lecturer explained that he once asked the president of a huge international organization, "What do you do in a boring meeting?" This wise leader leaned back, pondered a moment, and thoughtfully responded, "I don't know that I have ever been in a boring meeting. I can always learn something on timing, or word choice, or watch how the meeting is impacting the room or an individual. I can learn who I should talk with after the meeting, compliment, or redirect." That simple story imparts great wisdom on initiative and impact. Take a deep breath and reengage in the meeting or conversation in which you find yourself.

M—Moments and Momentum Matter

Within my first two years of practice, I heard priceless advice in an acceptance speech at the Women Attorney Association of Topeka's Justice Kay McFarland Award ceremony. Judge Marquardt, of the Kansas Court of Appeals, explained that she found herself many years ago in law school as a single mother with four boys. Her mantra was W.I.N. To be successful she had to do "W"hat's "I"mportant "N"ow. She said sometimes it was important to stay and finish a brief, other times it was important to be in the bleachers at a kid's practice. And sometimes "W.I.N."ing meant studying in the bleachers.

It truly only takes a moment to realign and ask yourself, "Am I choosing to 'W.I.N.'? Am I doing what's important now?" If we do this, not only will we be as successful as possible, but we also will find peace. I am learning that if there is anything that steals life and time, it is guilt. I contend that I can often be at peace and not be "balanced." I like the process of finding balance from chaos, not necessarily the end product. I think most of you are the same because you are lawyers, and finding balance (not necessarily being in balance) is fundamental to who we are as professionals and as people.

Probably the most halting and humbling experience I have had was about a week after I became a lawyer. I was in church and responded to a comment another woman had made. I later walked out of the room and overheard this woman say, "Did you hear that the lawyer said I made a good comment?" To me, I was the same little girl who they had always known, but to them I had changed. I was now a lawyer, and my evaluations carried weight and elevated another woman's self-esteem. I learned there that moments matter.

As lawyers, we are unquestionably seen as leaders. Our realism, our pragmatism, and our attention to detail often may suck the wind out of a room, whereas presenting our ideas with more thoughtful wording could actually add life and excitement. This can often be done by exchanging one little three-letter word with another; instead of "but" use "and." This is probably the largest time-saving tip I have to offer. There is something positively powerful in the word "and." Even when I am vehemently opposed to an idea, if I start my response with the word "and" before discussing my reservations, the conflict usually resolves quickly and to everyone's satisfaction (saving hours of negotiating through hurt feelings and bruised egos, extra conference committees, and retasking or even having to scrap an otherwise good plan, project, or settlement).

I am grateful for momentum. I often feel that I am spinning my wheels or even running backward. I encourage you to start an accomplishment journal. On New Year's Eve, my mother had us write down our accomplishments of the past year and our goals for the new one. We would then roll up our accomplishments and goals and put them in a paper towel tube, which mom called our time capsule. Each New Year's Eve, we would pull out all the time capsule tubes. Looking at the time capsule, I could see that I was progressing, even when I would otherwise swear to my mother I was not. Progress was visible in my handwriting, my projects, my desires, my goals, and my schooling. The paper towel tube time capsule is now a tradition for my own family, along with my personal daily gratitude journal, and a Super Woman yearly recap journal from my husband.

E—Energizing Enthusiasm Equals Exponential Effect

To this day, there are many who tell me that they continue trying and progressing as if they were still reporting to my mom. She would take an index card and write the important things and dates of people whom she met and follow up to see their progress. She accepted others where they were, but knew they had so much more in them. When a meal was needed, she already knew their favorite pie, soup, or main dish. She listened and was excited for your progress. Somehow she didn't "take" your excitement, but she gave it back along with an extra helping of "Of course, you are doing great, and I can't wait to see how much more you will do!" or "That is unbelievably awful, and you are dealing with it. I am so proud of you, you are amazing."

Enthusiasm is energizing, and it is contagious. Although we cannot create time, we can create energy, which is more empowering. We must work with energizing enthusiasm to make time our friend. Mom's last lesson to me was taught in the front row of the church at her funeral, when I turned to see the overflow curtains opened and the chapel full to the back of the room with nonfamily members who had traveled many miles and even from many states to pay tribute. This uneducated, stay-at-home mom who died at forty-three taught the exponential effect of energizing others to do good and to be good. Go and do likewise.

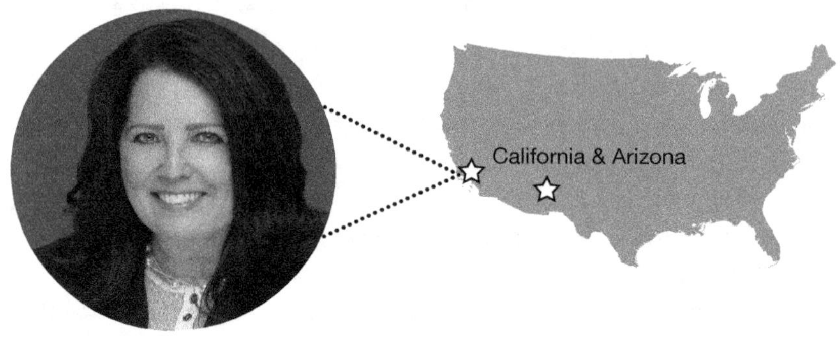

Her Story

Teresa M. Beck

Career

Partner at Lincoln, Gustafson & Cercos, where I practice Civil Litigation Defense.

Education

San Diego State University; University of San Diego School of Law, *magna cum laude.*

Best Advice

"Love bears all things, believes all things, hopes all things, endures all things. Love never fails." 1 Corinthians 13, 7–8.

Personal

Married twenty-six years, with three college-age children.

For more information about Teresa

www.lgclawoffice.com

"Darkness cannot drive out darkness; only light can do that. Hate cannot drive out hate; only love can do that."

—Martin Luther King, Jr.

Issues relating to work-life management and work-life "balance" are of huge interest to me. One of the goals of my career is to share the experiences of as many women as possible with other women, to help all women have multiple visions of female success. It is my hope that by sharing our stories and our best advice, women will learn from the experiences of their colleagues so that more of us stay in the practice of law, and more of us will advance in our careers into the highest levels of the profession. I truly could talk endlessly about things like the adventures of pregnancy and maternity leave, advancement tips when children are young, how things change as our kids grow up, how our views of business change as our families grow, how we can (like many of our male counterparts) thrive with our careers and with our families, what it's like to work through adversity, and more. The list is never-ending!

Presented with the opportunity to reach so many women through this book, I asked myself what is the single most important message I can pass on to other women. I realized that I must share how critical my spiritual foundation has been to me; the importance of anything else I could write about pales in comparison. I feel called to share my spiritual journey with my sister women attorneys in hopes you might recognize your path in my story and know there are kindred spirits in our profession, or perhaps you will be inspired to start building your own spiritual foundation. Either way, in my opinion, building your career on a spiritual foundation is the single most important thing you can do to prepare yourself for a successful career.

Lawyers don't often talk about their spiritual or religious beliefs, and for good reason. We don't want anyone to think we are overstepping proper professional bounds, and perhaps even more, we don't really want to get *that personal* with our colleagues. I am convinced that despite a seeming code of secrecy about the subject, the majority of us do in fact have a spiritual foundation, whether it is Christianity, Judaism, Buddhism, Islam, Hinduism, or some other belief system. If we could have an open conversation about our spiritual lives, I am certain you would hear many stories similar to mine, about how diverse lawyers with diverse belief systems find that their spiritual lives are the foundation of everything. Although it is a bit uncomfortable for me to talk about this subject, the importance of the message compels me. Something that is at the core of the lives of so many is worth discussing. So without in any way suggesting that my story is the only one, or that my beliefs are the only correct ones, here is how I developed a foundation that became the core of my entire life.

In the Beginning

One of the most important pieces of my spiritual journey was finding a place of religion where my family and I could grow spiritually. This might have been a little bit easier for me than others because my father was a Presbyterian minister and a Navy chaplain. I was raised in the Presbyterian church and went to worship services and Sunday school regularly. I often accompanied my father when he gave Sunday services on ships docked in the San Diego Bay, traveling from ship to ship in motor boats. Then, like many others, I became distant from my spiritual foundation as a college student. Nevertheless, my husband and I were married in the huge Presbyterian church I grew up in, and each of our children was baptized there. The church was so huge, though, that our efforts to assimilate into the church as a family never really got off the ground.

Beginning Again

As our kids grew, my husband and I realized more and more that our family needed a spiritual home. We really weren't focusing much on ourselves. We found a church home *for the children*! (Little did we know how much the church would come to mean to each of us.) When the kids were about two, four, and six, something in our hearts shifted, and we began our church search in earnest. Every Sunday was a different church, but none felt like home. One morning I drove past a small Episcopal church with a big sign for Vacation Bible School. I was honestly thinking that VBS would give my husband (a teacher with summers off) a nice little break from the kids from

9:00 a.m. to noon for a week. I had always been intrigued by the beauty of Episcopal churches. We had attended services once or twice at this little church. Although we didn't feel it was our church home, VBS seemed like it would be fun for the kids. I could never have foreseen how this little church would transform our lives.

Discovering Treasure

Our kids enrolled in VBS. Soon we were all singing VBS songs with wonderful messages about love and faith, the kids were bringing home precious crafts they had made, and we were invited to church the following Sunday when the kids would be singing for the congregation. The church captured our hearts over the course of that week, and we have been members ever since. We began attending every Sunday. We made friends, and our kids made friends. I taught Sunday school, something that was not difficult for me to do because teaching is a lot like litigating—lots of thinking on your feet. We got more and more involved in our church. The kids were all confirmed by the local Bishop. As they became teens, our children joined the teen group and went to the youth meetings every Wednesday evening. They joined church music groups and are part of the only teen worship band I know of in the city of San Diego who can handle all of the music for an entire service including communion! The kids are now so connected and devoted to our church that it would be odd to miss a Sunday. They also sing in the choir when their schedules permit, and volunteer for VBS, which thanks in part to our family, continues to be a tradition in the church. When we moved to the physical home where we planned to stay, in the neighborhood where the kids would go to school and play sports and perform in community theater and so forth, our minister came to our home and blessed every room—even the bathrooms, which the kids thought was hilarious.

The Real Treasure

After years of attending church, seminars, Bible studies, a church retreat (called Cursillo—it is fantastic), watching the church tradition cycle through the year from Christmas to Epiphany Sunday, to Lent, Easter, Pentecost, and on and on, I realize now that church was really for me too. We have all learned about things like the fruits of the spirit (there is no law against love, joy, peace, patience, kindness, goodness, faithfulness, gentleness and self control—Galatians 5:22, 23), the spiritual journeys of the men and women of the Old Testament, and the birth, life, and resurrection of Jesus. Over the years, I have learned different lessons from these teachings, with the passing years allowing for a deeper and deeper understanding of how these lessons are important in my life, in the life of my family, and even in the life of my career. The people of my church have seen me through difficult times, prayed for family members, visited my mother and husband in the hospital, and quite literally (and figuratively) blessed my home. Our minister has led us through dark times (including giving Last Rites to my father-in-law recently) and has taught us things we could not learn anywhere else. Our kids have twenty extra sets of parents and twice as many grandparents to help guide them. I have learned to pray for my family, and even for lawyers who are driving me crazy. I have found myself in very difficult cases and have been able to make successful decisions about what to do based on my spiritual foundation. I have felt the presence of God in our lives many times, and I know that comes from the commitment we have made to our spiritual lives. Our church is where it all began.

God at Work

Because we don't talk about our spiritual lives at work, we can forget that our spiritual fundamentals can serve us at work. We shouldn't leave our spiritual lives at the thresholds of our offices. I recall many times when contentious cases with terribly difficult lawyers left me feeling there could be no resolution and my career was on the line; when a problem with a coworker or staff person seemed insurmountable; when the pressures of work were overwhelming; when I despaired about the future of my career and did not know what to do or where to turn. It is in these situations that a spiritual foundation has served me the most. When I have been able to step out of my problems in such situations and give them to God, I have been amazed at how options I had not previously perceived present themselves. (I like to imagine my problems all sitting in the palm of my hand, and then I raise my palm to my mouth and blow all those problems to God.)

Perhaps more important, it is my strongest belief that the answer to every problem is, quite simply, love. How can love possibly be relevant in the everyday life of a lawyer? It's not easy, but I try to deal with even the most challenging people and situations by developing an attitude of love.

Why It Matters

We are still at a point in history when the work of women attorneys involves unique challenges. For many of us, dealing with bias and the negative micro messages we hear frequently, both within and outside our jobs, can seem daunting. Without my faith to carry me through difficult times, I am not sure I would still be in the practice of law. Without an understanding of what is really important in life, I might focus too much importance on work issues. Instead, my experiences in church, and in my life because of what I have learned in church, have created a heart of love and gratitude and a spirit of happiness and positivity within my soul. These experiences have deepened my relationships with my husband and with my three kids. Attending church with your daughter playing keyboard and singing, your eldest son on the guitar and performing vocals, and your youngest son playing drums, singing stirring songs of faith, is just a wonderful experience. But that's not all.

It's Not Easy, but It's Worth It

Getting up every Sunday and going to church, taking the kids every Wednesday evening to youth group, participating in daily activities such as prayer and study to learn more and follow my spiritual path (not to mention giving of my time, talent, and treasures to the church), all require commitment and sacrifice. It was hard in the beginning. But after making the commitment for a short time, these things become routine. And the rewards keep growing. I have learned how to rely on a power greater than myself, how to forgive, how to search for the will of God in my life, and all of these things have led me and my family to things greater than I had ever dreamed of or even imagined. God's plan for me has not always been what I had been planning for myself, but it has always been better. I take great comfort in knowing that there is a greater purpose for my life that transcends what I do as a lawyer. And getting down on my knees every week to pray keeps me grounded in humility and thankfulness.

Life's Not Perfect

Our Facebook society leaves many people feeling that their lives don't measure up. The lives of our friends and colleagues we see portrayed on Facebook often seem perfect, and hard times rarely seem to touch the lives of our Facebook friends. The fact is that every person faces difficult times, and I am no exception. Having a spiritual foundation helps me get through the hard times. Over the course of my career, I have faced the death of my brother from AIDS, the births of three children who each had lengthy stays in the Neo-Natal Intensive Care Unit, kids with learning challenges, and close relatives with drug and alcohol problems. I mention these things not to suggest I am amazing for getting through all of these problems, but to make it clear that I am just as needful of a spiritual foundation as anyone else, and in hopes that in my story you might find something that resembles your story, and know you have company.

Build Your Own Spiritual Foundation

My family's spiritual foundation is built on the Christian religion, but of course there are many other ways to build a spiritual foundation. It is interesting to me that in everyday practice the lawyers I know don't generally talk at all about their faith. I do know a few lawyers who have prayer groups in their private firms, and my Jewish partner regularly sends e-mails to the entire firm explaining the meaning of Jewish holidays. Other than that, though, the subject is somewhat taboo. We all want to be careful not to seem as if we are pushing our religion on others, and we certainly don't want to make anyone else uncomfortable. In a way, though, this is a tragedy because I suspect the vast majority of us engage in some form of regular spiritual practice. Whatever your spiritual foundation is, the important thing is to find one that you feel at home with that can serve as *your* spiritual foundation. It is my deepest hope and prayer that you find your spiritual foundation, or continue pursuing your spiritual journey, and build on it with commitment and sacrifice, which will bring *you* rewards beyond what you can dream of or imagine. And maybe even find a way to share your faith, and your spiritual journey, with other lawyers!

Going the Distance: Prioritizing Commitment to Health

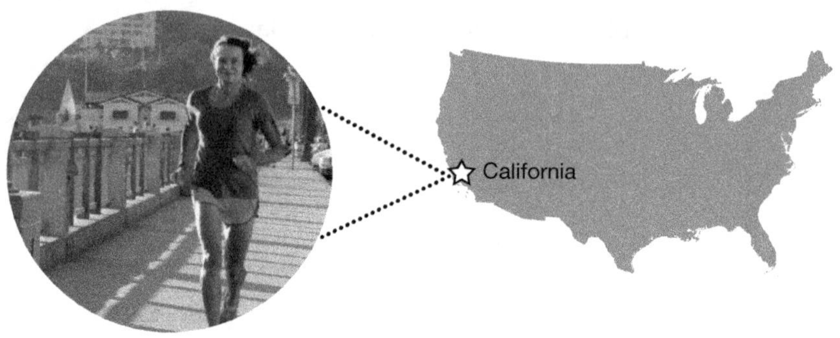

Her Story

Linda Somers Smith

Career

Partner at Adamski Moroski Madden Cumberland & Green LLP, where I practice business and real property law.

Education

U.C. Davis, BA in Economics, *magna cum laude*, Phi Beta Kappa; U.C. Davis School of Law, King Hall, JD.

Best Advice

You will be knocked down a lot. You will not always prevail, but you also will be supported and be given opportunities. Find and focus on the support and opportunities and let go of the rest.

Personal

Former competitive long distance runner, two times U.S. National Marathon Champion and U.S. Olympian, Women's Marathon, 1996. Awesome, supportive husband and daughter.

For more information about Linda

www.ammcglaw.com

The conventional belief among my peers is that I survive on Diet Coke, yogurt, and an occasional client lunch; but no one will dispute that I always make time for my health. I was asked to write this section because I have worked full time as an attorney for years, am an equity partner at a medium-sized firm (large by our community standards), have a family, and at the same time, until recently, pursued a professional running career. My running career includes winning two U.S. Women's Marathon Championships, competing in numerous world championship events, earning a position on the U.S. Olympic team in 1996 in the women's marathon, qualifying for the Olympic trials in the women's marathon a record seven times over the span of thirty years, and I have been inducted into the USATF Master Hall of Fame, Cal Aggies Athletic Hall of Fame, and RRCA Distance Runners Hall of Fame.

Competing as a long-distance runner is a time-consuming and selfish pursuit. Committing to the steps necessary to become a successful attorney, although not always selfish, is also time consuming. Ideally, I would have dedicated myself completely to one high-level pursuit, but working without having the outlet of competition did not work for me, nor did competing without the balance of a career.

What worked for me was doing both. Doing both, however, always required that I balance my schedule and plan in advance. The legal community loses a lot of talent because of its emphasis on billable hours. Fitting in a workout by coming in late, leaving for a long lunch, or taking off early is two to three hours you could be billing. For those with families, the pressure is greater because it is two to three hours you might not have to spare.

Commitment to Self

Working and competing, while also managing the other areas of my life, would not have been possible without a consistent commitment to my mental and physical health. In the end, caring for yourself is a commitment like any other, but there is tremendous pressure on women and attorneys to commit to others, leaving ourselves last.

Ironically, however, if you do not commit to taking care of yourself, in the long run you will be a less happy, healthy, and productive person. Like any commitment, you must override short-term concessions and focus on the long-term goal. You have to make the choice to care for yourself, which includes focusing on healthy eating and exercise, and prioritize these choices in your life. This focus is no different from the challenge facing every first-world worker, so some of my comments are no different than commonsense advice you might find on any health website. What I can offer is how focusing on choice and self-awareness can help you implement those recommendations for healthy eating and exercise.

Daily Choices

Practicing law is difficult and demanding. To me, the profession requires the mental dedication of a marathon runner. You train and build your strength daily if you want to reach your professional goals. You cannot be a happy person and maintain a long-term commitment to a career in law unless you choose on a daily basis to do those things that avoid burnout and frustration. If you do not choose every day to take care of yourself, you are bound—as many female attorneys do—to one day decide to give it all up. Women do not stay in the legal profession as long as men nor do they rise as high. I believe part of the reason for that is because when you try to be the best at everything, and do not take care of your personal health, there can really be no other choice.

I do not have a magic formula. There are days when working out seems ridiculous, on balance, given the other demands of the day. When I was competing with a competition on the horizon, the desire to do well in the competition balanced the nagging voice telling me to bill more hours, get more done at home, and spend more time with my family. When I retired from competition, I had, for the most part, trained the nagging voice to back off permanently, though it is still there. Giving into that nagging voice would have been easy and hard at the same time: easy in the moment, but I would have lost so much satisfaction over time. I spent many nights, weekends, and vacations working to make up for hours spent at the track or gym. I have forgone vacations and social events and been less involved in my family's activities than I would have liked to have been, and there are times when my legal career was not a top priority. Although I may not be able to hit an ideal balance each day, I strive to hit the balance over time.

For those of you who do not have the external pressure of having to stay fit and eat well as a second job, the nagging voice does not have to necessarily win out. Even though I no longer compete, I work out daily, whether by running, walking, swimming, or lifting weights. I do this because, without physical movement, I know the accumulation of the days at work and hours billed will otherwise overwhelm me and my family. In other words, I understand the accumulation of steps in taking care of myself is essential to my survival and ability to perform adequately.

Making the Time

If your goal is to maintain your sanity and health—a sound mind in a sound body—you have to make the time. The nagging voice that makes you turn off the alarm clock instead of going to the gym, or the voice that says you will be better rewarded if you attend a bar lunch rather than working out, may be right in the short run, but it may not be better in the long run.

Eating right and exercising are crucial for attorneys. Regardless of where you are on the spectrum from hating your legal career to loving it, you need to have a stress outlet. Lawyers earn a higher wage than most other careers. People pay us, sometimes insane hourly rates, not because they necessarily like us but because the work we do is hard. You cannot be a good attorney without paying attention, networking, researching, and continually "practicing." Though there are times when a case presents itself squarely within my comfort zone, almost every situation involves a combination of facts that require work, reflection, then more work.

Unhealthy Choices

We sit most of the day, we are constantly on the phone or in meetings or court, and we ignore our posture, aches and pains, and weight as we reach for the most convenient food available. All of these lead to healthy-billable-hours success but to an unhealthy physical state.

The Benefits of Commitment to Health

What daily choices can you make? I can outline some strategies I use, but the best advice I can provide is to remind you that because work and family control your time, you have to actively control your commitment to health. Each day of that commitment builds upon itself, and healthy decisions become a way of life without much thought. You will be a better friend, parent, spouse, and coworker, and you will find the stress release of physical exercise prevents you from falling into unhealthy patterns of stress release, such as seeking instant gratification through, for example, drinking or overeating. The beauty of committing to this process is that it becomes self-fulfilling. Once you have a program and commit to it, you fill in the day around it. Simple things, though cliché, do work. Here are strategies that have worked for me:

1. **Bring a healthy lunch to work every day.** It does not have to be complicated—yogurt and fruit work. Having healthy options immediately available provides a safety net so you do not seek the quickest and oftentimes least healthy alternatives. It also saves time when you do not have a lunch commitment, leaving time to fit in exercise.
2. **Avoid alcohol.** Attorneys have a high rate of substance abuse for a reason; alcohol and other substances offer immediate gratification. Luckily, I have not been tempted to overindulge because my outlet has been exercise. I have solved many problems, conquered anxiety, and structured transactions during my many miles on the roads. Alcohol is a negative stress reliever, whereas exercise results in a positive impact on your mind and body. I am not advocating giving up alcohol, but there is a reason athletes do not drink before competition—it is incredibly hard on your brain and body and not conducive to peak performance. If you are the type that needs empirical evidence, keep a log of alcohol consumption, exercise, and your overall energy levels—you will see the profound difference for yourself. Better yet, skip the empirical evidence and just go for a walk.
3. **Find an exercise option that works for you.** I am a strong proponent of sports and physical activity for everyone.

The physical activity should match your preferences. If you hate an activity, you will not stick with it, so try not to force yourself to pick the most popular activity. You may not have a body or mind for distance running, and I do not have the body or mind for power sports. Find what suits you; there is something for every one of us. If you have trouble with motivation, hire a trainer or set up group events where your absence will be noted. If you have trouble working out alone, plan group workouts and set times to meet people so you have some external pressure to show up. If someone is waiting for you, or if you have a set class, you can't tell yourself "just ten more minutes" until it is too late.

If you do miss a day or a week, do not use that as an excuse to give up. The worst thing you can do is let your frustration sink into "impossible thinking" where you decide that you "just don't have the time."

4. **Sleep.** I always get a bit sad when someone tells me they sleep only four hours a night. When faced with those who do not need sleep, it is easy to feel lazy. The four-hour-a-night sleepers, however, are an exception. Most people need seven to eight hours of sleep. As long as you consider sleep unproductive time, you fall into a common trap that cutting into sleep is an easy solution. Every athlete who competes knows and values the importance of sleep. Athletes tend to brag about sleeping ten hours a day plus daily naps. Granted, unless you are training heavily, you might not need the extra sleep, but sleep is restorative, physically and mentally.

Exercising and healthy eating are not only about optimal athletic performance but about an optimal life for anyone. We spend so many hours sitting and dealing with high-stress situations. Without physical movement on a regular basis, we are bound to burn out or seek unhealthy alternatives that perpetuate stress. You cannot rely on others to ensure your health. Only you can select a path that helps you be more productive, less stressed, and more likely to meet the challenges of a legal career and enjoy life during your career and beyond.

REFLECTIONS

1. Do you utilize your calendar effectively to manage your professional and personal commitments? What does your calendar say about your commitments and values? Is there room to improve your ability to prioritize? Are you carving out time to be present for the things most important to you?
2. Do you live life deliberately? Do you feel in control of your career path?
3. Do you believe it is possible to have a thriving career in litigation while also making family your top priority? Are there role models at your firm who are doing this?
4. Do you struggle with the feeling that time is passing too quickly along with the constant strain that there aren't enough hours in a day? What strategies have helped you more effectively manage your time?
5. Have your time-management strategies changed as you advance further into your career? How so?
6. Do you feel as though you are living life to the fullest? Are you taking time to smell the roses?
7. Did you choose your practice area? Did you have an opportunity to do so? If so, did practical considerations play any role in your practice area selection?
8. Do you have any time blocked out on your calendar as "just for you" time? What about "just for your significant other and you" time?
9. Are you satisfied with the spiritual side of your life? Do you practice a religion? Have you consistently been involved in practicing your religion?
10. Are you finding meaning in your life? What do you feel the meaning of your life is?
11. Are you taking care of your physical health? What steps can you take to improve?
12. What are you doing to manage your emotional health? Brainstorm options to improve.

6

MAINTAINING PERSPECTIVE

The Importance of Aligning Personal Goals with Professional Aspirations

Introduction

"Your playing small does not serve the world. There is nothing enlightened about shrinking so that other people won't feel insecure around you. We are all meant to shine," says author Marianne Williamson in her essay "Our Deepest Fear" from *A Return to Love: Reflections on the Principles of a Course in Miracles*. In this chapter, we explore where our personal goals and our professional aspirations intersect. From choosing a career path in line with your values, to choosing an innovative career and alternative work arrangements, to firm management philosophy, these stories provide insight into how women lawyers can play large, and shine. Then, as Marianne Williamson concludes, "as we let our own light shine, we unconsciously give other people permission to do the same."

Choosing a Career Path in Line with Your Values

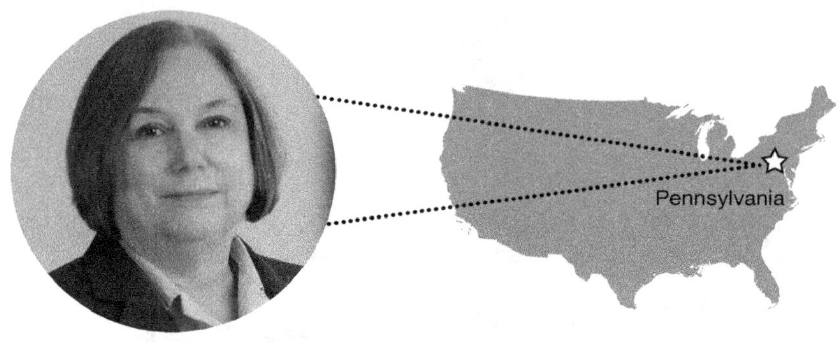

Her Story

D. Alicia Hickok

Career

Chair, Appellate Team, Drinker Biddle & Reath LLP; deputy counsel for Pennsylvania's Appellate Court Procedural Rules Committee.

Education

Texas Christian University, BA; University of Pennsylvania, JD.

Best Advice

Contentment is a gift. It does not come from the absence of challenge but from knowing that you are in a place where you can derive joy from the ways in which you make the lives of your colleagues and your clients better.

Personal

I am blessed with a wonderful, patient husband, three children, and two grandchildren. I love to garden.

For more information about Alicia

www.drinkerbiddle.com

The title of this essay was given to me, and it is at once powerful and somewhat misleading. It certainly is the case that my choices have been driven by my values. But those values have not always pointed to a clear direction, and they have frequently left me conflicted and struggling with fear and self-doubt. As well, my path has not been a drive from a starting point down a straight road, bounded by values on either side to prevent my turning to left or right. Instead, my path is forged every day, sometimes by deliberate and affirmative decisions, sometimes by passive acceptance, and sometimes by simply refusing to look at alternatives. If someone told me when I was fresh out of college doing antitrust economic research in downtown Los Angeles that I would be a lawyer in 2016, I would have said "of course." But I never would have guessed the kind of law I would practice, or where my career would take me, and when.

That said, there are certain ways of life—perhaps some would call them values—that have been constantly before me. Growing up, my family backpacked a lot. Backpackers have certain persistent mottos: observe always; be a good steward; leave each place better than it was when you arrived; if you do not know what turn to take, mark your path with what we called ducks (three stones stacked in a triangle) so that those coming after you will know where you have gone; never let anyone backpack alone; and make certain you are carrying your fair share. Backpacking often means climbing a mountain via switchbacks, appearing to traverse the mountain interminably, but gradually increasing in elevation as well.

My undergraduate degree is in international affairs, and I graduated from college thinking that a master's in international affairs combined with a law degree would build nicely on my undergraduate studies, and that economic research was a good job to have during the months until I started law school. Being very young and stubborn, I believed that path could come only through one joint program at one university. When I was wait-listed there, I decided to look in a different direction. Eventually, that different direction took me to Oregon, where I met and married my husband while working as a paralegal for an antitrust lawyer in Portland. I had my first two children while my husband was in graduate school there.

Devotion is a key value to me; I struggled with how I would work and pursue a career while being the mother my young children needed and the wife my husband needed, given his very odd hours at that time. I also knew that my children were a gift from God, to be treasured and cared for. I wanted to be a good steward of that gift. After much deliberation and prayer, my husband and I determined that I would stay home with our children and not start law school until my younger child started school. Taking a "switchback path" rather than climbing straight up a mountain certainly is not the right choice for some (or for most) people. That said, some of the most precious times I have had in my life were engaging with my little ones, fueling their imaginations and answering their questions, sharing books and blocks and baking, and learning to know them as they grew and became the people I love so much.

It turns out that switchbacks are not an easy choice. Many people viewed my decision as betraying all that prior generations had fought for. I understood what those generations had done. I knew that my grandmother had graduated from the University of California at Berkeley at the age of twenty with a 4.0 and a double major—only to stay home the rest of her life. And, I knew that her daughter, my aunt, was told when applying for jobs that the most she could ever hope to be was an elevator operator. She did not listen to them, though, becoming vice president of an employment agency. My mother was the first in her family to go to college—and was the first to get her master's and then her doctorate. My mother-in-law went to medical school and landed a prestigious residency; upon hearing that she was the one who had earned it, she was chased down the hall and yelled at for taking opportunity from a real (i.e., a male) resident. I was accused of turning my back on all of them and others, and I struggled with whether I was carrying my fair share. Ironically, I did not fit in with the values of the stay-at-home mothers I met either. I did not see my mission in life as being a homemaker; I simply saw it as critical for me to support my husband and pour myself into my children when they were young.

After my husband earned his graduate degree, the best place for him to work was in rural Oregon, and while there we had our third child. Our family was able to experience life in the foothills of the Cascades, with an antique apple orchard just across our stream and opportunities for imaginations to run wild that we had never experienced in Portland. By the time our youngest was ready to start school, my older two were ready to enter seventh and fifth grade, respectively.

The choice of law school was no longer just a personal choice. Indeed, the school I had applied to years ago did not even make the list of possible law schools because I could not reconcile that program and where it would lead with what I perceived as my obligation to my children. I mentioned earlier that my path was sometimes the result of deliberate choice and sometimes the result of refusing to look. This was both. I deliberately chose where to go, but I refused to look at the school that was once my only choice. Although my decision was driven by values, it was also driven by a perception of the importance of stability that now appears misguided. My daughter has lived in India for a number of years and travels the globe working on international privacy issues, taking my granddaughter with her wherever she goes. Both of my sons are looking at graduate studies abroad. It brings me great joy to know that where I was tentative, they are secure; where I was afraid, they can plunge in headlong.

But fueled by fears of selfishness and what would happen if I moved my children around too much, I looked instead at schools in places where they would have opportunities to pursue what was important to each of them and where my husband could find work that he would feel fulfilled doing. Creating a matrix to ensure that everyone's desires were accounted for led me to the University of Pennsylvania Law School. It turned out to be the ideal school for me, a me that was no longer very young and stubborn, but was instead older than everyone else and juggling emerging adolescents, a young child, and guilt. Guilt that I was no longer baking all of their bread, no longer attending all of their school and after-school functions, no longer engaging in all of the creative things I had done when they were younger. I juggled those demands and emotions against an insatiable desire to get everything I could out of law school. I loved (and love) Penn, with its collegial atmosphere and outstanding professors, and I loved (and love) studying law. I was warned not to expect firms to hire me; I was, after all, the same age as some of the people who would be interviewing me. Perhaps some firms looked askance at me, but there were enough high-quality firms that wanted me that I had to winnow and sift to decide where to spend my second-year summer.

I almost chose a firm with an international focus, but once again I dismissed my desires as selfish. In choosing to stay in Philadelphia, I asked people I knew in various parts of the legal community which of the firms I was considering they would choose. When a former plaintiff's attorney told me that Drinker lawyers always litigated with integrity and a public interest lawyer told me that Drinker lawyers both made and kept very real commitments to pro bono work, I knew where I wanted to spend my summer.

When I graduated, I was blessed to have a wonderful clerkship and then to work for the same firm at which I summered, a firm that has provided me with many mentors. They have taught me that I work for a firm built on a tradition of partners standing firmly alongside even those with whom they disagree. They have encouraged me to develop my voice, a voice that I have learned is not actually "my" voice at all. Instead, it is the voice of each client, channeled through the facts and law to speak to judges—or to resolve differences through settlement. I cannot express how grateful I am that they did not (and still do not) make me walk alone on that journey.

The firm has given me the opportunity to do many things I could not have done if I were in-house or on my own: serving as deputy counsel for Pennsylvania's Appellate Court Procedural Rules Committee, teaching part-time at Penn; and filling various roles in the ABA. Each allows me to work with wonderful people to build what ultimately will be a better legal system. Most of all, though, I have the opportunity to be involved with associates and counsel as they are developing their own voices and learning how to be the people they are and bring who that is to the practice of law. What I am looking at is far different from what I thought I would be looking at when I graduated from college; but there is nothing I would rather do than what I am doing.

Returning to the backpacking metaphor, when I was asked to write this essay, I wondered if there was any point in putting a duck in the path. I am, after all, in very many ways an odd one, with a strange path full of seeming switchbacks and with steps motivated at times by values muddied by fear and self-doubt. I hesitated because every person—and especially every family—should identify for him- or herself the best way for each member to be fulfilled. That won't look like my path, just like my path does not look like my mother's, my mother-in-law's, or my aunt's. Their stories are more linear: They wanted to go somewhere, and they did. My story does not read like the tale of one who had a dream and pursued it relentlessly and in the end achieved it—except that it is.

Maintaining Strength and Passion to Fulfill Even Unknown Dreams

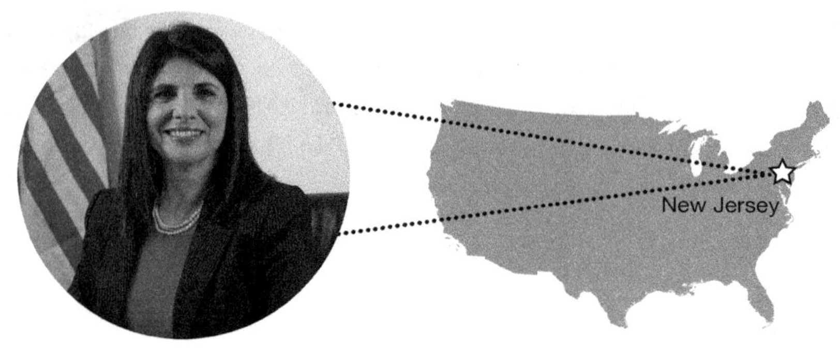

Her Story

Jodi L. Rosenberg

Career

Founder of Law Office of Jodi L. Rosenberg, LLC.

Education

University of Michigan, BA in Political Science, 1990; Boston University School of Law, JD, 1993.

Best Advice

Always over-prepare; you'll look great and feel confident.

Personal

Mother of Brandon (eighteen), Jordan (fifteen), and Sydney (twelve).

For more information about Jodi

www.jodirosenberglaw.com

> *"Love many things, for therein lies the true strength, and whosoever loves much performs much, and can accomplish much, and what is done in love is done well."*
>
> —Vincent van Gogh

Most people cannot make a living doing what they love. The lucky ones include professional athletes, rock stars, and me. Unlike A-Rod and Bruce Springsteen, I did not pursue my dream career of being a Broadway performer. However, I have achieved my dream of having a life filled with purpose and balance. My wish for my children and future generations is that the rigor of today's educational system and the immense pressure to succeed do not deter the exploration of outside interests. I have learned that being well rounded is both emotionally satisfying and career enhancing. To me, that is true work-life balance.

I grew up with a love of theater. I performed in school musicals and attended a performing arts overnight camp throughout my childhood. I took many years of voice, dancing, and acting lessons. There always was (and often still is) a Broadway show tune playing in my head, and my car radio is tuned to the Broadway music station. Although I had friends who succeeded in show business, I did not think I had the raw talent or the drive to make this a career. Instead, I decided to focus on my studies and look for a different vocation. However, I hoped to always keep musical theater in my life.

In high school, I worked hard and maintained good grades. The typical extrovert, I was very social and loved connecting with people. When it became time to choose a college, I chose the University of Michigan because it seemed to have the perfect balance of great academics and school spirit. It was the perfect choice for me.

Like most of my friends and peers, I did not know what I wanted to do for a living. I attended college "undecided," which was probably more acceptable thirty years ago than it is for today's students. I eventually chose to major in political science, and I also enrolled in acting and film classes to nurture my artistic side. By my senior year at college, I was still unsure of what career to pursue. Having spent every summer during college working on Wall Street, I had the opportunity to work on the New York Stock

Exchange immediately after college. At the same time, a law career seemed obvious given my political science and theater background. As both attorneys and performers need to listen, process, communicate, and improvise, I considered law school.

At age twenty-one I was confused about what to do, but I was sure about my personal values and beliefs. I knew that I wanted both a family and a career, and I knew this was still no easy feat for women. I wanted to choose a career in which I could take time off or work part time when I had children, and be able to manage both career and family. Whatever direction I chose, balance was as important as the career. I knew from my summer employment that women were not as welcomed as men on Wall Street at that time, and that working part time was not possible in the financial sector. If I became a lawyer, I believed I could remain one even if I took time off to have children or to pursue other interests. I chose law because it felt right for me based on my personal goals.

While in law school, I continued to pursue my love of theater by performing each year in Boston University School of Law's Legal Follies. Although the intensity of rehearsing for a show was difficult with a demanding law school schedule, I found that I accomplished more when busy and tightly scheduled. I also found the comedic escape of the show to be a welcome break from my studies. I was very fortunate to be able to combine my personal and professional interests.

When I graduated from law school and moved back to New Jersey, I worked as a litigation associate in a large firm. It was a far cry from the television series *L.A. Law*, and my courtroom experiences were few and far between. I spent much of my first few years reviewing voluminous documents and summarizing deposition transcripts. I was not in love with the law, but I was learning, and I was paying my dues. No matter how busy I was at work, I always scheduled outings with family and friends during my free time. I also found time to perform in shows at my local community theater. These activities kept me feeling balanced and fulfilled.

When I had children, I found a way to work part time and spent ten years balancing family obligations with working as a litigator in a large New Jersey law firm. I felt very successful on both fronts and felt lucky to be able to have it all. I was the first litigator in my firm to work part time and was viewed as a trailblazer. I was able to try cases and produce elementary school plays at the same time. Sometimes it was more of a juggle than a balance, but on the whole it worked well.

As I love connecting with people, and I am not one to shy away from a leadership opportunity, I became the leader of the largest networking group in my town. The Workmom Group of Millburn/Short Hills operates a very active listserv and holds networking and social events. Under my seven-year leadership, the group has grown from 200 members to more than 1,350 members. Members of the group can instantly seek the expertise of other working moms in town who are striving for work-life balance. Our members help one another as if they are sisters. For example, if one member sends out an SOS late at night for poster board long after the stores have closed, she will likely find several members willing to help her within minutes. Women stop me in my hometown all the time and tell me what a lifesaver our network has been to them. We help one another with everything from last-minute child care to rides home from New York City when the trains are not running. It makes our township of 20,000 residents seem like a small village. I receive no compensation, and sometimes moderating this opinionated and active group can be very challenging, but it has also been incredibly satisfying and would later help me professionally.

My carefully structured work-life balance was threatened when I lost my job in 2009. I was counsel to a large New Jersey law firm, and my position, like many others, was eliminated during the Great Recession. I had been at the firm for nearly fifteen years, and I had all three of my children while working there. Leaving the firm was not part of my master plan. I was the trailblazer, and the trail had ended.

The timing turned out to be perfect. I was rehearsing for *Bye Bye Birdie* with the New Jersey Volunteer Lawyers for the Arts. We are a unique group made up solely of lawyers and judges that puts on a biennial performance of a musical for charity. Losing my job was a setback, but being part of the show was the best way to move on. Everyone in the group wanted to help me and the other lawyers who were in transition. The sole practitioners in the cast encouraged me to hang a shingle and shared their knowledge and resources. One of the cast members who practiced criminal law had more work than he could handle and hired me on a per diem basis while I was deciding what to do. It was in this safe and sincere environment that I was able to embrace the thought of going out on my own.

A few months later, with the advice and support I received from my fellow cast members, I started my own firm. I hung a shingle in my own hometown and gave up commuting. My husband and three children were thrilled because my hours could be as flexible as their schedules required. With all of the technological advancements since I started practicing law, it was much easier and less costly than one would think to set up and maintain a solo practice.

It took some time to be able to generate clients and income, but it was the best professional decision I have made as a lawyer. I told everyone who would listen what I was doing and asked them to spread the word. My credibility as the Workmom group's leader resulted in a flood of new business. The members saw me as a strong and capable leader, and they felt confident in referring my services. I found clients much easier than I could have imagined. Again, my acting experience and interpersonal skills were a huge help. When I had more work than I could handle, I hired one of my fellow cast members on a part-time basis. It has been almost seven years, and I feel immensely proud of what I have accomplished. I may not have made the choice to go solo had I not lost my job, and I now truly love being a lawyer and a business owner.

Not only has my law firm flourished due to my community involvement, but I have also gained the respect of my township's political leaders. I was selected as the candidate for the one open seat on the Millburn Township Committee, and after months of campaigning, I was elected. My theater background was once again useful in making speeches, campaign videos, and personal appearances. It all felt very familiar and comfortable. I was even awarded "Rookie Campaign of the Year" by my county's political leaders. Who would have thought that my volunteer work, leadership, and numerous connections would put me on the road toward becoming the mayor of my hometown? It is exciting to see my political science background, my love of theater, and my legal background all coalesce.

Now that my oldest son will be attending college next year, I empathize with the pressure for today's teens to need to know what they are going to do to earn a living. Based on my experience, I firmly believe that a career in law offers a breadth of options and allows one to pursue outside interests. I would not hesitate to encourage my son to choose law if he so desires. I also believe there are several paths that can make one feel happy and fulfilled, whether inside the legal field or in other professions. What is most important is that my children have the opportunity to honor their values and nurture their strengths while pursuing their passions. To me, that's the true path to success.

Creating a Niche: The Importance of Diversity and Inclusion

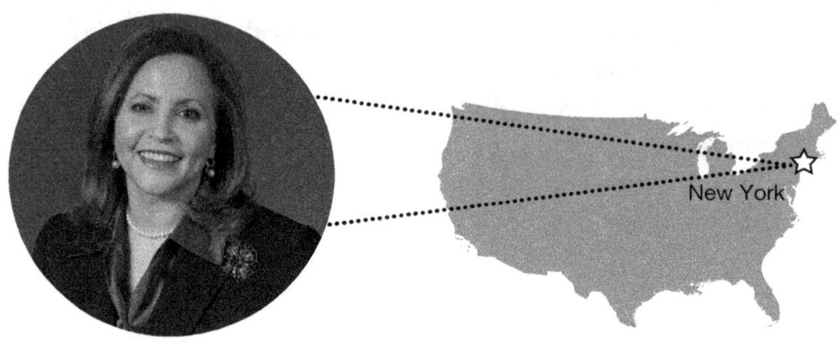

Her Story

Betty Lugo

Career

Founding member of Pacheco & Lugo, PLLC, the first Hispanic women-owned law firm in New York.

Education

Brooklyn College of the City University of New York, BA, *cum laude*; Albany Law School of Union University, JD.

Best Advice

Keep positive and believe in yourself. Always be thankful, professional, and respectful. Honor the past, respect the present, strengthen the future.

Personal

President, Puerto Rican Bar Association; HNBA, past regional president, founding member, 100 Hispanic Women, Inc.; NYSBA active member, past chair of Diversity Committee.

For more information about Betty

www.pachecolugo.com

"Uniformity ceases to be a good when it becomes a uniformity of oppression."

—Judge Benjamin Cardozo

I am the sum total of all of my experiences and influences. I am a proud American. I learned as a young woman that the last four letters in the word American read "I Can." I was raised to be strong, independent, and to seek justice for all. I learned early on about the importance of education and success. As the youngest of six children raised in a female-headed household, my mother, Juanita Lugo Martinez (from Ciales, Puerto Rico), taught us that "with a strong faith in God above you, there is nothing you cannot do." My father, Miguel, was a "Borinqueneer" Korean War Veteran, 65th Infantry Division. My grandparents were farmers in the mountains of Puerto Rico who struggled to raise a large family and instilled strong values of self-esteem, respect, equality, and justice. Although I did not grow up with my father, I consider myself a warrior and the proud descendant of great warriors who fought for the survival of family and our great country.

I believe my career started before I was even born. I was the only child in my family born in New York. As my mother carried me in her womb on her trip to New York, she also carried her anxieties, dreams, and hopes for a better life of education, employment, and opportunities for our family. I grew up in the Bedford Stuyvesant/Williamsburg section of Brooklyn when it was quite rough. My mother owned a small store, and we assisted her by translating for customers from English to Spanish. We all grew up fully bilingual, a tremendous asset today. I often helped Mom's customers by going to different government agencies to translate and advocate for them. I learned about diversity firsthand as I lived in a mixed neighborhood of all races, religions, and cultures. As a result, I developed into a proud, strong, independent, and determined woman. I graduated third (out of 890 students) from Norman Thomas High School in Manhattan.

In 1980, I met my best friend, Carmen Pacheco, who eventually became my business partner. We met in a Philosophy of

Law Class at Brooklyn College, City University of New York. We immediately developed a strong bond and friendship. We even discussed our future plans to attend law school, become lawyers, and start our own law firm in a big building in Manhattan. After graduation, we each went our separate directions. I graduated from Albany Law School, and she graduated from St. John's University School of Law. We kept in touch even though our careers continued on different paths. She worked at a Wall Street firm, and I worked at the Nassau County District Attorney's office (first Hispanic woman).

After three years as an assistant district attorney, I practiced as a litigation associate at a Long Island law firm, and I tried many cases. I was the only female associate, and knew I would never make partner. In 1991, while working as an associate at a major Wall Street firm, Carmen experienced the disparate treatment of being a Hispanic woman. Carmen then came up with the idea to start our own law firm, and we had many discussions thereafter. Our friendship continued, and with careful planning and preparation and with the advice and support of our families and Judge Irma Vidal Santaella (first Hispanic female Judge in New York), we became partners in a Wall Street firm by starting our own firm. It was our family values, religious beliefs, and reputation for excellence that brought us together and has kept us together.

On January 27, 1992, we opened the first Hispanic women-owned law firm in New York at One World Trade Center, Pacheco & Lugo, PLLC. We are three days apart by birth and both Geminis, so we were called "The Twin Powers in the Twin Towers." We have been very blessed and survived the first attack on the World Trade Center in 1993 and then moved to Wall Street. In 2002, we purchased our own building in Brooklyn, New York, and will celebrate the firm's twenty-fifth anniversary in 2017. Our respect for our families and our communities has made us successful at achieving our goals.

In the beginning, we created a niche with banks, lending institutions, consulate offices, and government and nonprofit groups. We incorporated many nonprofit organizations and chambers of commerce that were needed in the Hispanic and small business community. With our bank clients, we were able to create a link between the Wall Street community and the Hispanic community, and we assisted in building the economy in our communities as well as with the international community. Our Hispanic backgrounds along with being completely bilingual have been tremendous assets in creating our niche. Our respect for community, culture, diversity, and inclusion has opened many doors in our professional careers and advancement. We have represented individuals, companies, and organizations of many diverse backgrounds and religions from just about every continent. Our success comes from our ability to respect all cultures and to listen carefully in order to service the needs of our clients.

Our success also stems from our expertise, me as a litigator and Carmen as the "Wall Street lawyer." As a litigator, I am trained to have a keen instinct, ethics beyond reproach, to find inconsistencies and, at times, to go for the jugular with passion. Carmen, as a Wall Street lawyer, is trained to be cool, corporate, smooth, stoic, and respectful. The Wall Street mentality is to "never let them see you sweat"; you need to be "corporate" and act just as a lawyer—without regard to the person you truly are. You are encouraged to never act with emotion or passion.

In litigation, you take on a different persona. It is necessary to be strong, but it is better to be assertive than to be overly aggressive in getting your point across. As a woman, you make a better point by being assertive than aggressive. I am very proud that in 2014 my law firm, Pacheco & Lugo, PLLC, received one of the top verdicts in a construction labor law case in New York. This is huge, especially because we are a Hispanic women–owned law firm and won against all odds; others had told us to settle for a lot less. It was the belief in ourselves, inner strength, and confidence that resulted in our great verdict. Faith is the true equalizer.

I am currently president of the Puerto Rican Bar Association in New York (one of the oldest ethnic bar associations in New York, founded in 1957). The PRBA is an inclusive organization of lawyers, paralegals, and other professionals and was started at a time when people of color were not allowed to join the existing bar associations. Our members are from different ethnicities, genders, races, and religions. Our mission is to promote justice and advance diversity in the legal profession. I am personally involved in many bar associations and recommend that others become involved as well. We all have a commitment and a sense for equality and justice.

As a guide for success, I put together some of my own pearls of wisdom that I have learned and practiced throughout the years:

1. Put God first always.
2. Seek guidance and share guidance with others.
3. Respect others. Do unto others as you would have them do unto you (the Golden Rule).
4. Advocate assertively not aggressively.
5. Work hard, give it your best. Do not cut corners.
6. Listen carefully.
7. Have the courage to do the right thing.
8. Put your heart and passion into whatever you do.
9. Speak softly but strongly; roar when necessary.
10. Always remember where you came from.
11. Honor your past, family, and the trailblazers who opened doors for you.
12. Do not leave others behind.
13. Recognize hard work—not just greatness, because greatness is relative.
14. Say thank you.
15. Do not take others or anything for granted.
16. Smile and be friendly.
17. Do not complain, and do not gossip.
18. Keep it real.
19. Fight for equality and justice.
20. Mentor others.

For the legal profession to embrace true diversity and inclusion, we must become involved. "Honor the Past," "Respect the Present," and "Strengthen the Future" are my mottos. We must honor our trailblazers, thank our mentors and those who are promoting the positive aspects of our profession that strengthen all of us, and mentor others who need our help. Law and the legal profession do not exist in a vacuum. As lawyers, we stand at the forefront and act as the catalyst for positive change in our society. We must continue to respect one another. We all need to make a positive difference. Engage and involve yourself in the community; help those who are in a bad position. Volunteer and help someone resolve a difficult situation. I guarantee it will make you grow personally, professionally, and spiritually. You will be well respected by your clients when you take a position in favor of doing the right thing for our profession. When I started my firm, it was because there was no diversity. Today many corporations and law firms value the importance of diversity, but we must still assist and teach them how to truly engage and work on the "inclusion" part of diversity and inclusion. The best way to do this is by being ourselves: confident, smart, and strong, and by delivering results.

I have assisted thousands of clients and mentored thousands of individuals; business owners; high school, college, and law students; young lawyers; and professionals. My greatest satisfaction is seeing these people reach back and help someone else in need and continue the chain. We must continue to lift each other up and continue to help increase the number of socially conscious and caring members of our society. Embracing and engaging with each other for a better society and legal profession is truly rewarding.

The Road Less Traveled: Pursuing an Innovative Legal Career and Life Path

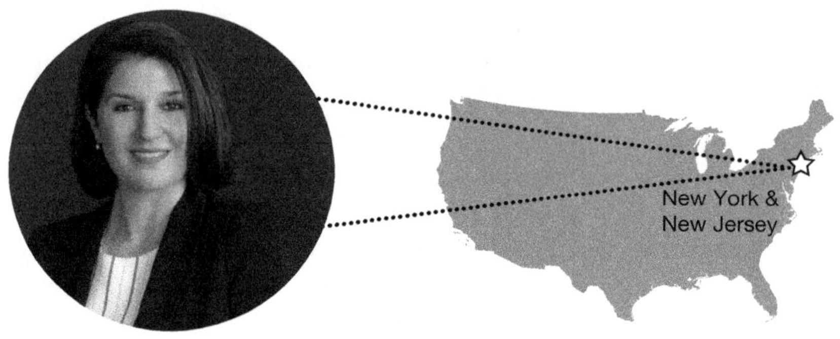

Her Story

Alison G. Greenberg

Career

Owner, Law Offices of Alison Greenberg, LLC, where I practice employment law and commercial litigation.

Education

University of Pennsylvania, BA; Seton Hall University Law School, JD.

Best Advice

Start out where you can get the best training and always be accountable. Hold onto your personal goals, and know that you can pursue them, if not sooner, later.

Personal

Breast cancer survivor.

For more information about Alison

www.Agreenberglaw.com

As a kid, I wanted to be a lawyer for idealistic reasons. When I was graduating from college, I decided to go to law school due to strong encouragement from my father. Looking back nearly twenty years later, the traditional lawyer track at a big firm would eventually position me to be an independent lawyer and to have the practice of law that I had idealized.

For ten years, I worked at McCarter & English, LLP, a highly respected firm in Newark, New Jersey. I practiced commercial litigation and employment law, getting experience in different industry areas. The cases I enjoyed the most involved issues of right and wrong, whether representing an individual in a partnership dispute or a hospital seeking to unwind a joint venture based on allegations of fraud. The employment cases had an actual human story underlying the case. They involved narratives of injustice that required corrective and remedial action. Yet opportunities to represent people in these types of matters were few and far between at a big firm.

At the age of thirty-six, I found myself with, for all intents and purposes, a wonderful career. I achieved the goal of making partner and worked with a wonderful group of men who mentored me and supported my advancement. Proverbially speaking, I "had it all." Yet something was definitely missing. In some ways, I no longer felt as connected to my firm. I knew I had never intended to work for a large firm my entire career. At this point in my life, I realized I needed to pursue a vocational path that was more meaningful to me.

In my spare time, I met with a career coach, and that process helped me to analyze what I was looking for in my next move. Figuring out what was important to me, to my authentic self, guided my life moving forward. What had kept me at that firm for ten years was fear: fear of making a drastic life change, fear of failing, and, of course, fear that I would not be as financially stable doing something else.

During this time, I was living in Greenwich Village and began attending community board meetings in my neighborhood. A focus of concern was the proposed redevelopment of a local hospital, which would entail the demolition of several historic buildings and mean years of construction in a residential neighborhood. Attending meetings after work, I became informed about the issues of importance to the residents and small business owners. I became acquainted with people in my immediate neighborhood and throughout the downtown area. Eventually, I was appointed to the community board and had to vote on consequential issues. We discussed and debated real estate development, historic preservation, quality of life and safety concerns, the environment, the arts, and local politics. Becoming friends and colleagues with a vibrant group of people enriched my life in ways, I realize now, that my life had not been enriched before. This new association provided me with the feeling of community that perhaps was missing in my workplace. I was subsequently inspired to join other civic groups and causes in lower Manhattan.

In becoming aware of and investigating matters that meant something to me, I began to meet people who were making a difference in the community—people I admired and with whom I shared common interests. It also became evident to me that I was not ready to give up the practice of law, attend graduate school for an urban policy degree, or suddenly work for the mayor's office. I needed a change, a new direction, but one still somewhat within my wheelhouse: law. I appreciated the camaraderie with my work colleagues, and I knew how crazy it seemed for me to walk away from the job security offered by my partnership at a major firm. But I believed I could be personally fulfilled and perhaps even more effective working in an environment that would give me the chance to pursue the types of cases that fit my evolved "mission." Working with my career coach was instrumental in finding the courage to take calculated risks and to move on.

Those few cases in which I represented the underdog were the most memorable and significant to me. I wanted to, and needed to, build my own client base, helping individuals who enabled me to be the type of lawyer that my idealistic child self always dreamed of being. Going solo suddenly made the most sense because it would force me to be independent and become more civically engaged. Perhaps eventually I could find like-minded attorneys with whom to build a practice.

Being a solo practitioner has, for the most part, fulfilled my goals. I have become more experienced in employment law in New York and New Jersey, helping clients to achieve their goals in court and through out-of-court resolutions. I attend networking events and take time to meet with other lawyers and entrepreneurs, which has helped me build a solid referral base. Individuals who face discrimination in the workplace, or who run into tricky contract issues, or who come up against work-related obstacles that they cannot solve on their own now know to contact me. I do my best to help, whether through counseling, negotiation, or litigation. This work has greatly enriched my life and reinforced my sense of purpose.

Over time, I have joined local political clubs, become actively involved in a historic preservation advocacy organization, and spent a lot of time strategizing with lawyers and community members to fight a major redevelopment project that has made its way through the New York state courts. I genuinely feel that I have made a difference where I live, but I still have much work to do.

I have experienced a number of different work environments: from being employed at a large firm to working on my own, and everything in between. The past eight years have given me greater insight into the experiences of my clients, whether individuals or corporate entities. I have gained a deeper appreciation for what it takes to run a practice and for the importance of finding the right people with whom to work. Along the way, I have built and maintained important friendships with other lawyers and members of my community—people with whom I have common alliances.

Perhaps this is the subject of another essay, but also through the practice of law, I have found that my friendships with women litigators have provided perspective and balance in what can otherwise be a very antagonistic industry. We tend to share common career goals, philosophical views, and personal convictions. I cannot overstate the importance of these relationships; a strong sense of community and friendship exists with these women.

We enter the practice of law with goals and expectations. Pursuing a somewhat less-than-traditional path within a regimented, traditional practice can be challenging, but it can also be enriching and rewarding. Looking back, I am so glad about each step along the way, and I am glad that I did step off the conventional path to pursue my personal goals.

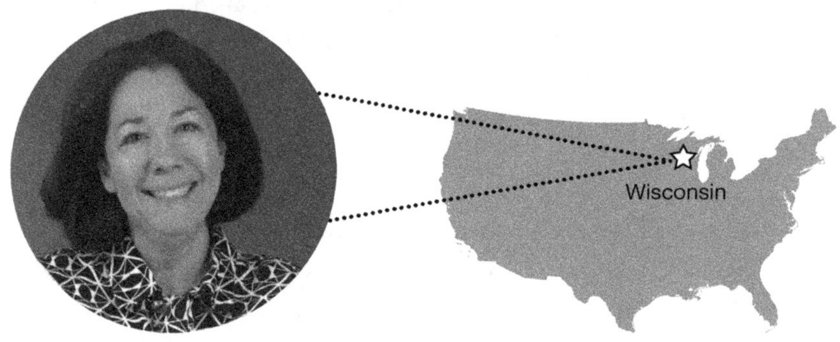

Her Story

Christina Plum

Career

Staff attorney at Wisconsin Court of Appeals, and adjunct professor at University of Wisconsin Law School.

Education

Marquette University, Honors BA in Journalism, *magna cum laude*; University of Wisconsin Law School, JD, *cum laude*.

Best Advice

Your education and lawyering skills will continue to develop and evolve over your entire career. Be sure to regularly seek out new educational and professional experiences to foster that growth.

Personal

Married to a law school classmate, with one teenage daughter.

I was in my third year of practicing law when I sought out my first alternative work arrangement. After leaving a job at a large Chicago law firm, I was interviewing for a nonprofit legal services position in northern Wisconsin. The new job seemed a great fit for me: I would provide outreach and representation to Native American elders concerning retirement and public benefits. The job would call on my skills as a lawyer, a public speaker, and a one-on-one communicator to directly serve a population in need. Excited about the possibilities, I was tempted to accept the job offer on the spot, exactly as it had been presented. Instead, I hesitated.

I had recently left my law firm job in search of greater work-life balance; I wanted to spend more time with my extended family after the unexpected death of my mother. I also hoped to continue to serve the profession as an active bar association volunteer in the State Bar of Wisconsin Young Lawyers Division. So I carefully considered how to ensure that the new job would be a crucial part of my professional life, but not my entire life. Ultimately, I proposed that I work four days a week, with flexibility to float my day off so I could travel two days one week and work five days the next week as my other obligations required.

To my surprise and delight, the employer agreed to my proposal and reduced my salary accordingly. With my reduced schedule working for a nonprofit law firm, I was making one-third of what I made at the Chicago law firm, but I was able to pursue my professional goals as a lawyer and bar leader and also to spend time with the people I cared about most.

After several years, I returned to full-time work. First, I served as a law clerk for an appellate court and then as a court commissioner for a state trial court, where I presided over small claims trials and initial hearings in family law cases. But my need for an alternative work arrangement arose again when I had my daughter. My husband and I relocated to southeast Wisconsin to be closer to family, and I was thrilled to find part-time work as an adjunct professor at the University of Wisconsin Law School. My part-time status allowed me to not only continue to develop as a lawyer and teacher but also to spend more time with my daughter in her early years and to focus on the American Bar Association Young Lawyers Division, which I chaired in 2005–2006.

In the years that followed, I worked in private practice with my husband and for the Wisconsin Court of Appeals in Milwaukee. Five years ago, I moved from a full-time role as a law clerk to a part-time staff attorney for the court. I currently work three days a week, and, as my family, friends, and coworkers can attest, it is a terrific fit for me. My work is challenging; I use my analytical, research, and writing skills to review cases in a high-volume court. I continue to teach public speaking at least one semester a year at the University of Wisconsin Law School, and I have remained active in the American Bar Association. The fact that I have two days off each week has made teaching and volunteering possible. It has also been a great benefit for our family—I can take care of appointments and errands during the week, leaving us more time for fun on the weekends.

I love my current alternative work arrangement. However, as I look back on my career, I'm aware that each time I've elected to work less than full time there have been trade-offs. I certainly make less money than many of my peers, both because I work fewer hours and because I have chosen lower-paying jobs that are especially accommodating to part-time scheduling. In addition, the jobs I have chosen—in part because they offer flexibility—have also been low-profile roles: community outreach, adjunct teaching, and working behind the scenes for an appellate court. To interact with large groups of lawyers and influence the legal profession and society in general, I have had to look beyond my day job, to work with bar associations and other community organizations.

Over the years, I have been fortunate to find employers who were willing to accommodate my desire for alternative work arrangements. As a teacher and a volunteer, I have served as a mentor and sponsor for lawyers at the beginning of their careers, and many have asked me about my experiences. They question whether part-time and other alternative work arrangements are worth accepting and how to pursue them. In response, I share with them my experiences and offer these suggestions.

First, I strongly believe that new graduates need to be prepared to "go hard" the first three to five years after law school. I encourage them to think of those years as their legal residency.

Those are the key years to learn how to practice law, to build a network, and to discover the work that interests and excites them. Those are also the years to build a professional reputation. If at the end of those years you're seen as a competent, committed lawyer, you'll be more likely to be in a position to negotiate an alternative work arrangement if that is what you desire.

Speaking of desires, my second suggestion is to consider—very deliberately and over a period of months or years—what you hope to accomplish as a lawyer and how that fits in with what else you want out of life. It's tempting to scoff at the idea of creating five- and ten-year plans, but when you talk with many successful lawyers, you'll hear how they did just that. Part of that planning process will be to consider whether telecommuting, working part time, taking a sabbatical, or seeking other alternative work arrangements is a high priority for you, and then consider how those desires may be affected by your other aspirations. For instance, if your goal is to be recognized as a brilliant lawyer with a national practice and tons of trial experience, you may find that goal challenging to achieve if you choose to pursue alternative work arrangements. There are examples of people who can disprove that proposition, but most would agree that it is difficult to rise to the top of a profession without devoting an extraordinary amount of time and energy to doing so. Once you have deliberately considered and weighed a broad range of goals, you can set about creating a plan for achieving them.

My third suggestion is that if you are considering an alternative work arrangement, be sure to explore the full range of alternative work arrangements before you approach your employer or prospective employer. I have spoken at length here about part-time work, but alternative work arrangements also include changing the times you will start or end your workday, working remotely, taking a year off, periodically taking extended vacations, and a host of other options. A quick Internet search for alternative work arrangements in the legal profession reveals tremendous efforts that the American Bar Association and state, local, and specialty bar associations and law schools have made to explore this issue. Invest time in reviewing the many reports and recommendations they offer before you develop a proposal and approach your employer.

Fourth, remind yourself to be patient. By definition, if you are seeking an alternative work arrangement, you are asking for something outside the norm. You are more likely to get the enthusiastic "Yes!" you're seeking if you have put in significant time with an employer and shown your commitment to the firm and the profession, as well as your value to the team. By being patient and seeking work that allows you to demonstrate those things, you will put yourself in the best position to get the affirmative answer when the time comes. In addition to being patient and diligent about gaining experience that will make you invaluable, you will also need to be patient during the time it takes for your employer to contemplate your proposal. Frequently, the employer will need to consider how granting your request will affect other employees and whether other employees will be inclined to seek similar accommodations if they are provided to you.

If you are proposing an alternative arrangement to a prospective employer, your preparation needs to be significant, as it is rare to find a job advertised that offers part-time hours, telecommuting, or other alternative arrangements. You'll be selling your skills and qualifications and, at the same time, making the case why the employer should approve an alternative arrangement from the outset.

Finally, my advice is to be grateful. If you are fortunate to secure an alternative work arrangement, appreciate that you have been offered an opportunity that is not available to everyone. Be sure to regularly evaluate whether it continues to work for you and for your employer, and make adjustments proactively as needed.

Law Firm Management: Make Your Firm the Place You Wish It Could Be

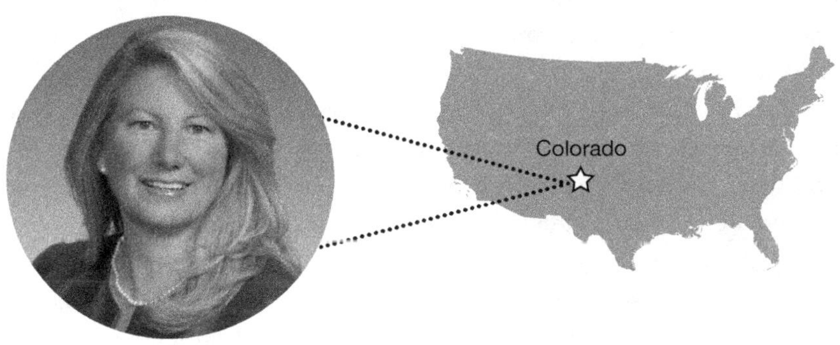

Her Story

Maureen Reidy Witt

Career

Trial attorney/partner at Holland & Hart LLP, where I am a Product Liability, Employment, and Commercial Litigator.

Education

Gonzaga University, BA in English and German, 1977, *magna cum laude*; Notre Dame Law School, JD, 1980.

Best Advice

Remember what matters: Family is more important than any career objective or opportunity.

Personal

Proud single mother of four amazing children.

For more information about Maureen

www.hollandhart.com/mwitt

I was greeted by a sea of navy blue and gray suits, accented with deep red or blue striped club ties, and dotted by the occasional perfectly folded handkerchief peeking neatly out of the breast pocket of a blazer. The facial expressions that met me weren't warm and welcoming but cautious and curious, possibly even concerned. "Who was this young woman accompanying the chairman of Holland & Hart's Management Committee?" their eyes seemed to be asking. Is it his secretary, assistant, or paralegal, perhaps? Why is she here with him at the annual meeting of the managing partners and chairmen of the Seven Sister law firms? The information shared here is confidential, strategic, and forward-thinking. Why would he bring along a woman—and such a young woman at that?

Those are some of the thoughts that were likely running through the minds of the managing partners, financial partners, and chairmen of the management committees of seven similarly sized but geographically diverse (and therefore noncompetitive) large full-service law firms in the fall of 1988 when I attended my first of their annual meetings to discuss firm management, pending issues, and future plans. I was thirty-two years old and recently named the managing partner of Holland & Hart, where I have now been practicing for thirty-five years. At that time, Holland & Hart had more than 100 partners, 100 associates, and approximately 500 total personnel in eight offices throughout the Rocky Mountain West and in Washington, D.C. In addition to the managing partner, who functioned much like the chief operating officer of the firm, Holland & Hart had a five-member Management Committee comprised of one member representing each third of the partnership delineated by seniority, one member representing the regional offices, and a chairman considered to be the head of the firm. That structure is still in place today. The Management Committee met at least monthly, made all policy decisions for the firm, and determined all partnership compensation. At that time, every member of the Management Committee but one and the chair were male.

As managing partner, I was not a member of the Management Committee but set their agendas, attended all of their meetings, made executive decisions with the chair, and handled the day-to-day operations of the firm. I later served a term on the Management Committee, representing the middle third of our partnership.

Throughout my career, I have served in numerous other management roles, including serving as the firm's first financial partner (essentially CFO), a position I recommended that our Management Committee create during my tenure as managing partner. Today, our firm has grown to more than 250 partners, 243 nonpartner attorneys, and 1,000 total personnel, with fifteen offices in the Rocky Mountain West and in Washington, D.C. One of my closest friends serves as the current chair of the Management Committee, which now consists of two women and three men. She is the second female chair of the firm. One other woman served as managing partner several years after I completed my term. The four of us, the two women who have served as chair and the two women who served as managing partner, have been the very best of friends since we joined the firm within a year of each other in 1980 and 1981 as associates just out of law school.

Against that backdrop of management experience, I share my thoughts about the impact of law firm management on the careers of law firm lawyers and on the value of participating in firm management to affect positive change.

Is Your Firm's Management Philosophy Conducive to Your Career Path?

In deciding which law firm to join, few lawyers, especially those just out of law school, think twice about whether the firm's management philosophy and approach is conducive to their career and personal goals. Most, like me, are just grateful to have a good job. But your firm's management philosophy can make a big difference in your career and in your life.

I was fairly confident when I joined Holland & Hart that I wanted to be a trial lawyer. After a required rotation through other departments, I settled into the litigation group. I learned quickly how lucky I was to be at our firm. Partners and senior associates took time to discuss strategic decisions, explain edits they made to memos and briefs, and afford me opportunities to be on my feet in court as often as possible. The firm hosted in-house training seminars and encouraged participation in programs such as the National Institute of Trial Advocacy. Although changing circumstances and normal attrition meant that not every associate who started at Holland & Hart stayed at the firm, those of us who did felt that the firm wanted us to grow and succeed and was dedicated to supporting us in that effort.

The firm also fostered associates' development in areas of firm management, starting with committee and task force assignments and building to positions of significant responsibility. The first committee I joined as an associate was called FITPOLCOM. The acronym stood for "Fun In The Practice of Law Committee." We were in charge of choosing, coordinating, and hosting the social events for the firm. I moved from that committee to the Recruiting Committee, which involved traveling around the country interviewing law student applicants and participating in hiring decisions. From there, I joined the Associates Committee, which was designed to facilitate associates' input and involvement in the firm, address associate issues, and determine associate compensation (the associate members of the committee did not participate in compensation decisions). The firm created task forces to tackle specific issues, and I served on a number of those as well. All of those opportunities helped prepare me to become the managing partner at a young age, when I was a very new partner. Probably the greatest exposure and training, however, came when I served on our very first Strategic Planning Committee, which developed a five-year strategic plan for the firm. That experience was the stepping stone to serving in the highest level of management at our firm.

While I was progressing as a lawyer and a potential leader in our firm, I also got married and wanted to start a family. When I joined Holland & Hart in 1981, the firm did not have a maternity or part-time policy. Another associate in my class, who later became the first female chair of our law firm, took the initiative to get a group of interested women lawyers together to draft and propose a maternity policy and a part-time work policy for child care. After some negotiation and tweaking, and after overcoming some negative reactions, those policies were adopted. Since then, the firm has expanded the part-time policy to encompass situations and needs other than child care, created paternity and adoptive parent leave, and developed a number of other family-friendly policies. We also have a sabbatical program that allows partners to take three months off with full pay every five years. The vast majority of our partners take advantage of the sabbatical program, which is the key to its success. No one feels like a dilettante for leaving for three months, and no one feels put upon by carrying another partner's load for a while.

These policies, and the firm's philosophy that undergirds them, made my career-family balance possible. I raised four children while maintaining an active civil trial practice involving cases in jurisdictions across the country. I combined maternity leaves and sabbaticals, took a one-year unpaid leave of absence when my children were young, worked part time for several years, and basically cobbled together every way to make it work that I could. I don't mean to make it sound easy. It was never easy. It would not have been possible, however, if my firm and its management were not open-minded, flexible, and supportive. In the same vein, I never would have been asked to serve as the managing partner in 1988, as a thirty-two-year-old woman, if my firm was not egalitarian, progressive, and willing to take risks. I encourage you to look for, develop, and sustain similar attitudes and approaches in your firm.

One way to be part of that development is to participate in law firm management, which will afford you the opportunity to ensure that your firm adopts the attitude, approach, and policies you would like to see. It's not for everyone. Many lawyers far prefer to focus on their practice and avoid management like the plague. But for others, the idea of holding a leadership position in their firm and shaping their future is very attractive. I polled colleagues in our firm who have held significant management roles and offer our collective thoughts, both positive and negative, regarding participating in firm management.

Some of the advantages of participating in the management of your law firm include:

- Having a voice in all important firm decisions, even those that do not rise to the level of a partnership vote.
- Getting to know and appreciate your colleagues and their practices in much more depth than you would otherwise.
- Learning about the business of the practice of law, including finances, profitability, policy making, and compensation,

which helps you understand and relate to the real-world pressures on clients.

- Raising your personal profile within the firm and, often, in the community, regionally, or even nationally, which can help your career in numerous ways, including enhanced business development.
- Having a positive impact on the retention and advancement of women attorneys and lawyers of color.
- Proposing and supporting policies and practices that make your firm a better and more enjoyable place to work.
- Observing which professional habits and practices lead to the greatest success and which ones are problematic, so that you can learn from them for purposes of your own practice and for training younger lawyers.

Participating in the management of your law firm is interesting, challenging, and fun. If you work closely with other partners in management, you will form unique and lasting friendships that you might not have developed otherwise.

Participation in firm management can have some disadvantages, however, even if you and your firm achieve your goals. Some of the potential downsides include:

- Being in a leadership or management position over your partners and peers can be difficult and, at times, isolating.
- Maintaining an active law practice while spending time on firm management can stretch you and your time to the maximum extent. Often, you have to step away from the bulk of your practice for a while and then rebuild it later.
- Making compensation decisions affecting your colleagues can, on occasion, put stress on your friendships.
- Being responsible for decisions that affect the future of your firm can weigh heavily on you both during and outside of work hours.
- Being willing to make difficult decisions and face conflict head-on is stressful.
- Balancing firm management, any semblance of a law practice, and raising children or dedicating appreciable time to your personal life can be extremely challenging.

Participation in firm management is demanding, and you need to constantly strive to be at your best: patient, willing to listen, thoughtful and understanding yet decisive, professional, capable of maintaining the utmost confidentiality of matters when necessary, and honoring the trust your partners have placed in you.

Developing Leadership and Management Skills

Often, developing leadership skills and assuming a management position in your law firm is the most direct and effective way to implement change and foster progress. Many lawyers have no business training or background, and they come to management positions without some invaluable skills. If you aspire to be in management, look for opportunities to learn about law firm finance in advance, study and understand existing firm policies and compensation systems, and develop a collaborative style that works for managing equals as opposed to subordinates. You should also cultivate strong written and verbal communication, public speaking, and presentation skills. If possible, work with those who can mentor you in developing the attributes of a leader, and seek opportunities within and outside of the firm to lead increasingly greater efforts and projects. Welcome the opportunities presented to you that invite you to be a leader.

Timing

There is no way to pinpoint the ideal time to serve in firm management, both in terms of your personal career path and to be most effective in promoting important policies and perspectives. It is extremely hard to participate effectively, however, when you have young children who need your time and attention or when your legal practice is all-consuming or at its peak. Choosing to embark on a management role when you are not truly available to dedicate the time, effort, and energy it requires is a disservice to you and to your firm. Carefully consider when the time is right for you to become involved. I was married but did not have children when I was managing partner, and I reduced the time devoted to my practice significantly in order to serve in that role. Fortunately, I was at an early enough stage of my career that I was able to rebuild my practice at the conclusion of my term. I waited until my children were in middle school and high school to serve on our firm's Management Committee, but that only worked because the demands of being a member of the committee were far less than being managing partner. Numerous factors will influence your own choice to participate. The important thing is to be thoughtful about your decision and timing.

Leadership

Finally, remember you can always be a leader in your law firm whether you hold a significant management position or not. You can lead by example in your law practice, exemplifying professionalism, expertise, and care for your clients. You can lead younger attorneys by mentoring them along their career paths. You can take time to train associates in the practice, management, and life skills they need to succeed. You can lead bar association committees, community boards, and other enterprises. You may need to be elected or selected to serve at the highest levels of management in your law firm, but you yourself choose whether to be a leader. Either way, decide what will work best for you considering your personal work-life management challenges and opportunities.

REFLECTIONS

1. Give some thought to your career path. Has it been a straight line, or more of a crooked path? In what ways have you succeeded? What were the low points, and how did you rise from them?
2. Have you helped others on any of the paths you have followed? How?
3. What help could you have used that you didn't get?
4. Do you feel connected to your current position? Are you content?
5. What are your other interests?
6. Could alternative work arrangements work for you? Which ones?
7. What is your firm's management philosophy? How do you know? Is the management philosophy consistent with your values?
8. Consider assessing your strengths with the Strengths Finder program at http://strengths.gallup.com/Default.aspx.
9. Consider working on defining your personal purpose at http://cherylbachelder.com/resources. Cheryl Bachelder is the CEO of Popeyes® Louisiana Kitchen, Inc. and a leader in what she calls "dare to serve: leadership." Provide your e-mail and download the Journey to Personal Purpose.

7

GETTING BACK UP

Managing Crises along the Journey

Introduction

Things sometimes go wrong. Sometimes, they go very wrong. Robert Collier, an early twentieth-century self-help author, in *Riches Within Your Reach!* noted: "Sooner or later comes a crisis in our affairs, and how we meet it determines our future happiness and success."[1] An internet search reveals that Henry Kissinger clearly noted that "there can't be a crisis next week. My schedule is already full."[2] Lawyers can generally relate to Kissinger's notion of busy weeks and not being able to handle any more crises. Crises come in many forms, however, and do not arrive on schedule.

In these essays, lawyers share some challenges in their lives and explain how they reestablished lives of balance, conquered alcoholism, coped with illnesses such as brain tumors or kidney stones, dealt with job loss or teen pregnancy, and found their

1. Robert Collier, Riches Within Your Reach! (TarcherPerigee 1947).
2. Henry Kissinger, The New York Times Magazine (June 1, 1969).

spirituality. These women faced challenges and handled them with grace, integrating their personal and professional goals with their values when their careers unexpectedly skidded off track. We hope you are inspired and find your own courage in these stories, as we will all inevitably face challenges over the course of our careers.

Becoming an Alcoholic in Private, Living in Recovery in Public

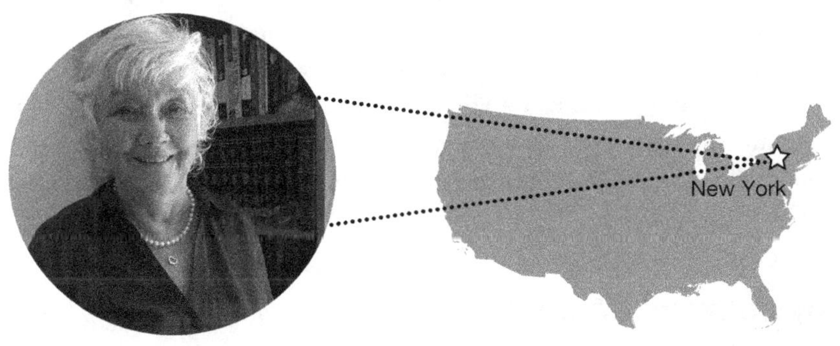

Her Story

Hon. Sarah L. Krauss (Ret.)

Career

Retired judge of the New York City Courts, presently under contract as an outreach consultant for the New York State Bar Association Lawyers Assistance Program.

Education

Wayne State University Law School, JD.

Best Advice

Pick a career path that gives you not only a sense of pleasure and accomplishment but also one with good mentors and real autonomy.

Personal

Married to my sweetheart from law school after forty years apart. My daughter is a veterinarian technician in northern California and has been happily married for twenty-eight years.

After years of drinking, I stood on the cusp of losing all the gains I had made in my legal studies and chosen career in government service. With the assistance of friends and relatives already in recovery, my life took a better turn as I got sober and began a recovery process that has held me in good stead for more than thirty-three years. At a certain point in the recovery process, I came to the realization that staying anonymous in the legal community was not going to be very helpful to the lawyers and judges, the law students and their family members, who might benefit from hearing a story of recovery just as I had. This essay is the story behind that process.

My Path from Addiction to Recovery

Until that turning point, my life was on a steady decline. This decline began slowly and progressed insidiously. Over time and probably without much notice, I began drinking more and more. At one time, I could drink with friends on a Friday night and maybe even on a Saturday night, but by Monday I would be back into my responsible mode. Then, slowly, the weekend drinking increased and began to creep into weeknights, and eventually I found myself drinking during the day, especially when my responsibilities—law school, studying, single parenting, and showing up for work—became overwhelming.

I had married very young and had a child, but I was determined to get an education and make something of my life. As young marriages often do, mine began to unravel. Curiously, as my marriage deteriorated, I found I had a desire to achieve, in part because I knew I would have to take care of myself and my young daughter on my own. As my marriage ended, I worked full time in the court system while attending law school at night. In the short span of five years, I had transformed myself from a young dependent housewife into a disciplined, motivated superwoman. I could do anything!

Regardless of my desire to achieve, I continued to drink. The drinking subtly became a more important part of my days than I realized. I drank to relieve the stress of working, studying, class attendance, and child care. The problems such drinking created seemed to pale in comparison to the story I told myself. I was a single working mother who planned to join a noble profession—I was going to be a lawyer. I was on the ladder up, a trailblazer, a woman on fire, a successful woman in the seventies.

For certain, my relationships with family and friends became strained and, as time wore on and the drinking took over more of my life, necessary relationships with family and employers were, to say the least, no longer cohesive and were often chaotic.

People could not depend on me to show up in a responsible and timely manner. My work and studies began to show a steady decline. Like many with this problem, I was unaware of the damage drinking was doing to my life and relationships.

I found many reasons to blame circumstances and others for needing to drink: for relief, for relaxation, to reduce the stress and fear I was feeling. Through this false sense that I was all right and could handle the drinking and everything else, I couldn't see the toll my behavior was taking on my family or work responsibilities. At the time, I thought I was handling all of these responsibilities well.

My life plans underwent a radical change owing to the end of a cherished relationship related to the excessive drinking and the perception that it was other people's fault that I was so unhappy. I graduated from law school and moved to a new city. I had a variety of legal jobs there. I made new friends. I had a new boyfriend and a renewed relationship with my daughter. With the new situation, I had hoped that this time I would be able to control when and how much I drank.

That didn't happen, and I began to recognize that my drinking was out of control. The only thing I thought about throughout the days at work and nights partying or at home was my next drink. As more people told me that I could have a problem with drinking, I stopped drinking in public. I preferred to spend evenings alone in the privacy of my home where I could drink without facing the consequences of blackouts or unruly emotional outbursts. I felt safer there because I was afraid of where I might end up in a blackout.

By then, I was having a hard time focusing, making good decisions, getting to work on time, or even taking proper care of myself or anyone else. I was unable even to pay attention to my now young teenage daughter. The consequences of failed relationships and now unmanageable responsibilities piled up and became a mountain too high to climb. Unfortunately, this provided many reasons (although not rational ones) to continue drinking.

Increasingly, the shame and fear became overwhelming. Soon I began to have bouts of believing that I'd be better off dead. During my darkest hours of failed relationships, chaotic life circumstances, and uncontrolled drinking, I did attempt to end my life. Fortunately, those attempts were not successful.

Friends began to talk to me about the excessive drinking and my erratic behaviors, offering suggestions for help. Seeing a psychiatrist, a psychologist, and taking prescribed antidepressants did not have any effect on the drinking. Many attempts at getting sober—stopping drinking for long periods but using other substances to "take the edge off"—resulted in progressively more unmanageability in my life. After some improvement when I had first stopped drinking, the use of drugs began to take its toll. Again I found myself in a morass of unpredictable chaos, and my work and relationships began unraveling again.

Perhaps because the consequences were too much to face, the guilt too much to bear, or death too frightening to stomach, when I heard someone speak of recovery it stirred something deep inside. Miraculously, I was able to not only hear the message but to surrender to the possibility of sobriety and recovery. This provided the opportunity to change the destructive course I was on and opened up a whole new life to me. A period of detoxification and rehabilitation treatment followed this surrender, and I began to walk a different path. This initial period of sobriety was followed by intensive years of attendance at support groups and a sustained period of sobriety while working with others, both in and outside the legal profession.

My Role as a Messenger to the Bar

About twelve years into recovery, I wrote my story for the *ABA Journal*. With that publication, I willingly surrendered my anonymity to assist my colleagues who were dealing with the disease of addiction. The decision to reveal the details of my own alcoholism and recovery was not an easy one. Some of the ramifications were difficult to deal with, but I do not regret my decision for one moment. After all, those who had the courage to tell their story had brought me to recovery and saved my life. How could I not do the same in hopes that I might help someone in return?

The extreme shame and stigma experienced by lawyers, judges, and law students created a critical urgency to put a face to the problem—my face. I was also acutely aware of the role a demanding profession played in this disease.

With the gift of hindsight, I share highlights of my journey as a messenger of recovery. Sharing serves to keep my sobriety strong and may influence those who are at that crossroad of revealing their condition or in the middle of a substance abuse experience and need a word of encouragement and hope.

In 1994, I became a commissioner with the ABA Commission on Lawyer Assistance Programs[1] (CoLAP) through the encouragement of another attorney in long-term recovery who was active in CoLAP. It was because of this commission appointment that I first publicly shared my story of addiction and recovery to a group of my peers.

I agreed to speak to a roomful of women bar leaders about CoLAP. It was a last-minute decision, and I was left with little time to prepare. I quickly realized that sharing my story would ultimately be the best way to educate them about CoLAP's mission. I would have to reveal to them that I was an alcoholic. This decision gave me pause, especially when I saw many of my New York State colleagues in the audience, but I knew it was important to show them what a lawyer and a judge in recovery looked like: healthy and successful. Who better to deliver this message? I was one of them, a bar leader who had just completed a year as the vice president of the Women's Bar Association of the State of New York and had previously served as the president of my county women's bar association, but different, possibly, because I had overcome the challenge of active alcoholism and had remained in the legal profession and was now willing to talk about my struggles with this disease.

It was following this presentation that I wrote my *ABA Journal* article. A few years later, I shared my story with the Board of Trustees of the Brooklyn Bar Association and participated in a

1. *See* http://www.americanbar.org/groups/lawyer_assistance.html.

mock intervention for New York administrative judges as well as the Executive Committee of the New York State Bar Association. All of this put my private story on public display but served a critical purpose of demonstrating that recovery works.

Since finding sobriety and then finding the courage to share my story of recovery with those in the legal profession, much has changed with regard to the universal message to legal professionals about addiction and the incidence of mental health issues in our profession. Today all lawyer assistance programs offer education on how to recognize and intervene when someone is impaired. These educational programs continue to be offered for free or for a very low cost on subjects related to mental illness, addiction, and lawyer well-being. The assistance that the state lawyers' assistance programs offer is also free and confidential.

Personally, sobriety afforded me the privilege to serve for more than seventeen years as a judge in the Civil, Criminal, Supreme, and Family Courts of New York City. In addition, I had the honor of serving on CoLAP as chair of the Judicial Assistance Initiative and, later, as the overall chair of CoLAP. Volunteer work on state and local lawyers-helping-lawyers committees and on behalf of my colleagues became critical to my own well-being and gave me an opportunity to be on the cutting edge of the lawyer assistance program development throughout the United States. There are many courageous judges, lawyers, and law students among us who are not only in recovery but have also lent their time and energy to this effort, who have publicly acknowledged their struggles with addiction and mental health problems, and who have maintained their recovery while contributing their formidable skills and talents to the legal profession. The willingness to admit what has happened to us while continuing to demonstrate, through our own professional accomplishments, that a recovering attorney is a responsible member of the profession, as well as the willingness to volunteer to educate our colleagues, has done much to reduce the stigma of addiction and mental illness for judges, lawyers, and law students. But more important, we are able to get effective assistance to those who are suffering and dying every day from these very treatable illnesses.

Reestablishing a Life of Balance

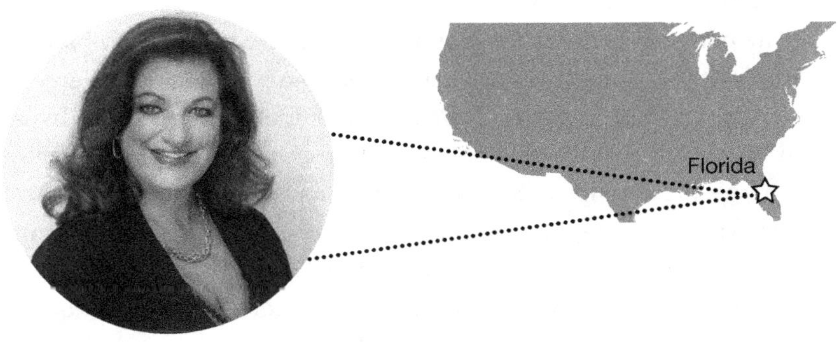

Her Story

Mayanne Downs

Career

As of September 1, 2016, I became president and managing director at GrayRobinson, practicing commercial litigation, appellate law, and high-stakes domestic matters.

Education

University of Florida, BA; University of Florida College of Law, JD.

Best Advice

For someone interested in pursuing a leadership role, my advice is volunteer, volunteer, volunteer. There's always nonbillable work to be done. Do it, do it well, and become indispensable.

Personal

Two children, Barry, a musician in Nashville, and Savannah, a law student at the University of Florida.

For more information about Mayanne

www.gray-robinson.com

It took a health crisis, a near-death experience, and a coma to focus my attention on the importance of a balanced life. It was a critically important lesson, and I'll never forget it. It changed me in a fundamental way.

The entire episode started as a fairly routine medical problem—a kidney stone, something that happens to about thirteen percent of men and seven percent of women at some point in their lives. Smaller stones usually resolve without treatment; larger ones may need to be broken up with shock waves or removed surgically.

My kidney stone, however, turned out to be a little more stubborn than that. It got stuck and would not move, which led to sepsis, a severe bacterial infection of the bloodstream. In quick succession, I ended up in the hospital, then in the intensive care unit, and ultimately in a medically induced coma. Doctors told my family that I only had a twenty-five percent chance of survival. I survived, but the experience profoundly changed my life and the way I think about nearly everything. It made me realize just how unbalanced my life had become.

"Well, of course it changed you," you may think. "You probably had some very serious bargaining sessions with the Almighty. 'Get me out of this one, and I'll live a better life, I promise.'" But the truth of the matter is that I was blissfully unaware of the precariousness of my position. In fact, I was unaware of everything. My family, friends, and colleagues may have been anxiously gathered around my bedside, but I was in la la land for much of my seventeen-day ICU stay. In a way, the consequences of my illness were visited upon everyone but me. I did not get to experience them until later.

That is when I learned what the whole experience had meant. Not so much to me, really, but to the others in my life—my family, of course, and those people close to me, but also to many others who were on the fringes of my existence. People who did not really have much reason to care so deeply about what had happened to me, but who did anyway.

It was their stories that made me pause and think about how I had been living my life. During my lengthy recovery period and even to this day, it has been those stories that have dominated my thinking. Here are a few of them.

- Family members, friends, and colleagues gathered around my bed while I was in the hospital. Many of them, of different faiths, prayed for my recovery. Evangelicals, Episcopalians, Jewish Kabbalah, and spiritual healers were all there praying. Even a Reiki master laid on healing hands. At times, there were so many people at my bedside that the overflow had to gather in a nearby conference room.
- While I was in a medically induced coma, my colleagues on the Florida Bar Board of Governors gathered for a dinner in Tampa with their spouses. Robyn Sasso, wife of Governor Andy Sasso of Clearwater, passed out knitting needles and gave some fast knitting instructions. Then they all prayed as they worked together on a prayer shawl for me. When I left the hospital after my seventeen-day stay, that prayer shawl was wrapped tightly around my shoulders.
- A lobbyist thought it would cheer me up if she organized a manicure event in my room, and she invited a number of people to come by with different nail polishes. The nurses would not let them in, but I loved the idea. It still brings a smile to my face when I think about it.
- A young girl, developmentally disabled, drew me a picture that was hanging on the wall in my hospital room when I awoke from the coma.

When I regained consciousness, I discovered that people I had never met had been involved in my recovery as well. As time went by, I met people who told me that I was on the prayer list at their church, or that they had organized people to pray for my recovery. I am not a traditionally religious person, but those stories had a great impact on me.

The stories I heard about the impact my illness had on others made me do quite a lot of reexamining. The experience caused me to look back on my childhood, on those who raised me, on the things that had happened to me over the years, and to put them in an entirely new perspective.

Recovery was a time of great reflection because I could not do much else. After getting home from the hospital, the first thing I realized was that I could not navigate the three steps leading up to my house—I was not physically strong enough. I felt weak and tired and did not do much of anything except rest. My long period of rest gave me plenty of time to think about life and how grateful I was to be alive. I thought about how I could live my life better, and how I could share my experience with others.

I always believed life was important and had meaning, but I began to see life in an entirely new light once I realized that I had come very close to losing something so incredibly valuable. My illness turned out to be a great opportunity to learn. Some things I had learned from my father many years earlier helped with that. He was very focused on approaching life by challenging assumptions, and he worked hard to understand and analyze and observe the things around him. He was a real maverick in the way he thought about things.

My father was a very attentive parent and not just in the traditional ways. A couple of times a month I would wake up to find a piece of paper on my bed with a picture drawn on it. That picture would lead me someplace else where I would find another paper with another picture. Then there would be another, and another. He loved to design these "treasure hunts without words." They were always designed to teach me to think. I would believe that I had figured out some great truth without realizing that that was exactly what he was trying to teach me. From him, I learned to think about things a little differently. And that gift from him—the ability to think critically and in a solution-driven way—helped me to understand what my illness had really been about, what life should really be about, and what changes I needed to make in my life to benefit from those lessons and ultimately lead a more balanced life.

Lesson 1: Life Isn't Just About You!

I'm not going to tell you that I did not think about myself and about what had happened to me once I came out of my coma. But what I really thought more about was all those other people who had been affected by my illness and my near-death experience—the shawl-knitters, the picture-drawers, and the people who prayed for me. I thought about my family members, and what life could have been like for my son and daughter. I thought about my colleagues, my law clients, and even about the strangers I might have been able to help somewhere down the road. What I learned was not to minimize the impact you have on others.

Lesson 2: Life Isn't Just About Work

My relationships now are much different than they were before my illness. In fact, my pre-2007 life is different from my post-2007 life. Work always used to come first; now people and relationships do. In the past, whenever I had thought about self-improvement, I had thought mostly about improving myself professionally—going to school, reaching this or that professional milestone, adding more letters after my name. I have to say that since my illness I think very little about those things. Now I spend a lot more time and energy thinking about relationships, loved ones, friendships, and about people who might benefit from my time or help. The nonfamily things I do I commit to only if I love it and believe the work will make a difference.

Now, don't get the wrong message; I still love my work, love the law, and believe that much of my ability to help others comes from my legal training and experience. Work did not become unimportant or meaningless; it simply has assumed a somewhat different place in my perspective.

In fact, one of the things I learned from my illness is just how amazing the profession of law really is. Every profession is special in its own way, but the law provides assistance to others in a very interesting way. It provides professional and personal service that is unparalleled. Go to any community and start looking at all the local charities and public activities that are taking place, and I guarantee you will find lawyers deeply involved in all of them.

But time has to be set aside for other important things. There has to be time for family and friends; there has to be time for reflection. Living a good life means participating, not standing on the sidelines. There is a yin and yang that is important to successful living and that is the very essence of a balanced life: "balanced" should never mean giving up one for the other.

Lesson 3: Don't Be Afraid to Love or to Be Vulnerable

When we grow up and reach a certain age, or we experience something eye-opening and important for the first time, we may feel uncomfortable when we recognize our vulnerability. Young people have a very definite sense of invulnerability, a belief that bad things happen only to others. In that same way, we do not like to believe that bad things can happen at random. But my near-death experience was a random thing that could have happened to anyone.

Like a lot of people, I used to believe that stoicism was a virtue in times of trouble or pain. But ultimately stoicism does not work. The answer to vulnerability is not stoicism, but love—the kind of love that others showered upon me when I was near death.

My pre-2007 self was very emotionally distant. I did not like huggers, and I was made uncomfortable by open displays of affection. My post-2007 self understands that love is more important than all that, and I make a constant effort to get over my natural reserve. It is not always easy, but I try.

Lesson 4: There Is Value in Routine

Why do people clean out their closets when they are feeling stressed? It is a way to apply order to a place where there was none. It is an exercise in healing. Routine can also satisfy the need for order when recuperating from a traumatic event or health issue.

I tell my children that there can be value in saying you are sorry even if you do not entirely mean it, because those words have a healing power of their own. In the same fashion, I think there is healing power in getting back to your routine even if a part of you is not ready for it. If you find difficulty in walking, just put one foot in front of the other; before you know it, you will be walking again.

One thing I still struggle with is the notion of working hard versus taking time for rest. I do value my free time, my family and friend time, and my time for reflection like never before. But I also believe in the "fake it 'til you make it" axiom. After my recuperation, I probably returned to work earlier than I should have. Sometimes it's important to get back on the horse after it throws you, even if the bumps and bruises are still throbbing. I also think that my recuperation was helped by getting back to work and getting back into the routine that seemed so familiar and even comforting.

Lesson 5: When in Doubt, Persevere

You may not be able to defeat the bad things that happen to you, but you can probably outlast them if you just keep plugging along. I realize that this may not be the most glamorous bit of advice you will ever be given, but I have come to believe that the best thing one can often do in the worst of times is to simply keep on going. If it is a particularly bad day, just do whatever you have to do to get to the end of it. Tomorrow will be a new day, a clean slate.

My recovery was long and painful, and at times I never thought I would overcome the fatigue and the weakness that I felt. But eventually I did, and I owe it all to simply persevering and keeping the outlook that tomorrow would be better.

Lesson 6: Know That What Seems to Be a Setback Is Really an Opportunity

People are sometimes surprised when I talk about my illness in positive, almost glowing terms. But the truth is that I now look back on that experience as the single best thing that ever happened to me. I have come to believe that bad things usually end up as good things in disguise, even though that may not be easy to see at the time. That kidney stone and the resulting near-death experience had great value, and that is what I always talk about when I speak about my experience. I describe it as a great gift; audiences seem to be moved by that, and I cannot tell you how happy that makes me.

Another thing that causes great happiness in me is something that I used to turn my nose up at—platitudes, feel-good posters, and upbeat messages of all kinds. I used to feel pretty smug about such things and thought they were sappy and hollow. Since 2007, I have felt very differently about the feel-good messages that you might see on a greeting card or posted on Facebook. I now find them inspiring because I know that the messages, although often a bit simplistic, contain powerful truths. Instead of ignoring those little messages, or turning my nose up at them, I now try to weave them into my life; I consider them little reminders from a higher power. I try to use them to make me a better lawyer, a better parent, and a better friend. Sappy? Well, maybe they are, but I try to allow myself to accept the message, and I find that it helps me.

Sometimes I struggle with patience and acceptance. To deal with those defects of character, I try to be aware of the opportunities that I know life will send my way for dealing with those things. We all experience heartache and disappointment, but these things are simply part of living life and are an opportunity to grow. In my post-2007 life, I embrace that and try to remain positive.

Lesson 7: Take Time to Reflect

I find great comfort in reflection, and I try to make lots of time for it in my post-2007 life. Call it deep thought, call it looking inward, call it meditation, call it journaling, or call it prayer, it is a way to plug into my unconscious to find peace. I find this time has great healing power. I used to think that such things were a waste of valuable time; not anymore.

Life has a way of sending us the experiences that we need. If your life is populated with little pockets of intolerance or misunderstanding, you are probably going to find a time when you will bump up against circumstances that will challenge those beliefs. Do not ignore them; this is life's way of sending you opportunities to better yourself.

Caring for the Sick: Brain Tumors, Billable Hours, and Balance

Her Story

Dina R. Richman

Career

Member at Cozen O'Connor, where I practice insurance coverage and litigation.

Education

Pomona College, BA, *magna cum laude*; UCLA School of Law, JD.

Best Advice

Find people you like working with and stick with them.

Personal

World traveler and proud aunt.

For more information about Dina

www.cozen.com

It is often said that if you don't have your health, you have nothing at all. I learned that the hard way. In April 2009, I was a second-year associate at a large litigation firm. Like most new associates, my biggest concerns were doing a good job and billing enough hours. That all changed one Monday morning as I was driving to work and my cell phone rang. I looked at the caller ID and saw that it was my dad. It was not unheard of for him to call me early in the morning, but it certainly was unusual. When I picked up, he said, "Hi, Dina. I just wanted to let you know that I'm going to the emergency room. I'm having some neurological symptoms and want to get them checked out." He explained that he was having weakness on the right side of his body, to the point where he was having trouble writing. Being a doctor, my father rarely sought medical treatment, so I knew that something must be seriously wrong. I offered to go with him to the hospital, but he told me to go into work and he would update me later. A few hours later, he called me with the news—he had a brain tumor. The doctors could not tell from the MRI what kind of tumor it was, but it was large and had to be removed as soon as possible. He went to see the head of neurosurgery at UCLA that same day, and he was scheduled for surgery a few days later.

The initial operation lasted eight hours. When it was over, the surgeon had good news and bad news. The good news was that the operation had gone smoothly with no complications, and they had been able to remove much of the tumor. The bad news was that the tumor was a Glioblastoma Multiforme (GBM). GBM is a malignant, aggressive, and nearly always fatal type of brain cancer. With treatments available at that time, the five-year survival rate for GBM was five percent, and the median survival was only one year. I was not so naïve to believe that he would miraculously be cured.

Over the next few months, my father underwent several rounds of chemotherapy and radiation. Like most patients undergoing such treatment, he was nauseated, weak, lost his hair, and lost weight. Even more concerning, his neurological symptoms continued to get worse. Shortly after his surgery, he was no longer able to drive, and he was soon unable to walk without assistance. My sister and I rotated "dad duty" and picked him up from work (incredibly, he still insisted on working), brought him home, prepared dinner, ran other errands, and spent time with him. Some of my best memories are of watching the NBA finals on TV that year with my dad (the Lakers won). It was a blessedly normal moment in an otherwise tumultuous time.

Yet my job did not just disappear. As soon as my dad was diagnosed, I talked to the partner with whom I was primarily working. He was more than understanding. He told me family should be my number one priority, and I should not worry too much about work. Thankfully, that was not just lip service. The firm allowed me unfettered flexibility with my schedule, never questioning when I had to leave early or work from home. My coworkers regularly asked how my dad was doing and were always willing to lend a sympathetic ear.

But I could not just ignore my work—my type-A personality would not let me slack off. There was only one thing I could let slide—myself. I told myself that I was young, healthy, and there would be plenty of time "later" to relax or have fun. For the time being, I would keep calm and carry on.

That attitude only worked for a little while. As winter approached, I developed a minor cold. It started to get better, but turned into a minor cough, and back to a head cold, then a slight fever, and so on. For several months, I was always slightly under the weather. Nevertheless, I told myself I had to keep soldiering on. I already felt bad about how much time I had taken off from work, and more important, my dad was getting worse. Even though it was not good for him to be around someone with a cold, he still needed help, so I wore a surgical mask around him and washed my hands constantly. Eventually my body could not handle it anymore. One day at the office, I started coughing uncontrollably. It felt like a gorilla was sitting on my chest. I was supposed to go to a meeting that night but felt so ill that I went home instead. I took my temperature: it was 104. The next day, my fever was no better, and the coughing was worse. I could barely breathe. Even walking from my bedroom to my bathroom was exhausting. I went to the doctor, who took a chest X ray and diagnosed me with pneumonia.

Even though I felt miserable, getting pneumonia had one bright side—it forced me to rest. Because my dad's immune system was already compromised, I was forbidden from being around him until I was completely recovered. I also could not return to work until I had the doctor's clearance. I spent about a week in a feverish daze, coughing and watching "Saved by the Bell" reruns. Even when I was well enough to go back to work, for a few weeks I could not overexert myself or I would start coughing and wheezing. Thankfully, I recovered, and for a little while things were calm.

Unfortunately, while I was getting better, my dad continued to deteriorate. In March, the doctors confirmed what we already knew—the tumor had substantially grown again. Having tried all the conventional treatments, my dad looked into various clinical trials that might be available. He was finally able to get into one at UCLA. For the trial, they would operate again and try to remove as much of the tumor as possible and then make a "vaccine" from the tumor tissue. The surgery was scheduled for June 11. It was supposed to last five to seven hours but ended up taking around twelve hours. The tumor was larger than they thought; the doctor called it a "whammy."

When I first saw Dad after the surgery, he was woozy and confused, but that was to be expected. I had high hopes that he would be noticeably better the next day as he had been after his initial surgery, but he was not. When the next day came, he did not recognize anyone. He thought it was 1999 and he was in Europe.

Two days later I walked into his hospital room and he said, "Hi, Dina!" I have never been so happy to hear such a simple phrase. Sadly, it is the last thing I remember him saying to me, because that afternoon the hospital put in a feeding tube and he could not talk. The day after that, my dad got pneumonia and the hospital put him on a ventilator.

The neuro-ICU became my second home. We did not want my dad to be alone, so my sister and I, and occasionally other relatives, had shifts at the hospital. On weekdays, I would wake up, go to work until about 3:00 p.m., go to the hospital until 8:00 or 9:00 p.m., when he would fall asleep for the night, go home and sleep, then start the cycle over again. Because of the feeding tube and ventilator, my dad could not talk and could barely move. We could only ask him yes or no questions that he would answer by blinking or a hand squeeze. He had always loved to read, but now he did not have the ability to hold a book. After a few days in the ICU, I offered to read to him, and he gladly accepted with a double eye blink. I began to read *Trojan Odyssey*, by Clive Cussler, one of his favorite authors. Every day, I would arrive at the hospital, tell him about my day, and then read a few chapters of the book. It was a welcome distraction for both of us. Not being a doctor or a nurse, there was not a lot I could do to help him from a medical perspective, but reading to him was something I could do to help him psychologically. As hard as this whole period was, I will always treasure those quiet afternoons that were just me, my dad, and *Trojan Odyssey*.

We kept hoping that my dad's pneumonia would improve and he could be weaned off the ventilator and go home, or at least leave the ICU. That never happened. Instead, the brain tumor was rapidly growing again, which made him ineligible for the clinical trial. The doctors told us he probably only had days or weeks to live. I spent most of the last two weeks of his life at the hospital. I went home only to sleep and did not go to the office at all. He died on a Friday night, and on Monday I went back to work—not because I could not take time off but because I wanted to be distracted.

Most people who become lawyers like to be in control, and I am no exception. Unfortunately, we cannot control most things in life. I could not control that my dad got brain cancer and died at the age of fifty-six. But I could control how I reacted to it and how I rebalanced my life to deal with the situation. I did not balance it perfectly, as I wore myself so thin that I contracted pneumonia. But I had to adjust my priorities and make the best of the situation. Little things like going for a walk or having a good meal (fortunately the hospital had a great cafeteria) made a huge difference in maintaining some semblance of balance. I did not make my hours that year, but I do not regret a single moment I spent with my father.

My Spiritual Journey

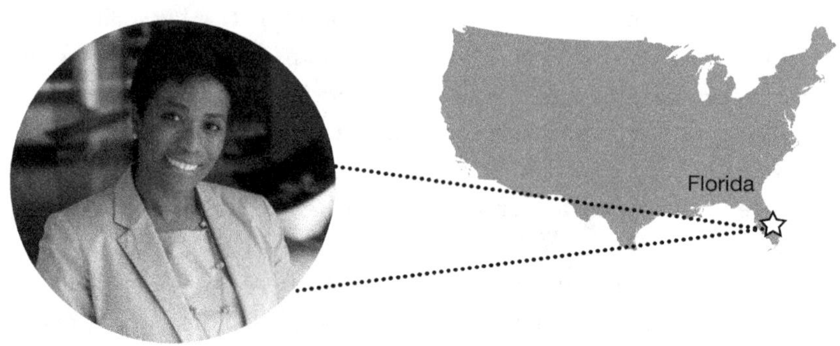

Her Story

Marlene Gordon

Career

Vice president, general counsel, Bacardi North America Corporation; Global Lead Bacardi Women in Leadership Initiative.

Education

University of Chicago, BA in Economics with Honors; Northwestern University School of Law, JD.

Best Advice

Career development and growth are important, but don't lose yourself or your identity in the process. Don't give up on your dreams, and always live your life on your own terms.

Personal

Married for twenty-seven years to my childhood sweetheart; college and law school age children.

For more information about Marlene

www.sfbwmag.com/2015/12/inspirational-journey

"Because God has made us for Himself, our hearts are restless until they rest in Him."

—Augustine of Hippo, The Confessions of Saint Augustine

Running on Empty

In December 1999, I had a rude awakening. I became sick. Not sick like I was going to die, although at the time I felt like it. I was in-house counsel at a major multinational corporation, working long hours, managing what was a crisis of massive proportion for the company, raising my two boys—then twenty-two months and seven years old, respectively. I was running on empty. I hardly had any time for my husband and zero time to take care of myself. In the midst of all this, my illness started innocuously enough. I was at work—after all, where else would I be—and I developed a major headache. I managed to make it through the day and left the office "early" around 6:00 p.m., to go home, take some aspirin, and go to bed. I forewarned my husband and my aunt, who was my live-in nanny then, "You have kiddie duty tonight because I have a major headache."

I made it home, took a shower, turned off all the lights, and attempted to go to bed. The problem, however, was that my headache refused to go away, and it stayed with me for days. After popping aspirin with no relief, I made an appointment a week or so later to see a doctor. I didn't even have a regular doctor—after all, who had time for such a meaningful relationship? My job, my kids, my husband, and my extended family were just about all the relationships I could handle. After searching through the providers listed in my health insurance book, I found a doctor and went to see her, telling her that I had been having a headache every day and that I needed something to make it go away immediately. "I am too busy to be sick," I remember telling her.

Time for a Time-Out

The doctor told me that I was suffering from chronic tension headaches, and she promptly honored my request and wrote me a prescription for Fioricet, a prescription given for tension headaches.

Yes! I was eager to continue my harried life—pain-free. However, my body simply would not cooperate. Even though I took the medication as prescribed, I did not get much relief. Things got worse. As the days and weeks progressed, I started to get panic attacks and began suffering from anxiety. I worried about everything:

> "What if I get on that plane to go on that business trip and it crashes, what would happen to my children?"
> "What if my baby wandered out of the house and drowned in our pool?"
> "What if my mother got sick and died?"

I went back to the doctor and she increased the Fioricet dosage. That was her treatment solution. Dutifully, I continued to take the medication and put all my hope in the increased dosage to cure my woes. Much to my discontent, the headaches only got worse. Now I not only had headaches but also nausea and a lot of stomach discomfort. Convinced that I had a brain tumor of some sort, I made an appointment to see a neurologist. The neurologist was like no doctor I had ever seen before. He sat me down and started to ask me a lot of questions about myself:

> "Do you exercise?"
> "What's your diet like?"
> "What do you do for fun?"
> "What do you do for yourself?"

I looked at him like he had two heads. Seriously, I thought, "What do I do for fun?" I could not remember the last time I had *any* fun. I barely had time to brush my teeth and comb my hair, and he wanted to know "What do I do for myself?" After fumbling over my words for a few minutes, I looked at him sheepishly and said, "I don't exercise; my diet is horrible—I barely have time to eat, and when I do, it is hardly what I would consider a nutritious meal. I do not do things for fun. I work and take care of my family, and that means I don't have time to do anything for myself."

He looked at me with that serious look that doctors give their patients when they think they are about to say something profound and said, "It sounds like you are under a tremendous amount of stress. Everyone deals with stress differently and has a different tolerance threshold. Your chronic tension headaches are the result of your body asking you for a time-out. Listen to it." In the end, he and I worked on a plan of care that included biofeedback therapy, meditation, committing to an exercise program, developing healthy eating habits, and taking time out of my hellish schedule to find some time to do something for me—and only me. My husband was very supportive, and we reached an agreement that Saturdays would be my day to do whatever I chose to do. This began my journey to physical recovery.

Finding Myself

Around this time, I also began my journey to spiritual recovery. I use the word "recovery" in this context because I grew up with a spiritual background but it took a backseat after I left home to go to college. I frequently went to church, read my Bible, and prayed during my formative years. However, beginning in college, through law school, and the early years of my marriage and motherhood, my spiritual side was placed on the backburner. I had told myself that I was a superwoman: I could do all things through me; I got all my strength from me, myself, and I. I persuaded myself that there were no mountains so high that I, in my misguided mind, could not climb them on my own. In sum, I was self-sufficient with a capital "S." *I* was in control of me.

It took these months of headaches, nausea, and losing confidence in my body and my mind to go full throttle at all times for me to realize that *I am in control of nothing.* God placed these physical discomforts on me to "wake me up" physically, mentally, and spiritually, and looking back I am so very grateful that I suffered simply from headaches, panic attacks, and anxiety. His divine "wake-up call" could have been so much more dramatic, if not catastrophic.

Fast forward to the present day, and I listen to the hit song *Wake Me Up*, by Avicii. The lyrics totally resonate with me because of the journey I took to spiritual recovery. The verses talk about finding one's self without realizing one was lost to begin with, and trying to carry the weight of the entire world with only my two hands. The lyrics reminded me of that time in 1999. Now that I am older and wiser, I know that I never have to go it alone again.

After agreeing on my "Get Well Plan," or, better yet, my "Coping with Stress Plan" with the neurologist, I earnestly began to do the things I agreed to do. I religiously went to my biofeedback sessions; I became a gold card member at my local nutrition store. I started to exercise and lost some weight, and I would meditate nightly before I went to bed. By the spring of 2000, I was on my way back to physical recovery, and my chronic tension headaches, panic attacks, and anxiety slowly subsided.

Yet I still did not feel right. I felt like my wings had been clipped. Something was missing. My belief that I was superwoman had proved to be false. I no longer trusted that I could do all things on my own strength. And if this wasn't true, then what was true? I still had this feeling that I was missing something in my life, and I had a deep longing in my heart. In a nutshell, I was *restless* in my spirit. I remember driving to work and thinking, "what is this life we are living all about?"

Finding Peace and Learning to Value Relationships

In March 2000, I embarked on a new journey to develop a personal relationship with God. In other words, I started my spiritual recovery. The catalyst, of course, was rooted in the physical debility I was recovering from and my now clear understanding that I was not, and never would be, wholly self-sufficient. My need for God to play a prominent role in my life—if not the most prominent role—became crystal clear to me when my pastor quoted Saint Augustine who said, "Man is restless until he rests in God!" It was like BINGO! Fireworks went off, and I had the answer to the restlessness I was feeling in my spirit. I had clear evidence that I could not go it alone, that I needed help, and now I knew exactly where to go to get that help. God, my Father and the Creator of the universe, was the source of my help.

I began to think long and hard about my life, and I became very honest with myself. I admitted to myself that I spent all my time honoring my obligations and did not spend a lot of time truly enjoying myself. I realized then that I had been trying to find pleasure, and even comfort, in worldly things—my job, the car I drove, the home I lived in, the vacations I took—in other words, all the physical things money could buy me. The reality was that I was genuinely disappointed that I was not *totally and completely* happy, at peace, or comforted by all these things. I had never before acknowledged or understood that these worldly things *alone* could not give me the total contentment and sense of spiritual peace that I was yearning. I began to pray and earnestly ask God to give me a sense of peace, a peace that surpassed all understanding. The answer to that prayer came with the realization that I could only get that sense of spiritual peace if I developed a personal relationship with God. God gave me the wisdom to understand that I had been totally consumed with the notion of honoring my obligations. All I had time for was to go to work and give fifty percent of who I was to my employer, and then go home and give the other fifty percent to my children, my husband, and the rest of my family. I simply had *no time* for anything else. I was living life in "overdrive" without any spiritual nurturing and development, and that led to my restlessness.

My spiritual journey began with the development of an understanding of the following three things: (1) that I needed to have *faith* in God; (2) that I needed to live my life with *hope* (that blessed hope that we are assured of); and (3) that life is meaningless without *love*. I came to understand that I could not achieve *spirituality* on my own, and to achieve peace I needed to "rest in God." The question then became, "How do I rest in God?" I began to read the book *Experiencing God*, by Henry T. Blackaby and Claude V. King, and from that book I developed the understanding that to rest in God I needed to experience Him in and around my life. The authors helped me to understand that it was not enough to know "about" God, but that I needed to know Him by developing a personal relationship with Him where God revealed Himself, His purposes, and His Ways to me, so that I could then experience God working through me. Prior to reading this book, I had always believed I had a relationship with God, but in truth and in fact, I did not. I did certain acts that intimated that I had a relationship with Him. For example, I had accepted Jesus Christ as my personal Savior at age thirteen; I was baptized during my pregnancy with my second son back in 1998; I read my Bible occasionally; I went to church occasionally; I said prayers; and I did good things for others. Despite all of these things, there was no personal relationship between God and me.

I started to really ponder the nature of my relationships, those that were good and those that were not so good and needed improvement. I reflected on when I first started seriously dating my husband. I remembered how much time I spent getting to know him better. I remembered how I wanted to know his likes, dislikes, and what made him tick. I remembered how I spent every effort trying to do things to make him happy. I remembered how much time and effort I put into nurturing that relationship with him. After expending all that time and effort, the end result was that I came to rely on him and he came to rely on me. We shaped each other's lives, affected each other's moods, and influenced each other's outlook on life. We began to plan our lives together and dream of the things we wanted to accomplish together. We wanted to be a part of each other's future.

I also considered all the other personal relationships in my life, for example, my relationship with my parents, my brother, my children, extended family members, and close friends. I thought about how each relationship influenced my life. I thought about the time and effort (or lack thereof) that I put into each relationship. I realized that I had devoted the time to nurture and maintain all of the important relationships in my life, and I saw the benefits.

With that backdrop, I began to think about the time and effort I had put into my personal relationship with God. It was utterly and completely disappointing. I realized that I had failed to take the time to truly know God. I could not hear when God spoke to me. I could not identify God's activity in my life. I was not willing to let God completely influence my beliefs, character, and behavior. I did not always want to respond the way God wanted me to respond. I was clueless as to what God wanted to do through my life; and very rarely had I asked Him to speak to me and guide me. Remember, I believed I was superwoman. As they say, I was large and in charge. I needed no one's guidance until I fell flat on my face.

I began to pray and ask God to interact with me in my life. I told Him I wanted to hear Him speak to me; I wanted to see, welcome, appreciate, and celebrate His activity in my life. I wanted

Him to completely influence my beliefs, character, and behavior. I wanted to respond to His activity in my life the way He wanted me to respond. I wanted to know and understand what He wanted to do through my life. I asked, no begged, Him to use me for His purposes. I wanted His guidance and direction. I completely surrendered to His will. I humbled myself before my Creator. I devoured His Word. I began attending church and Bible study classes, and I even took a college level theology course. I learned. I prayed. I lived out what I learned. I shared what I learned. I became a teacher to others. I developed a personal love relationship with God.

In May 2000, a coworker gave me a pamphlet simply titled *A One Hour Retreat*. The retreat required that I take one hour, go to a quiet place, and meditate on God. The premise was Jesus and his example of prayer. Jesus prayed all the time, and he always took the time, no matter how busy he was, to go off quietly and talk to his Father. It outlined the prayer of Jesus in the garden of Gethsemane, right before he was betrayed and ultimately turned over to his enemies to be crucified. Jesus was overcome with grief because he knew his fate. He told his disciples, Peter, James, and John, "My soul is crushed with grief to the point of death. Stay here and watch with me." Jesus then went off to pray, and when he returned he found his disciples asleep. Jesus said to them, "Couldn't you stay awake and watch with me for even one hour?"

So *A One Hour Retreat* required me to spend one hour alone with God. It was broken up into different sections. I do not remember each section specifically, but I remember the first ten minutes required me to thank God for any and every thing I could think of. I distinctly remember the last section. It was ten minutes of silence during which I was supposed to clear my mind and listen to what God was saying to me. After the first fifty minutes, clearing my mind and being completely still was relatively easy to do.

I know many people believe that God does not talk to His people anymore. That somehow that was something that He did in biblical times but does not do today. This is so far from the truth. What I have learned and what I learned on that evening when I did the one-hour retreat is that God speaks to us all the time. Most of the time, we are simply not listening. Other times, we are so out of touch, so out of tune with who God is, that even if we are trying to listen, we are not capable of hearing. Well, on that evening, I was listening, and I heard every word He said. And what He said to me are three things that I will never forget as long as I live:

1. "Show Your Love to Others."
2. "Love Me."
3. "Do Not Forget Me."

Now some may read this and think, "Why does she claim God said these things?" I make the claim because I had spent the prior fifty minutes meditating on God and His Word. I was calm, quiet, and at peace within myself and with my environment. My mind was completely clear. For those of you who have meditated before, you understand, I am sure, the complete feeling of serenity that comes as a result. So it was within this setting that those three thoughts came to my mind, one right after the other. I woke up (I do not mean literally because I was not actually asleep, but I felt so rested and renewed, it is as if I had just woken up) and immediately grabbed pen and paper and wrote the three thoughts down.

I am now convinced that those three thoughts were messages from God because they make no sense for me to think or say to myself. Although I might tell myself to show love to others, it does not make sense for me to tell myself to love me and do not forget me.

Ever since that evening, I have had a strong conviction to try to do those three things. I cannot say that I fulfill all three directives all the time. I, like everyone else, get caught up in the world around me, and I react to or internalize events that happen around me or to me not always in the way God wants me to do. Nonetheless, I have never forgotten the messages, and I always come back to them. And each time I fall off the horse, I get back on and keep trying.

Today I thank God for His intervention. I thank Him for loving me and for intervening in my life rather than leaving me to my own peril. Today, I am strong in my faith, and I am at peace with myself. I know who I am, and I know what I am not. I have been through many crises since the spring of 2000 when I embarked on my journey of spiritual growth. Each trial has only served to strengthen my personal relationship with God. I have lost my two best friends, one in November 2001 shortly after she delivered her first child, and the other in April 2009. My faith got me through those losses and then carried me through the prolonged illness and death of my mother, who was my biggest role model, my greatest supporter, and my truest friend, in September 2012.

I trusted God when my mother, then age sixty-two, suffered a couple of years of deteriorating health, false diagnoses, and then was ultimately diagnosed with the rare and genetic condition called Familial Amyloidosis. I continued to trust Him when my mother was told she needed a heart and a liver transplant and would relocate to Rochester, Minnesota, to be treated at the Mayo Clinic. My faith did not waiver for the months of waiting while my mom was on the transplant list and then received the transplants in October 2011, which led to nine months of hospitalization, kidney failure, dialysis, multiple life-threatening infections, and numerous times on life support. She was released from the Mayo Clinic and returned home to South Florida on her sixty-fifth birthday in June of 2012, and the last ninety days she spent at home. I trusted God through it all.

In closing, my personal relationship with God—my faith; living my life with the *hope* that only God provides; and my deeply rooted belief that life is meaningless without *love*—has brought me through some very dark days. My personal relationship with God has allowed me to be strong, resilient, and count this adventure called life as all joy, no matter the circumstances. I completely understand that without this relationship I do not have the strength to face and conquer life's challenges or to fully take advantage of all its opportunities. My personal relationship with God gives me the courage to live, the confidence to die, and the strength to face all that comes in between. My personal relationship with God has taught me humility and has stilled my restless heart.

The Unexpected Path

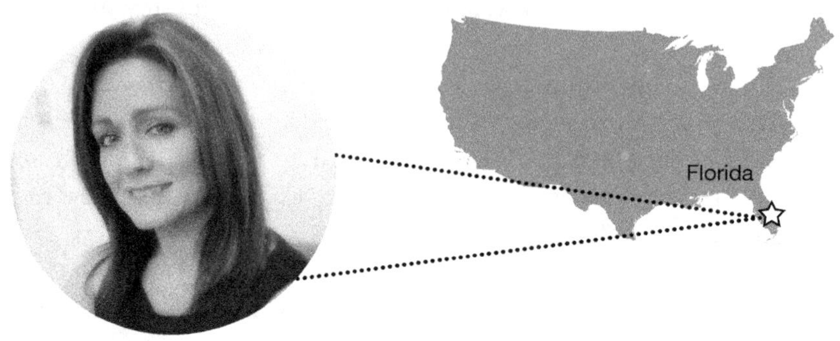

Her Story

Jennifer A. Lizotte

Career

Counsel, operations for Vistana Signature Experiences, Inc.

Education

University of Central Florida, BA in Legal Studies; Dwayne O. Andreas School of Law, JD.

Best Advice

Put into motion today the goals you have for tomorrow. You are today what you set forth to be years ago.

Personal

Mother of two adult children, one on the autistic spectrum, and proud grandmother of one.

For more information about Jennifer

www.linkedin.com/in/jenniferlizotte

My Story Begins

Sometimes I am most thankful for unexpected detours. Those detours molded me into the person I am and gave me my life's greatest gifts. My story starts in the family doctor's office with my mother. The doctor was telling my mother, not me, that I was pregnant. This should have been a joyous occasion, but when you are fifteen years old and the third of five children of ex-military, deeply Catholic, and hard-working parents, the scene is less than ideal. Although a hellion of a child (my mother's words), I was academically gifted and a great athlete. For as far back as I could remember, I wanted to be a lawyer when I grew up. Part of my childhood was spent in a small town just outside of Washington, D.C. My fondest memories of living near D.C. were visiting the Lincoln Memorial and field trips to Congress. Strange for a first grader, I know.

By the time I was fifteen, my father had retired from the Navy, and we were living in civilian housing in Florida. I started hanging out with the wrong crowd. I got involved with drugs, alcohol, and, of course, unprotected sex. I still remember that day at the doctor's office in detail, and later at home when telling my father my horrible secret. After coming home from the doctor's office, my mother told me to go tell my father the news. Both my parents worked full-time jobs, and my father worked long nights to support his five children. He was napping before heading to work that evening. I told my dad through the door of his bedroom that I had a problem and needed to talk to him about it. He motioned for me to come in and said, "Sit down honey, I am here for you." I told him I was pregnant. He was blindsided. I was Daddy's Little Girl. I was special in my father's eyes . . . until that day. The words he next spoke still haunt me to this day: "Get out. Get out of my room. I don't want to see your face." I was hurt, not from his words, but from the fact that I had failed him and my mother. I ran to my room and slammed the door . . . and then cried until my whole body ached. A few hours later my father came into my room and told me I was giving the baby up for adoption. It was not until I wrote my story on this very day that I realize my father did not go to work that night.

My Teenage Pregnancy

My future was set for me: my parents had unilaterally decided that I would give my baby up for adoption. The only other choice, of course, was to keep the baby, as abortion was not and is still not an option for me. My parents researched where to get assistance, and we ended up at Catholic Social Services. It was this nonprofit agency that told my parents about a local alternative school, and I soon enrolled and began taking high school classes at the BETA Center. My self-esteem was at an all-time low. I was disappointed in myself and disappointed I had let my parents down, but I trudged along in my mother's old clothing, trying to hide my pregnancy from everyone on the street.

I gave birth in March of my tenth year of school, two months shy of my sixteenth birthday. My mother held my hand the entire twenty-four hours of my labor, never leaving my side. I was surprised by the absolutely stunning baby girl that came from me. The entire birth experience and the miracle of life were much more emotional than I had anticipated, and it gave me strength. It brought back the drive and determination for which I was infamous as a child: a characteristic I thought I had lost through this experience. My parents called it "stubbornness," but that "stubbornness" pushed me to my next step. Despite my parent's belief that adoption was the right choice for me, I could not do it after looking into the innocent face of my daughter. I knew I had to concoct another plan.

Forging My Own Path

When my daughter was four days old, I was discharged from the hospital and made plans with Catholic Social Services to place my daughter in temporary foster care. I went home to my parents, solemn, but determined. As soon as I got home, I called a few friends and set my plan in motion. When my daughter was seven days old, I picked her up from foster care, packed my few belongings, and left my parent's home. I am forever grateful to my dear friend Donna and her husband for taking my daughter and me into their home.

I remained determined to finish high school. I missed so much school during the 1983–1984 school year that I had to attend summer school to complete the tenth grade. It was at the BETA Center while attending summer school (with my newborn daughter, Brittany, in tow) that I met a young recent graduate of Harvard University, David. He was my guidance counselor and administered the SAT that summer. There was no prep course, no planning or studying. I did not put much effort into the SATs. My dreams of becoming an attorney had vanished upon learning I was pregnant and then deciding to keep my baby. But when David sat me down to review my SAT scores, what he had to say was not what I expected: "Jennifer, if you are thinking of quitting school, I am begging you not to. With these SAT scores, Harvard and Princeton will be knocking down your door." I was shocked; what was I supposed to do? His words gave me my second boost of strength and ignited my stubbornness. I gave summer school my all and finished my tenth year of high school with straight A's. I found a job in the fast-food industry working thirty-five to forty hours a week, doing what I needed to do to support my small family. Then reality hit me: how could a single, teen mother attend high school and work at the same time? It was impossible. My responsibilities to my daughter were much more important than my dream of becoming an attorney. So I quit school right before eleventh grade.

Building My Family

Of course, my story does not end there, or you would not be reading this. Moving forward a couple of years, I met a wonderful man, and we married when my daughter was three years old. We moved to Fort Lauderdale, and I landed a job as an administrative assistant. Here I met another person from an Ivy League school who believed in me. Steve Weiss was my boss and had a doctorate degree in computer science. He gave me a gift one year for my birthday: a *Black's Law Dictionary.* On the inside of the front cover, he wrote: "If there was any one in this world who could learn every word in this book and understand it and in what context each should be used, it is you." At that time, I had no idea what a *Black's Law Dictionary* was or in what "context" it should be used! But there it was, my third boost of strength. I signed up to take the GED in 1988, two years after I was supposed to graduate from high school. A few months later, I registered for one class at the local community college: English Composition 101. I had no idea what to expect!

Starting College

I was scared. Scared of not being smart enough to be there, scared of the other students learning I was a high school dropout and a teen mom. But there I was, sitting in a classroom on my very first day of college. I remember actually trembling. My goodness, I did not even know how to take notes! As soon as the professor started speaking and I glanced at our syllabus (I did not even know what a syllabus was), I knew I was going to excel! This class was about creative writing! That I could do, and I completed my very first college class with an A.

Detours

But what I could not do was juggle *two* children and attend college—yes, two children. I was pregnant again (it was planned this time, just not expected so soon). I would once again forgo school for the sake of my family, but the one college class I had taken had lit the pilot light deep inside me and kept me fueled for the next chapter in my life. In February 1990, I gave birth to a beautiful blonde-haired, green-eyed boy: my Matthew. Matthew means "Gift from God," and my Matthew was definitely a gift from God. I knew Matthew was not going to be a typical child from the day he was born. At eighteen months old, my pediatrician told me Matthew was "mentally retarded." I did not believe her and promptly changed doctors. By the time Matthew was two years old, he had odd ritualistic behaviors such as obsessive cleaning. The teachers in his day care used to sing "Mr. Clean, Mr. Clean" when I dropped him off. He did not speak until he was almost five years old. I made appointments with every specialist in town to find out what was wrong. No one had an answer. The effects of my yearning to know took a toll on my marriage, and my marriage ended when Matthew was six years old and Brittany was twelve.

Back on the College Track

There is a silver lining to the end of my marriage: the Pell Grant! So there I was in 1995, a single mother of two, working full time during the day, and attending college at night. In the meantime, Matthew started kindergarten, and the school psychologist suggested Matthew may be autistic. Armed with this suggestion, it was the behavioral studies clinic in the local children's hospital that diagnosed Matthew as profoundly autistic. This time, however, life's punch was not going to stop me from continuing college.

I finished my associates degree in 1998 and immediately transferred to Rollins College. But don't let these black letters written on white paper fool you into believing this was not a struggle: the choice to attend college at night and work during the day was not an easy one. I wanted to quit many, many times. There were days when I just wanted to go home and sleep. But every time I felt this way, I just had to look at my children. I was doing this for them—they would see the benefits of hard work and determination. Plus, the increased earnings with a bachelor's degree would help care for Matthew in the coming years. Although Matthew progressed from moderate to high functioning on the autistic spectrum with Asperger's syndrome, it was believed he would never be able to live independently.

By the year 2000, I was also working in the corporate legal department for a large hotel company. The dream of becoming an attorney again grew inside me as I worked side by side with some of the most intelligent people I have ever met and on projects that tested the limits of my intellect. After some convincing from my supervisor, I completed the course work for a BS in Growth Management and Environmental Studies at Rollins and then transferred to the University of Central Florida in their legal studies program. I was told my potential growth as a non-attorney in the legal department would increase with a degree in legal studies. In one of my conversations with a favorite professor, Dr. Randford Pyle, I told him that I secretly still had some of my childhood dream to go to law school, but I had grave doubts, one being that "I was too old." As a response, he asked me, "How old would you be when you graduate law school, if you go?" I responded, "I will be almost forty years old; yes, I would actually graduate the year I turn forty." He then said, "Do you want to be forty years old and a paralegal or forty years old and an attorney?" Long, pregnant pause (no, I was not pregnant again).

Milestones

I graduated from the University of Central Florida in May 2002 (the same year Brittany graduated from high school) with my BA in Legal Studies and a minor in Business. I took the LSAT in August of that same year. I took a year off and enjoyed spending time with my son. But I was finally ready to pursue law school.

Meeting the Challenge of Law School

Out of the three local law schools to which I submitted an application, I was accepted to all three—with partial scholarships! I could not believe it. I am still in shock today. I was accepted. I WAS ACCEPTED!!! I could not wait to tell my parents. Twenty-one years after feeling like such a huge disappointment to my parents, twenty years after dropping out of high school, and sixteen years after my first college course, I was accepted to three law schools. This time, my family celebrated with absolute gusto.

I chose the school closest to my home that offered a part-time evening program geared for working adults. The next three and one-half years proved to be the most difficult I have ever endured. My sleep deprivation got worse, my stress levels increased exponentially, and so did my weight. Well, I think any 1L (or other freshman) can relate. But despite it all, in May 2008, the same year my son graduated from high school with his special education diploma, I proudly received my Juris Doctor degree.

Looking Back

I have learned that it is not the mistakes we make in our lives or the circumstances in which we often find ourselves that define who we are: it is our character, our attitude, and our determination in how we respond to those circumstances that mold us into who we become. Every action we take is a choice, and often a gamble. I had my doubts, but almost thirty-two years after hearing those words from my father in his bedroom, I know now that I chose wisely. My gambles paid off. Those gambles—and the gifts they brought to my life—meant everything.

Today I am a licensed, practicing attorney in the state of Florida. I have been with that large hotel company for more than fifteen years and have held the position of in-house counsel for the past six years. I have worked for and with attorneys who have embraced my life history and less-than-perfect past. My daughter, Brittany, is a single mother of the most gorgeous, intelligent, little boy in the world (yes, I am a proud grandma). Matthew still lives with me and has grown into a very respectable, caring, and intelligent young man. He has dreams of also attending college. I am in a committed relationship with a man who has endless patience for my ambition and determination. We even own a successful small business together. Needless to say, I still do not get enough sleep, but I could not be happier. And most of all, my family is proud of me. I have my self-esteem back, and I am, once again, the apple of my daddy's eyes (and my mom's too).

REFLECTIONS

1. What tools and techniques have you used to address stress and crisis as they arise in your life?
2. Do you have trouble with drugs and/or alcohol? Do you have loved ones with drug or alcohol problems? Consider seeking help from Alcoholics Anonymous Narcotics Anonymous, or Alanon.
3. How do you recognize that you're reaching a critical point and need to do something about what is happening in your life? For example, do you recognize signs that you are sick? Overstressed? Need a vacation?
4. What do you do for yourself? Do you meditate? Exercise? Journal? Scrapbook? Golf? Yoga? Do other fun activities?
5. What do you do for your significant other?
6. How do you care for yourself physically?
7. How do you care for yourself emotionally?
8. How do you care for yourself spiritually?
9. Is it the appropriate role of the workplace to address these non-work, life-style/health issues?
10. How do you handle eating properly? What can be done to make this easier, healthier, better?
11. How can you do better?
12. What was your last vacation? Was it fun? Relaxing?
13. How do you relax?

8

GOING THE DISTANCE

Maintaining Perspective throughout the Journey

Introduction

Elisabeth Kübler-Ross said, "People are like stained-glass windows. They sparkle and shine when the sun is out, but when the darkness sets in, their true beauty is revealed only if there is a light from within."[1] The challenge for women lawyers in the twenty-first century is to maintain their light even in difficult times so that we can go the distance and serve as beacons for the women lawyers who will follow in our paths. Moreover, if women lawyers are ever going to catch up to our male counterparts and enter the highest levels of the profession in comparable numbers, both in firms and in positions outside of firms, we must go the distance. The stories in this chapter demonstrate how women lawyers maintain perspective on the journey through their careers. These stories will challenge your notions of limitations on the success women lawyers can achieve.

1. *See* Jim Clemmer, The Leader's Digest: Timeless Principles for Team and Organization, p. 84 (ECW Press 2003).

We Have Come a Long Way

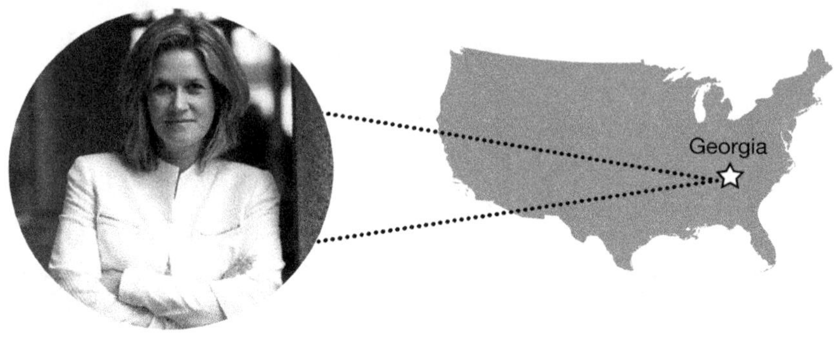

Her Story

Robin Frazer Clark

Career

Owner and founder of the Law Firm of Robin Frazer Clark, PC. I have practiced for twenty-eight years, and my practice has been devoted exclusively to plaintiff's personal injury.

Education

Vanderbilt University, BS; Emory University School of Law, JD. Published 162 articles in 84 different publications, with a total circulation of 3,122,569.

Best Advice

Spend more time with your family.

Personal

Married to William T. Clark, with two children, Chastain "Chaz" and Alexandria "Alex." I am also an avid golfer, carrying a nineteen handicap.

For more information about Robin

www.gatriallawyers.net or www.atlantainjurylawyerblog.com

Imagine a young female lawyer, having just returned to work from maternity leave, still breastfeeding her baby and having to try a jury trial in Fulton County State Court in Fulton County, Georgia. She is steadfast about continuing to breastfeed her baby even after returning to work. She politely asks the judge for periodic breaks in the trial to pump her breasts. The judge, a male, is taken aback. Suddenly his bow tie is too tight for the veins in his neck. "You want to do WHAT?!" he yells. Ultimately, he acquiesces, probably because he realizes giving in is simply more comfortable than discussing breast pumping with the young woman lawyer.

I was that young trial lawyer twenty-one years ago. I was reminded of the incident during a trial last year in DeKalb County Superior Court. During voir dire, the judge unabashedly announced, "We'll be taking a break at 2:00 p.m. so Juror 29 can pump her breasts." Just like that. No questions asked. No discussion. We've come a long way, baby.

How Times Have Changed

Times have changed for women lawyers. We have many trailblazers to thank for cutting the path for us, branch by branch. Let's take Justice Ruth Bader Ginsburg, for example. She was first in her class at Columbia Law School in 1959, but breaking with custom, Justice Felix Frankfurter refused to hire her as a clerk because she was a woman. She was a pioneer for gender equality at a time when most people had never even heard of that term. Ginsburg is reported to have said that her mother told her two things constantly. One was to be a lady, and the other was to be independent. So she started working for the ACLU, the only place she could get a job practicing law in the early 1960s, and began taking cases in which she could advocate for gender equality. Justice Ginsburg's daughter, Jane Ginsburg, who is now an intellectual property professor at Columbia Law School, said her mother was one of the few mothers back then who worked. Jane recalled: "I remember a friend of mine telling me that her mother said she 'had to be nice to Jane because Jane's mommy worked.' Like I had leprosy or something."[1] In 1972,

1. Stephanie Francis Ward, *Family Ties*, ABA Journal (Oct. 2010), *available at* http://www.abajournal.com/magazine/article/family_ties1.

Ginsburg founded and became the director of the Women's Rights Project of the ACLU, and all of her cases involved gender discrimination. Between 1973 and 1979, while running the Women's Rights Project, teaching law school at Columbia Law School, and raising two children, Ginsburg argued six cases before the United States Supreme Court.

Consider Sandra Day O'Connor. Justice O'Connor only took two years, instead of the customary three, to complete law school. Along the way, she served on the Stanford Law Review and received membership in the Order of the Coif, a legal honor society. O'Connor graduated third out of a class of 102, but she faced a difficult job market after leaving Stanford. No law firm in California wanted to hire her, and only one offered her a job—as a *legal secretary*. Ironically, a senior partner of that law firm, William French Smith, helped O'Connor's nomination to the Supreme Court years later as the attorney general. When O'Connor could not find employment in the private sector as a lawyer, she turned to public service and accepted a job as the deputy county attorney for San Mateo, California. Justice O'Connor was nominated in 1981 by President Reagan to become the first woman on the United States Supreme Court. In his book *The Nine: Inside the Secret World of the Supreme Court*, CNN legal analyst Jeffrey Toobin contends that Justice O'Connor has become the most important woman in American history.

And then we have our own trailblazers to thank right here in the Georgia legal community.

Before taking the Cobb County Superior Court bench, Judge Adelle Grubbs was a practicing attorney. On the Wednesday before Thanksgiving many years ago, she was arguing a divorce case before a male Cobb County Superior Court judge. It got to be fairly late, and Grubbs asked that court adjourn for the day. The judge was not going for it, until Attorney Grubbs is reported to have said: "Your Honor, you get to go home and relax and wake up tomorrow and enjoy Thanksgiving dinner with your family that your wife has prepared all day today. I get to go home tonight and clean house and polish silverware and get up early tomorrow and cook a turkey and an entire Thanksgiving dinner after having been in court all day today." After that, the judge simply quit holding court on the day before a holiday to be respectful to women lawyers.

We also have wonderful examples locally in Georgia. Our own Justice Hunstein was the first woman chief justice of the Georgia Supreme Court. Born into humble circumstances, Hunstein contracted polio when she was two, survived her first bout of bone cancer at age four, and lost her mother at age eleven. Her adolescent years were marked by frequent hospitalizations for cancer. Hunstein's father discouraged his six children from pursuing an education beyond high school. She married at seventeen, became a mother at nineteen, and was abandoned by her husband by age twenty-two. That same year, she lost a leg to cancer and was told by doctors she had only a year to live.

Struggling to find work to support herself and her son, Hunstein soon realized the value of an education. She went to college on a state vocational rehabilitation scholarship and to law school on the Social Security benefits she received after her former husband died. There were times when Hunstein could not afford to eat. Remarrying before graduating from law school, she soon had two daughters. She opened a private law practice in Decatur in 1977 and, spurred on by a county judge who repeatedly called her "little lady" in open court, Hunstein decided to run for the bench. She defeated four men and, in 1984, Justice Hunstein became the first woman elected to the DeKalb County Superior Court. She has served on the Georgia Supreme Court since 1992.

Probably my favorite story of Georgia women trailblazers comes from Judge Anne Workman, who, until her death, sat on the Dekalb County Superior Court bench. Workman's first attempt to get a legal job after law school was fruitless, but she recounted it very humorously. She had always loved criminal law and wanted to be a prosecutor when she graduated from Emory. She approached the district attorney at the time about employment in his office. Workman recalled:

> He told me in a very matter of fact manner that there were some places a woman did not belong and that a courtroom was one of them. But that was alright because I could have a baby and he couldn't. It was not the reasoning I had hoped to hear; but in one way it was helpful as it provided a considerable amount of focus and direction to me to prove him wrong. You take motivation where you find it. It

took twelve years, but in 1985 when I was sworn in as a state court judge, I saw him and reminded him of our long-ago conversation. I remarked that I must belong in a courtroom now because it had my name on it.[2]

Be Independent

These women cleared the path for us, branch by branch and briar by briar. There is no question that things are different now for women than they were for Justice O'Connor, Chief Justice Hunstein, or even for me for that matter. Much like the advice Justice Ginsburg's mother gave her, some of the best advice my father ever gave me was to be independent. He did not care what field I went into or what I studied in college, I just had to be independent. I have found that having a law degree is one of the best ways a woman can be independent. I am my own boss and have my own law firm. For me, this is the best way to practice law, giving me the most flexibility when I have wanted to watch my children's sporting events or other school activities.

There Is Still Progress to Be Made

A recent survey from the *National Law Journal* about women partners in large law firms is not that encouraging.[3] It showed that today about 18.8 percent of all partners, equity and nonequity, are women. That is up only 2.8 percent over the last ten years. If we just look at women equity partners, that number has been fixed at 15 percent for the last twenty years. This survey also proved that if a law firm has two tiers of partnership, an equity tier and a nonequity tier, women are more likely to be placed on the nonequity tier than men. The survey showed that women make up 17.6 percent of equity partners in law firms with only the one-tier track. Throw in a nonequity tier, and the women who are equity partners in firms with both tiers comprise only

---

2. Matthey McCoyd, *From the President: In Memory of Judge Workman*, DEKALB BAR ASSOCIATION NEWS, *available at* http://dekalbbarnews.com/from-the-president-in-memory-of-judge-workman/comment-page-1.
3. *A Current Glance at Women in the Law*, ABA COMMISSION ON WOMEN IN THE PROFESSION (Jan. 2017), *available at* http://www.americanbar.org/content/dam/aba/marketing/women/current_glance_statistics_january2017.authcheckdam.pdf

14.7 percent of equity partners. It is clear that the nonequity law firm model has become simply a convenient place to store would-be female partners.

Some say acceptance of women as equals in the legal profession is a matter of culture. That may be, but it has to be more intentional than that. I believe women must still make every effort to support and include other women because most men will simply not naturally do it.

Diversity in Leadership

Diversity of leadership—with proportional representation reflecting the makeup of any organization—is a key to that organization's ongoing health and strength. Although the State Bar of Georgia is comprised of thirty-four percent women, in 2013 I was only the second woman president in its history, and I was the only president also to be a mother. As I told one woman attorney, I am raising the issue now because in twenty years, when my daughter asks me why I did not do anything about this back in 2016 when I had the chance and the platform, I do not want to have to answer her, "I don't *know* why I didn't do anything." That is not an acceptable response. Women must support other women.

My mentors have all been men. There were not many women trial lawyers around twenty-seven years ago to mentor me when I started practicing law. Men have no idea what it is like to try a case while pregnant and having to use the bathroom every thirty minutes without being able to take a break. Or having to pump your breasts in the Fulton County Courthouse bathroom while waiting on a jury because you are still breastfeeding your child. But my mentors were all progressive men and my champions. In a 2010 *ABA Journal* article, Justice Ginsburg defined such progressive men as "people who think women should have equal chances to do whatever their talent permits them to do." My mentors realized the need to include women in our endeavors to strengthen our profession. Your mentors may be women, or you can be a mentor to another woman. It is extremely important to have mentors to show you the way, cheer for you on the sidelines, gut it out with you in the tough times, support you, encourage you, and give you a hand up.

Doing It All

How do women lawyers manage to do it all? I typically respond that women are natural multitaskers, capable of keeping numerous balls up in the air at once. The truth is I have an incredible partner, my husband (formerly, "The First Dude"), Bill Clark, who is without question one of the most progressive men I have ever known. Bill has never felt threatened by my success and has been my biggest fan. Justice Ginsburg felt the same way about her husband, and said in that 2010 ABA article: "That's my dream for the world. That a child should have two caring parents who share the joys and often the burdens. It really does take a man who regards his wife as his best friend, his equal, his true partner in life."[4]

Having It All

The media recently debated the question of whether women can have it all. I enthusiastically say "hell yes," and I'd certainly like to hear Justice Ginsburg's or Judge Grubbs's thoughts on it. But who is right? I believe we have many, many realistic role models for our younger women who are now trying to make their paths. I began my own law firm while pregnant with my second child and walked out of a very comfortable, reputable law firm without a single client to my name. I did it because I believed in myself and my abilities. I had always been told by my parents that I could do anything. As a mother of a twenty-one-year-old son and a nineteen-year-old daughter, I am extremely cognizant of the example I set for them professionally and personally. My daughter, Alex, wrote on Facebook that she thought her mom was an incredible role model. That was better than any victory I could ever achieve in court.

Paths to Success

My path has been to get involved in my profession at every level and at every opportunity, and it has worked for me. I recommend it to you as one potential path to success, both in your profession and in your personal life. There is no question your life will be

---

4. Stephanie Francis Ward, *Family Ties*, ABA Journal (Oct. 1, 2010), *available at* http://www.abajournal.com/magazine/article/family_ties1.

better if you really get involved in your world outside of your job and in your professional associations. Throw your energy into something unselfishly that has no logical relation to your practice. Roll up your sleeves and jump in. Or find some burning passion within the practice of law that you feel strongly about so that you can use your unique training as a lawyer to make someone else's life better. I have made friendships with many incredible people whose paths I might never have crossed but for working in the bar. My life is the richer for it. These people have set an incredible example of service and selflessness for me, and I am a better person just for having spent time with them.

We have a moral duty to help one another. A person should not only be about making money. Find your passion. Being involved in your profession gives you a greater purpose in life than just yourself. It will be your path to giving back. Getting involved in the bar and as a mentor makes you more well-rounded and gives you a more balanced life, and that is a desirable thing. The lawyer who is one-dimensional and does nothing other than sleep at night and practice law all day for twelve hours or more a day is a miserable person. There is no balance to her life, and trust me, no one wants to be around that woman. Ten years from now the lawyer without balance in her life will regret it.

Which brings me to my closing thought, and it is often my closing thought in every speech I give: "A Rising Tide Lifts All Boats." This is literally written on the wall of my office. I believe it, and it is that philosophy of mutual good and shared connections that has directed my entire career and my work on behalf of the Georgia State Bar. We are all in this together—women even more so—and we must mentor other women, encourage other women, and cheer each other on. By doing this for others, we will lift up ourselves unknowingly in the process. The more you help someone else, the more you help yourself. The less you think of yourself, the smaller your problems become.

Spurring Each Other On

When I was sworn in as president of the State Bar of Georgia, I had my Bible turned to Hebrews 10:22, and I think that passage is appropriate to share with you now: "Let's see how inventive we can be in encouraging love and helping out . . . spurring each other on." We must work together to remove barriers to inclusiveness. Each time a barrier is removed in the leadership of our courts, our legislature, or our profession, a door opens to a new generation of potentially great trailblazers, which might include the next Carol Hunstein, the next Sandra Day O'Connor, the next Ruth Bader Ginsburg, the next Adelle Grubbs, or the next Anne Workman. If you are one of the women who has benefited by someone pulling you through that door of success, it is now your turn to reach back your hand and help a sister through that door. Have we made strides in the last twenty years? Yes, without question. Are we at a point where we can simply declare that our work is done? Undoubtedly, no. We still have work to do. So let's get to work!

There Is No Right Answer, Right Path, or Easy Measure of Success: The Key Is How You Make the Journey

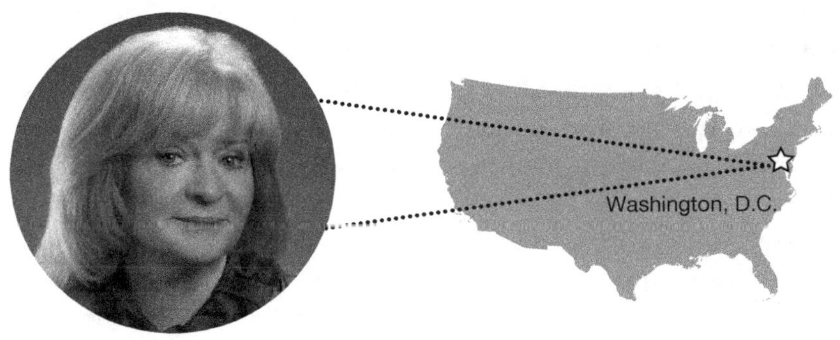

Her Story

Stasia Kelly

Career

Comanaging partner (Americas) and cochair of the Global Governance and Compliance practice at DLA Piper.

Education

Trinity University, *cum Laude*; George Washington University, JD, member of the Order of the Coif, and the *George Washington Law Review*.

Best Advice

Be open to adventure and be willing to take risks. Remember, even bad decisions can usually be used as a learning tool!

Personal

Best thing I ever did was have my twin sons, Michael and Brian. Balancing work and private life is hard, but worth all the effort it takes.

For more information about Stasia

www.dlapiper.com/en/us/people/k/kelly-stasia

This book is full of wonderful essays that will take you through the most important challenges of being a woman lawyer in the twenty-first century (which is not much different from the challenges in the twentieth century, but that is a subject for another time). The compelling insights offered in these essays will encourage you on your journey. I would like to tell you about what I consider the core foundational principles for the journey ahead.

The road to success is, as it sounds, a journey and not a destination. It is a marathon and not a sprint. Every journey is different, and success is measured through different perspectives. One abiding principle I have had for my journey is *stay true to yourself.* In the long run, it does not matter what your peers, competitors, and colleagues do to gain their success—it only matters that what you do reflects your own set of principles and values. We each have to look at ourselves in the mirror every day and be comfortable that what we are doing and how we are doing it stays true to our principles and beliefs. Otherwise, not only will you not be "successful," you will not be happy. In my view, part of the measure of success is being happy with how you have behaved and lived through the various circumstances in which you find yourself.

Do What Is Right for You and Your Family

Along the way on this journey, we are each presented with choices and forks in the road that we must navigate to reach that success we all want to experience. *There is no one way to navigate, and no one specific time to do something.* So often I have heard young associates at law firms tell me that they want to wait to have a family until they (1) are midlevel associates, (2) make partner, or (3) choose a practice area. In my view, there is no "event driven" moment for any career or family decision. There is only what is right for you and your family.

It Is Okay to Make a Bad Decision

So often I have seen lawyers, and particularly women lawyers, hesitate to take a job, change practice areas, go in-house, or make a similar decision for fear it will not be the right choice. As a result, they become paralyzed in their position, and the longer this lasts, the harder it is to make a different choice.

Not every decision you make in life or in your career will necessarily be the "right" decision, or even a good decision. So what? Fortunately, in our profession, unlike the medical field, no one dies when we make a bad decision. It is important to remember that most decisions we make are not irrevocable—if something does not work out, find something else that will work better. The key is to have the courage to make decisions and the wisdom to learn from decisions that turn out to be challenging. Some of the choices I made were clearly not the best from a number of perspectives, but I tried to learn from every decision I made and build upon those learnings for the next fork in the road.

All God's Creatures Are Equal

No matter how successful you are, what your title is, or how much money you make, you are still one person in the grand scheme of things. Treating our superiors and colleagues with respect usually is not difficult. But too often we forget that the folks who work for us—the driver who gets us to our destination on time and safely; the dry cleaner who makes us look as good as possible; the loyal assistant who filters difficult calls and protects us from unpleasant things in our day—are just as important (in fact, arguably more so) as any colleague or boss when it comes to being respectful. This is not only the right thing to do, it can be very helpful. More than once, I have been given important information or suggestions by a subordinate who went out of his or her way to be helpful. Subordinates and colleagues today could be bosses tomorrow. People remember the folks who were good and kind to them (and conversely those who were not).

There Is No Such Thing as Work-Life Balance; It Is All Life Balance

Every time I hear the phrase *work-life balance*, I cringe. This phrase makes it sound as though there is life and then there is work. To the contrary, it is all *life*, and the balance we all attempt to find in life should be viewed from this perspective. This outlook has always made it much easier for me to assess what is going on in my life and to make decisions accordingly. Sometimes my family took precedence, and sometimes I worked when I would rather be playing with my children. I always balanced the alternatives and chose what seemed to be best for what was going on in all aspects of my life at that time. Of course, we do not always make the best or "right" decisions along the way. But remember, these decisions are not irrevocable (see earlier principle). The more important part of this is to learn from your mistakes and move forward.

None of This Is Easy

If this journey were easy to navigate, we would not need the collective wisdom of others who have been down this path to help us along the way. We cannot, and should not, take this journey alone. We should take advantage of the wisdom and judgment of a colleague, a subordinate, or one of our children (out of the mouths of babes . . .). It is important that we learn from everyone around us, and to do that, we need to be able to listen and to be open to doing something a different way than we might choose. It is important to remain open to change, big or small, along this road.

Have Fun

Life is too short to take a job or remain in a situation in which we are not happy, or at least mildly content. Life can be difficult; being a lawyer can be difficult; and being a woman lawyer can be *really* difficult. You only have one journey to make. Do it as well and as happily as you can, and you will serendipitously make it happier for those around you, especially your family. This also means that we need to be good to ourselves. We need to listen to our own bodies and do what we need to do to keep the mind, spirit, and body in as good a shape as possible. For some this might be religion, for others yoga, and for still others a glass of wine, or some combination of these. Unless we take care of ourselves, we will not be able to take care of others or excel in a job the way we expect.

There Is No Finish Line

At least not while we are breathing and upright. Years ago, most people "retired" at age sixty-five and did not do much of anything after that time. Fortunately, we are living longer and healthier lives and can be productive beyond "retirement age." In fact, I think that phrase is becoming obsolete. We should always want to be as active in what we do as we were in any "job." It may and will be different, but it is all part of that same journey we are on.

My journey continues.

A Reflection by Oregon's First Woman Attorney General on How Far We Have—and Haven't—Come since 1972

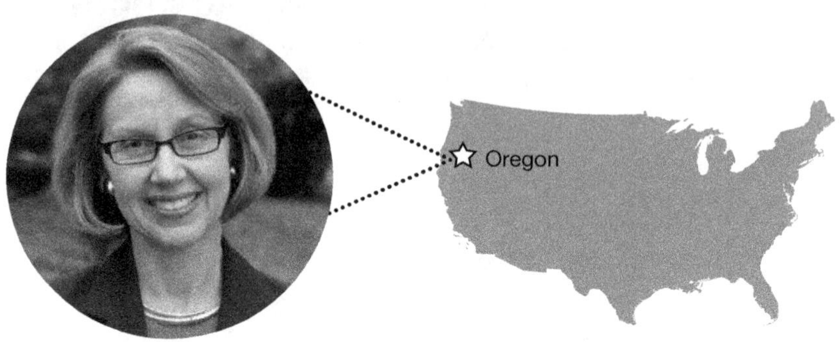

Her Story

Ellen Rosenblum

Career

Oregon attorney general, elected in 2012 to a four-year term. I am the first female attorney general elected in Oregon history, and I am currently running for a second term.

Education

University of Oregon, BS; University of Oregon School of Law, JD.

Best Advice

Always be more prepared than other lawyers on the case. Take care of yourself. Be generous with your mentoring. Take reasonable risks; don't be afraid to fail.

Personal

Married for thirty-four years to Richard Meeker. Two kids: Cate, a third-year pediatric resident at OHSU; and Will, a brand strategist for Astro Studios in San Francisco. One granddaughter, Charlotte Rose.

For more information about Ellen

www.EllenRosenblum.com

As Oregon's first female attorney general, I believe I bring a new and somewhat unique perspective to the job because of some of the experiences I've had that pertain to being female. Not unlike a mother bear protecting her cubs from harm, I view my role as protecting and advocating for the most vulnerable among us. I can also report that I enjoy this job tremendously, for the simple reason that what we do at the Department of Justice makes a difference in the lives of every Oregonian.

Each of us has our own narrative. For all of us, our personal stories shed light on what motivates us today and on our successes as well as our occasional defeats. So allow me to be a bit personal for a moment or two and share some of my story to explain why it's so important to promote justice, protect the vulnerable, and ensure equality—and why we in our profession should never let other concerns, no matter how pressing, undermine these core values.

I happen to be from a rather large family. I am the middle sister of three girls—and we were followed by five brothers! Dad was a law professor, and Mom, in her nineties now, was a social worker. Dinnertime was taken up with negotiations, often on behalf of younger siblings and often with a slant toward reaching fairness: Had due process and equal protection been provided? In that sense, my career as a lawyer started early.

Unlike a recent study in *The Atlantic Magazine*, asserting that the real problem for women and girls achieving equal treatment is their own lack of confidence, I did not suffer a confidence deficiency in my formative years. The opportunity to rule the roost over five strong-willed brothers, especially because our working mother put us girls in charge after school, provided me with (1) the chance to establish a power base, (2) assertiveness training, and (3) frequently, though not always, empathy for my siblings' predicaments.

I was also interested early on in the treatment of women in society and wrote a college thesis on working moms and their effect on their daughters' work-related aspirations. Although my parents were committed to gender equality, I learned that not everyone felt the same way.

When my law school class entered the bar, the legal workplace was not in the slightest ready for women, let alone working mothers. Even the fashion industry failed—utterly—to anticipate our arrival on the scene, and caused us to wear some of the most hideous outfits imaginable, as we tried to look like, uh, lawyers!

I started at the University of Oregon School of Law in 1972, and it was the *first* year to have more than a token number of women students. It was as if female college seniors had suddenly taken note that there were virtually no women lawyers and that perhaps we could do something about that. This was the Vietnam War era—and the feminist era. There was this pervasive—and wonderful—sense that the law was the best agent for social change. If we were going to change the world—and in those heady days we knew that was in the offing—we had to be lawyers. Before applying to law school, I worked as an aide to a classic male chauvinist school superintendent. That experience convinced me that I had better get on to my legal education quickly!

My class—and those at law schools across the country—increased the percentage of women law students virtually overnight, from about ten percent the year before to thirty percent in 1972. The University of Oregon School of Law reflected this sudden unforeseen jump—there were only two bathroom stalls for women. Worse, there were no female role models, and no women faculty except one adjunct professor in, of course, family law. There was but one female judge in all of Lane County, Judge Helen Frye, and only a small handful of practicing women lawyers, none of whom went to court.

As for the law school itself, no one knew quite what to do with us! Though there were important exceptions, such as Dave Frohnmayer and Laird Kirkpatrick, most professors had a dismissive attitude toward this new brand of student, leaving the Socratic dialogue to our male classmates. During my first year, I signed up for a mentor program. The law school put me with a downtown lawyer who first commented on my looks and then asked me what my husband would think when I was making more money than he was! Our Civil Procedure professor, former Dean Orlando John Hollis, simply could not countenance the use of what was then a new term—"Ms."—in his presence. He said it sounded too much like a bumblebee and forbade us to use it in his classroom.

Fast forward to the late 1970s, when I was made partner in my small Eugene law firm. My new partners took me out for a celebratory lunch at the Shadow Hills Country Club, with the result that I was forcibly evicted—physically pushed out of the dining room—because women were not allowed in the "men's grill." The Men's Grille, of course, was the only restaurant open at the club that day. (I don't believe my partners ever set foot in the club again, at which they were not members.)

Lest you think these sorts of slights no longer happen, as recently as three years ago, as I was completing my tenure on the Court of Appeals, I was mistaken for a secretary by counsel about to appear before me, I guess because I was a woman carrying a pile of briefs in the elevator. Imagine his surprise a few minutes later when I was one of the three black-robed judges who entered the courtroom to hear his argument!

Truth be told, I have had lots of advantages and professional opportunities and have benefited greatly from having been among that pioneering group of women of the class of 1975. I've been fortunate enough to blaze quite a few trails—including educating the esteemed federal judge Owen M. Panner on the necessity of nursing breaks for lawyers who also happen to be mothers of infants. In 1984, taking my newborn daughter Cate with me to eastern Oregon so I could continue to nurse her while I prosecuted a case was unheard of. Although I was fortunate and grateful to have Judge Panner's support of my dual roles as mother and AUSA, I'm also glad that Oregon women no longer have to depend on the kindness and understanding of their supervisors. It's now the law that many Oregon employers must provide breaks to accommodate breastfeeding mothers! I recently reminded that same daughter, Cate—now a mother of two-year-old Charlotte, and who also happens to be a third-year medical resident—of that law!

Because of the advantages I've had, I believe I have a dual role to help women—both those in the legal profession, where I remain dedicated to continuing the work of transforming the practice of law and promoting access to justice, and women in society at large. I firmly believe that the success of women in law is critical to the success and survival of all women, which is why I am so happy to be able to serve in a role where I can both promote women within the legal profession and use the law to advocate for and protect vulnerable populations, who all too often include women and children.

Make no mistake. Women have come a long way from the days I was escorted out of the men's grill, but we don't have a full seat at the table yet.

It is undeniable that women have made progress. We earn more college and graduate degrees than men. We now make up half of the workforce. We're closing the gap in the ranks of middle management. Some of that is undoubtedly motivated by empirical research showing that when companies employ women at higher rates, they do better than their competitors on every measure of profitability. Things are changing for the better every day because, as a society, we are starting to realize that men, children, and families all benefit when we give women the chance to succeed.

Even Federal Reserve Chairwoman Janet Yellen regularly speaks about economic inequality and describes economic opportunity as including having the means to raise children and access to education. As the first female Fed chair, she is also the first to emphasize its obligation to promote economic opportunity. That's probably not a coincidence. When women are part of the conversation, we arrive at different and, often, better conclusions.

That's something my new heroine, Senator Kirsten Gillebrand, also understands. Senator Gillebrand has championed eliminating sexual violence in the military and has issued a call to action in her new book for this generation to "elevate women's voices in the public sphere and bring women more fully into the decisions that shape our country." We need more women's voices heard at all levels of society—more women elected officials, and more women law partners! There is much work to be done, and we cannot be content with the progress, amazing as it has been, of the last half century. So I urge you to stick with the profession and find a way to blaze new trails for the women who follow in your footsteps—just look at the contributors to this book. It is my sincere hope that their stories provide you with inspiration and that you take a moment to reflect on how far women have come since 1972.

The Big Picture

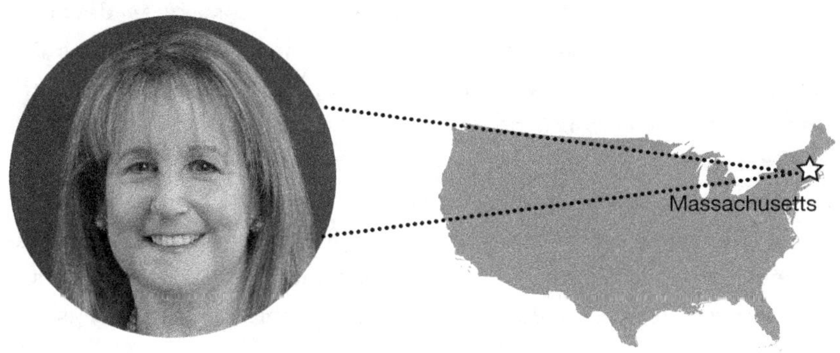

Her Story

Lauren Stiller Rikleen

Career

President, Rikleen Institute for Strategic Leadership. I provide speaking, training, and consulting services on strengthening multigenerational issues, women's leadership and advancement, and unconscious bias.

Education

Brandeis University, BA, *magna cum laude*; Boston College Law School, JD.

Best Advice

Be kind to others. Try not to let the craziness of your work-life challenges prevent you from enjoying the journey along the way.

Personal

Married to Sander Rikleen, a litigation partner at Sherin & Lodgen, with two millennial children.

For more information about Lauren

www.RikleenInstitute.com

I have been a working mom for twenty-eight years, married to a working dad. Our other titles have included law firm partners, zealous advocates, and community and professional leaders in a variety of organizations. Throughout, we have also been devoted children to aging parents and spent many enjoyable life-cycle, holiday, and other occasions with our siblings, nieces, nephews, and cousins. Oh, and I would be remiss if I left out the generations of golden retrievers who have been an integral part of our lives, including the four sitting near me as I write this.

In the writing, it sounds idyllic. In the living, of course, it is a far more nuanced picture. I have learned many lessons in the nearly three decades I have been a parent and a lawyer. It is an honor to share six of those lessons with you.

Lesson 1: Time Moves Us Along

Try to live each day understanding how quickly time passes. In retrospect, the years feel like they have raced along. The memory of the day-to-day struggles with work-life issues, career crises, and other bumps along the way fade and are seen with a different perspective when not in the immediacy of the moment. Recognizing how precious life is leads to the other lessons learned throughout the years.

Lesson 2: Embrace Everyone's Work-Life Choices

Stop judging yourself and others with respect to work-life choices. People need to make the choices that suit their own life circumstances, and those circumstances may change at different points in their lives. Know that you can pursue a career and be a devoted parent. These are not mutually exclusive goals. Never let anyone advise you otherwise, nor make you think that only certain careers mix with parenting.

It never ceases to shock me how frequently I hear parents criticize the life choices that others make. What I came to realize is that underlying these criticisms are deep-rooted anxieties about one's own choices: "If they can make it work by choosing such a different parenting path, how can my choice be correct?" "How can they be a good parent if they did not make the same decision to leave the workforce?" "How can they be a valued employee if they have kids at home, with competing demands for their time?" "How can that person leave behind years of education to be at home full time?" And on it goes.

Remember that someone else's decisions are not a challenge to your own choices. If someone does it differently, that does not make your decisions better or worse. They are simply different. It is time to end this debate that has no right or wrong answer, as the discussion itself leaves only anxiety in its wake. Everyone should have the opportunity to make work-life choices free of the judgment of others.

Lesson 3: Be Present with Your Children

There is no manual that tells us the best way to raise children. There are, however, certain immutable facts that need to play into the parenting choices you make. There is a difference between physical and mental unavailability, and your children will be a lot more forgiving of brief absences of the former than of the latter. Kids know when you are mentally not present, even when your physical form is next to them.

My lesson came when my daughter was young and complained that I was on the phone while in the car with her. Her annoyance and disappointment were searing in that moment and had a lasting impact, bringing about the desired change in my behavior. By the way, the joyous moment of payback came when she first tried to text friends while back in that same car a few years later. The "pay attention to me" rule continues to apply to all of us, which has made for wonderful conversations while driving over the years.

Lesson 4: Build Flexibility into Two-Career Households

If you are raising children in a dual-career household, it helps enormously if both spouses can be flexible in addressing family responsibilities and unexpected emergencies. Not all careers lend themselves to equity in decision making, but when they do, the overall family stress level can be reduced significantly.

My lesson on this topic came when I was in law school and arrived for a large class, only to see a sign on the door announcing its cancellation. At our next scheduled class, the professor began by apologizing for the inconvenience, telling us that his child woke up with a fever, which meant a parent needed to stay home. This required both parents to check schedules to determine who had the more flexible day.

The professor's wife was a law firm partner with a client flying in from another state; our professor had classes whose cancellation would inconvenience a lot of students. These working parents made their decision based on the fact that students can more easily be inconvenienced than a client who has been flying for hours for a meeting with a partner. By sharing this real-life example of what it is like to be working parents in demanding careers, the professor taught us his most valuable lesson of all.

Lesson 5: Embrace Ambiguity

Embrace ambiguity or it will forever haunt you. Life is complicated and often messy. Our great plans go awry or, as the old expression made famous by John Lennon goes, "Life is what happens to you while you are busy making other plans." The moments in life when we are not mired in uncertainty are rare. There is always something to worry about, a decision to second-guess, or a reason to feel guilty. Avoid making decisions at the moment you feel most in crisis.

There were many times when life circumstances collided with work responsibilities, and it seemed that there was no way to continue with my professional obligations. Each time, however, I was fortunate to have a husband who encouraged me to stay the course and gut instincts that were in agreement with that choice. Now that our children are settling into young adulthood, I am grateful that I chose to work through the ambiguity of life's circumstances and continue in my career. I am also mindful that others could make different choices under similar circumstances that would be the right decisions for them. *It is important not to be driven by the fear of the unknown in the choices you make.*

Lesson 6: Be Proactive in Addressing Gender Bias

Gender bias continues to exist, most often unconsciously, and it continues to thwart women's careers. To ignore this reality is a disservice to other women and to yourself.

I am saddened to hear men and women—at all levels of their career—counsel other women not to discuss gender bias, not to discuss pay equity, and to avoid looking like they are complaining about unfairness in organizational decision making. Problems do not get solved by wishing them away. Leaning in is a strategy that can take you only so far absent a workplace culture that is attentive to talent management, including issues of conscious and unconscious bias and equality in assignments, promotions, and compensation.

We can work together to strategically improve culture and solve problems without one person having to shoulder the burden alone. It undermines the hopes of those in the workplace for a fairer future if the advice in response to concerns about inequities is to ignore them.

After decades as a professional, I continue to be surprised by the fact that we are still talking about the same workplace challenges. The United States continues to lag behind most every other industrialized nation in policies that support working parents trying to manage work-life challenges. Pay inequality and barriers to leadership opportunities have been issues since women first entered the workforce. Although progress has been made, we are not where we should be and should not accept the status quo as good enough.

My life lessons come with battle scars and lots of second-guessing throughout the years. But with all the difficulties and high-stress moments, I am reminded every day that we must all continue our efforts to create a flexible and equitable workplace culture. As we watch our kids becoming young adults and see them navigating their own difficult workplace issues, it is clear that this work is not done. Achieving the goal of gender equity depends on what all of us do. I encourage men and women at all stages of their careers (because we need you all) to become active in your workplace, in bar associations, and in affinity groups to ensure that the next generation can benefit from the equality that has eluded us for too long. Meaningful work-life integration will be achieved when we treat it as a responsibility and an opportunity that belongs to all of us.

My Career in the Law: Reflections on the Challenges and Rewards for Women in the Profession

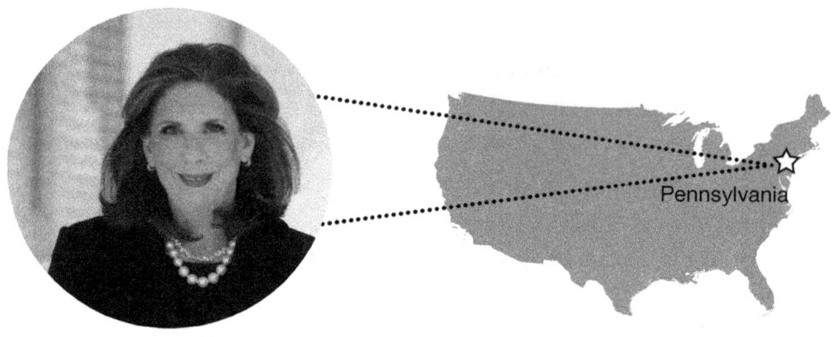

Her Story

Bobbie D. Liebenberg

Career

Partner at Fine, Kaplan & Black, where I focus my practice on antitrust class actions, complex commercial litigation, and white-collar criminal defense.

Education

University of Michigan, BA with Distinction; Catholic University Columbus School of Law, JD, *magna cum laude*.

Best Advice

Find a niche practice that will enable you to set yourself apart, and be proactive in seeking out writing and speaking opportunities to gain visibility in your firm and with prospective clients.

Personal

Married (forty-six years), three children, three grandchildren.

For more information about Bobbie

www.finekaplan.com

In the almost forty-one years that I have been practicing law, there have been dramatic changes for women lawyers. When I graduated from law school in 1975, women comprised only twenty percent of law students and fourteen percent of the lawyers in large law firms. Typical remarks made to women lawyers who interviewed for jobs included "we don't like to hire women"; "women lawyers belong in trusts and estates and family law, not litigation"; and "what are your plans for children?" Today, such remarks would be shocking, if not illegal.

The Few, the Proud, the Brave

The attainment of work-life balance for women lawyers in the 1970s was made exceedingly difficult by the virtual absence of formalized maternity leave and part-time policies. The paucity of women in the profession made it hard to find role models, mentors, and sponsors who could help women navigate the politics of overwhelmingly male work environments. Women were often excluded from the lunches, golf outings, and other social gatherings with clients—almost all of whom were male—making it more difficult for women to develop business. In addition, there were relatively few women in-house lawyers who could refer business to women at law firms. Although women dressed like their male counterparts—blue suits, white shirts, and the omnipresent floppy bow tie—they were often criticized if they acted as aggressively or displayed the same ambition as men. Given these constraints, it is no wonder that I and the other women lawyers of that era felt like the Marines: "the few, the proud, the brave."

Thankfully, women lawyers have made great strides since that time, and many have reached the highest pinnacles of the profession. Increasing numbers of women have become federal and state court judges, general counsel of corporations, deans of law schools, and heads of practice groups at law firms. A handful (approximately five percent) have even become chairs of their law firms, a notion that was inconceivable when I first started practicing.

Missing the Mark

Unfortunately, even though women have been graduating from law school in significant numbers for the past twenty-five years, we have yet to see these numbers translate into true equality for women in the profession. Hillary Clinton, who served as the first chair of the ABA Commission on Women in the Profession, was prescient when she wrote in the commission's landmark 1988 study that the increasing numbers of women lawyers alone would not ensure that they would advance and succeed at the same rate as men.

Stalled Success

Indeed, despite the overall progress since the 1970s, the annual statistics concerning the status of women in the profession bring a sense of déjà vu. The number of women equity partners continues to remain static at approximately seventeen percent, and *The American Lawyer* estimates that gender parity in equity partnerships will not be reached until 2181. Women still lag behind their male peers in compensation and the attainment of positions of real power and influence in their places of employment. A very disturbing trend is that the percentage of women attending law school has actually decreased somewhat since reaching nearly fifty percent ten years ago.

The attrition of women from law firms remains unacceptably high. Many women find it exceedingly difficult to fulfill onerous billable hours quotas and build a book of business while simultaneously raising a family or taking care of aging parents. Attrition takes a toll not only among women associates but also among more senior women. This is particularly true for women who either cannot advance from nonequity to equity partner status or who are deequitized after having become equity partners. The rate of attrition is particularly high for women attorneys of color, who face the "double bind" of both race and gender.

Policies for the Future

Today, nearly all law firms have adopted part-time and flextime policies, but the reality is that these policies are rarely used. Although ninety-six percent of firms have such policies, only six percent of lawyers utilize them and, not surprisingly, over seventy percent of those lawyers are women.[1] Distressingly, there has been

1. NAWL Foundation and the National Association of Women Lawyers (NAWL), *Report of the 5th Annual National Survey on Retention and Promotion of Women in Law Firms*, p. 15 (regarding Part-Time Policies) (October 2010).

a decline in the utilization of part-time and flextime policies by both women associates and women partners during the past several years. Although law firms pay lip service to flexible work arrangements, women lawyers have correctly recognized that actually using such arrangements will not lead to partnership. In fact, many law firms do not even permit part-time lawyers to be promoted to equity partnership.

Another significant change from when I began practicing law is that almost all firms now also have formal maternity leave policies. However, these policies have not resulted in a more hospitable workplace culture for women, many of whom continue to face an entrenched maternal wall bias. Women who had stellar reputations before having children experience persistent criticisms and negative evaluations concerning their competence and commitment after having children and are not assigned the types of significant matters necessary to advance in their firms. Consequently, in too many cases, women elect not to return to work after maternity leave, especially after their second or third child.

Women who have decided to return to the workplace after taking several years off to take care of their children encounter enormous obstacles when they try to reenter. Firms rarely have formalized on-ramp programs to help integrate them back into practice. Research repeatedly confirms that even women who successfully reenter the profession after a hiatus of several years find themselves disadvantaged in terms of compensation and promotion opportunities.

Clearly, all of these factors contribute to the continued "leaky pipeline" of women from law firms and adversely affect the number of women available for advancement and leadership roles. Despite various "women's initiatives" and other well-intentioned efforts to retain and promote women, law firms have been unable to take the steps necessary to stem the exodus of talented women. The resulting shortage of senior women in leadership positions and on significant firm committees, such as the management and partnership compensation committees, in turn perpetuates the continuation of policies that are inimical to the retention and advancement of women.

Combating Bias

Addressing this pernicious problem and seeking to change this paradigm has been a particular focus of mine for many years. One of the truly great benefits of a long career is the ability to devote substantial amounts of time to issues that you are passionate about and to help effectuate change. I was extremely privileged and honored to twice serve as chair of the American Bar Association's Commission on Women and also the ABA Gender Equity Task Force, as well as the Pennsylvania Bar Association's Commission on Women and the Philadelphia Bar Association's Committee on Women in the Profession. These organizations and I have worked to develop specific strategies, best practices, and model policies to combat the persistent implicit biases faced by women attorneys (particularly women attorneys of color) and to ensure that compensation, origination credit, and partnership decisions are fairer and more equitable, leading to increases in the number of women partners, leaders, and rainmakers.

I have spent a great deal of time on this effort because I am hopeful that more and more women will continue to enter and remain in the profession and reap the rewards that a long and fulfilling career can provide. I have to admit that with a busy litigation practice and raising three children, there have been occasional setbacks along the way. However, I have always enjoyed my work, which is extremely interesting and challenging. I have had the good fortune to work with lawyers I respected and who respected me. Despite working hard and devoting many hours to my cases and clients, my family has always remained my first priority. For example, I made it a practice to have dinner with my family and to be available to help my children with homework. This often meant working late nights after my kids were in bed, but this choice worked for me.

Looking Back

In a position now to look back and think about the tough times I faced and the decisions I made, I am so glad that I persevered even when it seemed impossible to continue to multitask and juggle so many responsibilities. You will often have to adjust your schedule to accommodate car pools and attendance at dance recitals, sports events, and parent-teacher conferences. But I am here to tell you that the memories of the stressful and difficult times will fade over the years, being replaced by memories of the many good times, both at home and at work. The enjoyment I have derived from my career made all the sacrifices well worth it, and my kids flourished and were proud of my accomplishments.

Given my own experiences, I offer a few tips that I hope will be helpful to you to achieve both personal fulfillment and professional success:

- *Don't try to be a superwoman.* The truth is that there is no such thing as someone who can "have it all." Set realistic priorities, taking one day at a time, and recognize that your goals may change as new opportunities present themselves. Take ownership of your choices, do not second-guess yourself, and try not to feel guilty when you are heading off to work or out of town. (I recognize that this is easier said than done.)
- *Get a support system.* Support of a spouse, partner, family member, and even a babysitter can be critical to success. In my practice, I had to travel quite a bit because many of my cases were around the country. I was extremely fortunate that my husband always has been my rock and helped to fill in when I was not around, thereby contributing to my success and happiness. In addition, it is important to cultivate relationships with mentors and sponsors, both within and outside your office, who can help champion you and increase your profile and visibility in the legal and business communities.
- *Take risks.* I have never been afraid to take a risk and try something new. This has entailed my venturing into new practice areas and leaving the security of a partnership in a large law firm to start my own firm. If you find yourself dissatisfied, stymied, or frustrated in your current practice, do not accept the status quo but instead try something new. I have found that change, although daunting, can be a very good thing, and sometimes your career unfolds in positive ways you could not have foreseen. By being flexible, proactive, and receptive to change, you can create new opportunities to advance and succeed on your own terms.

- *Give credit and take credit.* No one makes it on her own, so give credit to team members and to others who have helped you. Equally important, do not be reticent to take credit for what you have accomplished, and enlist others to tout your achievements and successes. Advocate for yourself just as vigorously as you do for your clients and just as vigorously as your male colleagues do for themselves.
- *Champion other women.* Women lawyers who have reached a certain level of success must help other women to succeed. As former Secretary of State Madeleine Albright has so aptly observed, "there is a special place in hell for women who don't help other women." You can lend a hand to other women lawyers by referring work to them, including women associates on a pitch team or a new matter, inviting women to speak at seminars or write an article, or sponsoring them for membership or leadership positions in bar associations or other organizations. My own career benefited greatly from having wonderful sponsors, and in turn I have personally derived enormous satisfaction by serving as a sponsor and mentor for many women attorneys. I have taken great pride in the development of a new generation of women leaders who will pick up the mantle of advocating for equality in the profession.
- *Have fun and enjoy your career.* Surround yourself with people who make you laugh. Try to figure out what you enjoy about the practice of law and how you can make your career more satisfying. It is far easier to cope with the trials and tribulations of the practice of law if you enjoy your work. What is great about a law degree is that it can serve as a passport to so many different professional opportunities and such a wide range of practice settings.

I hope to continue practicing law for many years. It is a profession in which I can truly make a difference, not only for my clients but also for society as a whole. I am happy that I never let anyone or anything deter me from pursuing my own ambition and achieving my personal goals for success. As I reflect on my career, women lawyers have certainly come a long way, and I look forward to witnessing the many accomplishments and successes of future generations of women lawyers.

REFLECTIONS

1. How has the workplace changed for the better in the last twenty years? What still needs to change?
2. Looking back on your career, have your supervisors or bosses helped inspire you to stick with the profession when your personal obligations became overwhelming? How so? Did you find both men and women willing to do so? How did you handle the situation?
3. Which of the stories in this chapter inspired you the most?
4. Did you find yourself relating to an author as she discussed her story?
5. Do you ever reflect on your career, what you've accomplished, and what you hope to achieve going forward? If not, do that now. Are you willing to share?
6. What are your non-law-related interests? What can you do to pursue them? How important are they to you?
7. Are you involved with a women's bar group? If not, why not? What can you do to support equality and flexibility in the workplace for women? Do you believe this is important? Why or why not?
8. How can you be a mentor or sponsor for another woman? Can you send business to another woman? Are you supporting other women? Why or why not?
9. What are three effective ways to advance women lawyers?
10. Think about and list three goals for your career and for yourself personally for the coming six months, year, and five years. Write them down, share them with a friend or mentor, or share them within a group discussion.
11. Finally, think about your story. What special experience can you share with other women lawyers? How can your story inspire others? Who needs to know about your story? Where is your story taking you next? Do you have a story to tell?